DIRTY MONEY

CLARENDON STUDIES IN CRIMINOLOGY

Published under the auspices of the Institute of Criminology, University of Cambridge; the Mannheim Centre, London School of Economics; and the Centre for Criminology, University of Oxford.

General Editors: Jill Peay and Tim Newburn
(London School of Economics)

Editors: Loraine Gelsthorpe, Alison Liebling, Kyle Treiber and Per-Olof Wikström
(University of Cambridge)

Coretta Phillips and Robert Reiner
(London School of Economics)

Mary Bosworth, Carolyn Hoyle, Ian Loader, and Lucia Zedner
(University of Oxford)

RECENT TITLES IN THIS SERIES:

Reinventing Punishment: A Comparative History of Criminology and Penology in the Nineteenth and Twentieth Centuries
Pifferi

Taking Care of Business: Police Detectives, Drug Law Enforcement and Proactive Investigation
Bacon

The Politics of Police Detention in Japan: Consensus of Convenience
Croydon

Dangerous Politics: Risk, Political Vulnerability, and Penal Policy
Annison

Punish and Expel: Border Control, Nationalism, and the New Purpose of the Prison
Kaufman

Dirty Money

On Financial Delinquency

VINCENZO RUGGIERO

OXFORD
UNIVERSITY PRESS

OXFORD
UNIVERSITY PRESS

Great Clarendon Street, Oxford, OX2 6DP,
United Kingdom

Oxford University Press is a department of the University of Oxford.
It furthers the University's objective of excellence in research, scholarship,
and education by publishing worldwide. Oxford is a registered trade mark of
Oxford University Press in the UK and in certain other countries

First Edition published in 2017
Impression: 1

Published in the United States of America by Oxford University Press
198 Madison Avenue, New York, NY 10016, United States of America

British Library Cataloguing in Publication Data
Data available

Library of Congress Control Number: 2016958906

ISBN 978–0–19–878322–0

Printed and bound by
CPI Group (UK) Ltd, Croydon, CR0 4YY

General Editors' Introduction

Clarendon Studies in Criminology aims to provide a forum for outstanding empirical and theoretical work in all aspects of criminology and criminal justice, broadly understood. The Editors welcome submissions from established scholars, as well as excellent PhD work. The *Series* was inaugurated in 1994, with Roger Hood as its first General Editor, following discussions between Oxford University Press and three criminology centres. It is edited under the auspices of these three centres: the Cambridge Institute of Criminology, the Mannheim Centre for Criminology at the London School of Economics, and the Centre for Criminology at the University of Oxford. Each supplies members of the Editorial Board and, in turn, the Series Editor or Editors.

Vincenzo Ruggiero's new volume, *Dirty Money*, is, as the title implies, a study of how money is transformed via human action into an instrument for the production of harm. Whilst money might superficially be thought of as a 'neutral tool', Ruggiero's book details how, consistently across time, money has perverted its neutrality. More specifically, the book focuses on episodes of what Ruggiero refers to as 'financial delinquency'. It further examines the ways in which a very broad array of observers—philosophers, theologians and criminologists—have shaped our understanding of these episodes and their causes and consequences.

In his opening chapter exploring the relationship between money and salvation in Christian thought and doctrine, we encounter many expected figures—from Dante and Bunyan to Max Weber—but also some surprises, including George Bernard Shaw, Wagner and Rabelais. Rabelais's economic vision saw debtors and lenders as interchangeable, and imagined a world in which credit and debt were so widespread and interdependent as to result in economic harmony. Ruggiero charts the gradual transformation of economic thought over the centuries, to a point where Walter Benjamin could suggest that capitalism had become a religion and economics its theology. Economics, Ruggiero argues, replaced 'sin' with 'crisis'.

These crises—from the Dutch 'tulip mania' of the 1620s and 30s, to the bubbles that erupted in Paris and London late in the century—were primarily interpreted as the result of the actions of unscrupulous individuals. By and large early criminologists had relatively little to say about such activity, the bulk of relevant commentary appearing in economic rather than 'criminological' writing. Beccaria drew attention to the ways in which the wealthy and powerful were protected by law, and distinguished between productive and sterile forms of financial activity; with irregular forms of conduct being attributed by Bentham to idiocy, calamity or the abuse of trust.

From the utilitarians, we journey to the 'century of railways, robber barons and financial distress'. British capital was heavily involved in the spread of the railways on both sides of the Atlantic and the railroad builders bought political influence, often through bribery, whilst both promoting the idea of market freedom and relying on state support and intervention. Their names—Vanderbilt, Carnegie, J.P. Morgan, Rockefeller, and Russell Sage among others—continue to resonate. Misconduct was rife and oversight was extraordinarily deficient. This was also the period that saw the emergence of Quetelet and the beginnings of statistical criminology, as well as Lombroso, Garofalo, Ferri and the rise of the Positive School. None had a great deal to say about 'financial delinquency', though Gabriel Tarde, with his focus on both technical and motivational innovation, at least offered ideas for analyzing and framing such conduct.

The early twentieth century saw the financial crash of the late 1920s underpinned by, among many other things, 'a flood of corporate larceny'. Moreover, the financial crisis led to widespread attempts to defray losses via fraud. Such activities naturally drew the attention of criminologists, notably the Chicago School and, in particular, Edwin Sutherland. It was he who observed that the 'law is like a cobweb; it's made for flies and the smaller kinds of insects, so to speak, but lets the big bumblebees break through'. Of the 70 corporations he studied, 40 were found to have publicly misrepresented their finances. Why then was it rarely accorded the status of 'criminality'? For Willem Bonger, it was simply because it posed an insufficient challenge to the social order.

Intriguingly, what follows is something of a gap in public attention paid to financial crime; Ruggiero speculates this may have been, at least in part, a consequence of changing media attention.

Financial delinquency, of course, continued unabated, with both the New Deal and the Marshall Plan offering extraordinary possibilities for exploitation. Increasing evidence emerged of corrupt relationships between politicians and the financial sector, as well as those involving the police and others in nefarious financial practices. The 1980s and 1990s saw the proliferation of financial delinquency and of initiatives to respond to it, together with heightened attention paid to the victims of such activities. The names read like a roll-call of shame: Milken, Savings and Loans, Maxwell, BCCI, Leeson and Barings Bank. The seeming ubiquity of malfeasance led to some shifts in criminological attention seeking, on the one hand, to combine elements of strain, labelling, and control theories and, on the other, to a greater focus on political economy and a critique of neoliberalism.

The financial crisis of 2008, and the regulatory response, are the next steps in Ruggiero's journey. New, unprecedented and widespread 'networks of greed' emerged in an increasingly deregulated environment, creating what Ruggiero refers to as a 'generalised Ponzi culture'. The limited impact of the regulatory reaction is depressing in the extreme, and Ruggiero offers considerable evidence to suggest that many of the measures proposed to prevent future crises were contested, amended, scrapped or neutralized, and that the growing influence of 'shadow banks', and the generalized failure of political control, has created a situation where attempts to control the financial sector look remarkably familiar to our doomed attempts to regulate illegal drugs markets. We live now, he argues, in a world of hidden wealth, where mobility, hybridity and fuzziness are the key characteristics of the fluid world of 'viral' money laundering. We inhabit a world in which the unscrupulous traders of the seventeenth century have been replaced by the transnational institutional vultures of the twenty-first. The future looks bleak. It is perhaps this that underpins Ruggiero's use of the term 'financial delinquency'. Whilst some might see a form essentialism in the use of such terminology, his intention is to 'draw attention to the harm these actors produce' for 'experience tells us that positive labelling and shaming (or positive moral entrepreneurship) have contributed to turning behaviours previously tolerated into unacceptable, revolting acts.' Given the rapacious nature of many of the harms that Ruggiero analyses, describing such activities, as delinquency seems almost an act of kindness.

As Editors we commend Vincenzo Ruggiero's book as making significant contributions to both the fields of white collar and corporate crime, and to the intellectual history of criminology. *Dirty Money* is to be most warmly welcomed to the *Clarendon Studies in Criminology* Series.

Tim Newburn and Jill Peay
London School of Economics
and Political Science
November 2016

Contents

1

Introduction

There are competing accounts of the origin of money. Some link it with barter, which supposedly was transformed by money from the exchange of things into the exchange of values implicit in them. Others object that barter, in the strict sense of moneyless market exchange, has never been a quantitatively important or dominant mode of transaction in any past or present economic system (Graeber, 2011; Martin, 2013). Money, we are told, originates from specific forms of fees such as tribute and sacrifice, including sacrificial payments, debts, fines, and donations to religious and political authority (Dodd, 2014). Examples from Greece are liturgies, 'the ancient, civic obligations of the thousand wealthiest inhabitants of the city to provide public services assessed in financial terms' (Martin, 2013: 62).

Was Adam Smith right in asserting that money is a neutral means facilitating commercial exchange and that monetary systems developed thanks to the desire of people to engage in trade relations? Or was Max Weber more acute in maintaining that money is a politico-economic institution ruled by an authority and, as such, bound to privilege certain interests and disadvantage others? A curse for Simmel, an instrument of freedom for the Koran, an abstraction conferring social power for Marx, money is a non-perishable good fit for accumulation and, while it circulates, it also manipulates those who do not own it.

Individuals who possess enormous amounts of money can be likened to army generals who use banknotes as troops. Zola (2014) described one such general attacking enemies and competitors, wasting resources in order to succeed in his aggression. The fever that devoured him turned into sleepless nights, when he marched his army of 600 million and led them to glory through extermination. Finally victorious, he found himself in the middle of disaster, having eaten others to avoid being eaten, but he also felt completely alone, supported only by his insatiable appetite. This extreme form of individualism posited by Zola, of course, might be tempered by the notion of 'homo negotiatus', who supposedly is not driven to personal interest, but to cooperation and coordination so that his interest overlaps with collective achievement (Ross, 2014). But isn't fraud too a negotiation, as victims are persuaded that they will gain something thanks to a common project? Fraudulent transactions abound in commercial and financial crises, where the confines of law and morality are overstepped, shadowy though those confines are. 'The propensities to swindle and be swindled run parallel to the propensity to speculate during a boom. Crash and panic, with their motto "sauve qui peut" induce still more people to cheat in order to save themselves' (Kindleberger, 2002: 73).

While not directly concerned with the origin and definition of money, this book is a study of how human action makes such 'neutral tool' or 'biased institution' the instrument for the production of harm. Its focus is, therefore, on dirty money, namely the illegitimate appropriation of financial resources by individuals and groups holding expert knowledge and, often, occupying positions of power.

The harm caused by the financial world could be explained through the low moral intensity prevailing in it: operators are too far removed from the effects of their action, like experts operating drones are a world apart from their human targets. Traders working in front of several computer screens are unaware of, or choose to neglect, the consequences of their number-crunching sales techniques (de Bruin, 2015). Competence, for them, does not lead to the appreciation of ethical issues, to the point that to call the financial sector unjust, in their view, makes about as much sense as calling the weather unfair. The harm caused by finance is a form of 'innocent fraud', perpetrated by individuals who are well paid to predict the unknown and unknowable: 'the financial world sustains a large, active, well-rewarded community based on compelled but seemingly sophisticated ignorance' (Galbraith, 2004: 48). Fraud is innocent, according to Galbraith, when it is not accompanied by a sense of responsibility or guilt, but is only engrained in the logic of value. Think of the guiltless trick enacted by Marcel Duchamp, author of the Mona Lisa 'improved', namely a Gioconda sporting a thin military mustache and a tiny goatee. In December 1919, Duchamp went to his dentist, Daniel Tzanck, and paid him with a fake cheque, wholly drawn by hand on a scrap of paper. Tzanck, who was also a collector and very active in Parisian avant-garde circles, knew very well he was accepting a precious Dada drawing, although not redeemable at the bank (Gay, 2007; de Duve, 2012).

Analytically located in the area of white-collar crime, the chapters that follow examine episodes of financial delinquency and discuss the way in which observers, including criminologists, shape an understanding of their causes and consequences. Manias, bubbles, and crashes are described alongside fraud and other forms of crime, including theft, in an attempt to uncover the relationship between financial conduct and its 'collateral' illicit by-products, be these the result of individual or collective acts. The financial sector itself, after all, is characterized by little firm knowledge and many uncertainties, by a form of ambiguity that makes it vulnerable to incursions by more or less respectable delinquents. It is the same ambiguity that surrounds fraud, which in order to be successful must not be recognized as such. The financial world offers numerous opportunities to blend licit and illicit conducts and to use deception, particularly for those who play a fiduciary role and are prone to exploit trust (Harrington, 2012). In trusted institutions, moreover, we find structures whose relationship to fraud is ambivalent at best, and often frankly complicit (Galbraith, 2004).

The following pages are inspired by views criticizing the translation of every good, affect, and being into money value. As Spinoza (1959) put it, money cannot be regarded as a 'digest for everything', because it changes the rhythm and spirit of life and affects the nature of social relations. In traditional societies, the rhythm of life was synchronized with seasons, births, deaths, mythical or practical events, while with money it is segmented into units, hourly rates, wages, interest, bonuses. According to Simmel (1978), money makes life more abstract and featureless, rendering it devoid of inner meanings. Moreover, money can be made invisible and non-existent to others: 'so the private individualistic nature of money finds its complete expression in the possibility of keeping it secret' (ibid: 385). Social relations become anonymous and are replaced by relations between computable values. Commodities themselves, along with their monetary value, take on an independent life, relating to each other rather than to those owning them (Marx, 1992). Ultimately, money expresses the violence inherent in social relations, and legitimizes power as the basis of its generalized acceptance (Aglietta and Orléan, 2002; Lordon, 2014; Dodd, 2014).

Anonymity, distance, calculability: these variables echo those commonly used in the description of white-collar crime, variables that we find in an unforgettable fictional example provided by Balzac (1966), when one of his characters ponders whether he would cause the death of someone unknown to him in exchange for a large sum of money.

We set off following the trajectory, in the Christian tradition, that led from a notion of money as a repugnant signal of greed and an obstacle to salvation to an important tool for securing salvation itself. St Francis had no more thought for money and gold than he had for stones, although he was aware of the threat hidden behind the fatal dictum: 'Render unto Caesar the thing's which are Caesar's, and unto God the things that are God's' (Buchan, 1997). By postponing the establishment of the kingdom of heaven, Christians could interpret this message to mean quite the opposite: accept and contribute to the establishment of the separate kingdom of mammon. While Aristotle found it abhorrent that money should give birth to money, Augustine had to concretely run a diocese and realistically deal with its material necessities: he was therefore adept at engaging with the trades of Babylon and could not escape *negotium* (Cacciari, 1996). Chapter 2, in brief, examines the relationship between money and salvation in the Christian consciousness.

In chapter 3 we shall see how love for money can turn into financial crisis. Focused on the Dutch 'tulip mania' and other bubbles that erupted in London and Paris, the chapter investigates the thoughts of early criminologists such as Beccaria and Bentham on the topic of finance and its criminogenic nature. It is in the economic writings of the two authors that several references are found to the subject matter, which is often only obliquely addressed through their analysis of luxury and usury. Financial crime was equated to accidents or calamities, or associated to unproductive economic conduct, idiocy, and abuse of trust. Surely, their depiction of the financial world appears as ambiguous as it remains today, although Beccaria and Bentham had to deal with an age in which the principles of economics still raised moral questions and were not, as they currently are, regarded as scientific or sacred.

Chapter 4 is a journey through the century of railways, robber barons, and financial distress. Investors, captains of industry,
and crooks were all participants in euphoric initiatives, which
led to bankruptcies and fraud, although guilt often tended to be
purged through the exercise of charity. The financial world, here,
developed its historical resistance against transparency, while
the law bowed to a notion of market self-regulation, therefore
establishing few obstacles to financial operators. Blaming smaller
dealers or petty embezzlers was common, although the major
culprits were singled out as the very victims of financial criminality, namely incautious and greedy investors engaged in what were
blatantly fraudulent exploits. The century also saw criminology
develop as a distinct discipline, and the chapter discusses the contributions of Quetelet, Lomborso, Ferri, Tarde, and others to the
analysis of financial delinquency.

If there is one financial crisis which persists in the collective
memory this is the crisis of 1929, when thousands gathered in
Wall Street confronted by police on horseback. Black Tuesday,
when Wall Street collapsed, is the theme of chapter 5, which analyses the causes and responses to the crisis from an economic and
a criminological perspective. Fraudulent schemes, mingled with
innovative financial strategies, created openings for swindlers
and adventurers, giving birth to definitions such as 'criminaloid'
and, in psychoanalysis 'coprophilia', an inadvertent return to the
medieval association of money with the excreta of the devil. The
work of pioneers such as Ross and Sutherland is focused upon the
contributions that forged the area of academic interest we designate as white-collar crime. Bonger also features in this chapter,
which documents a lively legacy we can still appreciate in contemporary studies of the crimes of the powerful.

Between the 1950s and 1970s attention given to financial crime
visibly declined. Whether this was due to the influence of the
media or to growing public tolerance vis-a-vis this type of criminality is still a matter for discussion. The crimes associated with
the Marshal Plan and the New Deal of the post-war period are the
subject of chapter 6, which is also concerned with the Eurodollar
crisis and the birth of treasure islands, the progenitors of offshore
financial markets. The analysis proposed by some psychologists
is discussed, alongside the work of Cressey, who perhaps polemically took an interest in embezzlers, excluded by Sutherland from
his research because they victimized employers not the general

public. The case of Equity Funding is explicated and accompanied by the reflections of Schur, who studied fraud from a sociological perspective. The chapter, finally, offers a series of insights derived from the studies of organizations and managers, which in that period complemented the analytical efforts of criminologists such as Geis, Pepinsky, Clinard, and many others.

We then move to the 1980s and 1990s, when financial crime was equated to rape. While the nascent neoliberal philosophy acquired maturity, financial delinquency, as examined in chapter 7, came to be regarded as a social problem due to public pressure and the unveiling of sensational scandals. The names of Drexel, Milken, Maxwell, and Leeson marked this period, along with cases such as the Savings and Loans crisis and the Bank on Credit and Commerce International. Sociologists and criminologists examined the relationships between individual financial delinquents and their criminogenic organizations, devoting increasing attention to the routine and the cycles of offending. Trust, techniques of neutralization, non-natural persons and labyrinths of agents, roles, and managers became the object of critical studies. The ubiquity of financial crime was a 'blessing' for criminologist, who developed increasingly thorough theoretical and empirical investigations.

WorldCom, Enron, Parmalat, and Madoff belong to the current century and feature together in chapter 8, where we encounter psychopathy, thrills, irresponsibility, anomalies, and inherent instability as the main themes and variables. After a concise florilegium of cases, the chapter deals with the financial crisis of 2008, offering observations and analyses from the criminological field. In response to arguments that the principles guiding the free-enterprise system are sound and that the crisis was precipitated by uncontrollable factors, networks of greed are described, involving bankers, politicians, and auditors. Financial delinquents are deemed metaphors of our times, facilitated by suitable targets and a lack of capable guardianship, while deception, abuse of trust, concealment, and secrecy constitute the main techniques they utilize. Corporate cultures and structures are studied in depth, while the financial system as a whole is equated to a mega-Ponzi scheme. In this chapter we reach the conviction that the long fight of religion versus mammon economics ends with the victory of economics itself as religion.

Stockholders are invited each year to the annual meeting, which, indeed, resembles a religious rite. There is ceremonial expression ... infidels who urge action are set aside (Galbraith, 2004: 34).

The regulatory proposals which followed the 2008 crisis constitute the subject of chapter 9, which looks at specific measures, binding or otherwise, purportedly designed to avert future crises. These measures, as we will discuss, were criticized or rejected for the constraints they imposed on the 'freedom' of markets, where freedom stood for normless conduct. When reluctantly applied, they were hollowed, disfigured, or diluted, therefore neutralized and deprived of their potential, if limited, efficacy. Partial and distorted applications of regulatory measures, however, were accompanied by the creation or expansion of grey financial areas impervious to regulation. The resulting 'different shades of grey' characterize now a financial world which accepts regulations only as far as they do not hamper a parallel process of deregulation. Financial markets, in this way, resemble illegal drugs markets, where enforcement in one place directs business elsewhere, producing a 'balloon effect' that bulges according to where it is squeezed.

Untouched by regulations, directives, and binding or unbinding memoranda of agreement, the growth of grey areas in the financial world mirrors the expansion of hidden markets hosting tax evasion, bribes, money laundering, and all other forms of dirty money which constitute the hidden wealth of nations. Chapter 10 addresses this hidden wealth, proposing a joint analysis of financial delinquency perpetrated by white-collar offenders and money laundering commonly attributed to conventional organized criminal groups. Zero-tax countries are visited which welcome a variety of actors irrespective of their curriculum vitae or criminal record: furtive money takes on its own identity regardless of who owns it. A mathematical form of morality takes shape and is embraced by individuals and groups located in networks where hybridity prevails, with respectable operators acting alongside respectable delinquents. The chapter concludes with the analysis of the specific criminal networks in which hidden wealth circulates and the fuzziness of those involved.

Some readers may be startled by the frequent, even obsessive use, in this book, of words such as 'delinquent' and 'delinquency' in relation to the financial world, especially those who are aware of labelling processes and refrain from describing all problematic conducts through the official terminology. I share with such readers an appreciation of critical views that there is no ontological reality in crime and delinquency and that criminal definitions change in time and space. It is indeed this change that concerns me. The delinquent label applied to the financial actors described in this book is intended to draw attention to the harm these actors produce: experience tells us that positive labelling and shaming (or positive moral entrepreneurship) have contributed to turning behaviours previously tolerated into unacceptable, revolting acts.

After reading this text for the umpteenth time, I feel humiliated, hurt in my identity as a critical scholar; I am infuriated for I am forced to put my 'radicalism' or 'extremism' in perspective. The reality of financial delinquency is far more radical and extreme than any member of the critical criminological community.

2

Money and Salvation

Whoever loves money never has money enough; whoever loves wealth is never satisfied with his income.

Keep your lives from the love of money and be content with what you have.

Better the little that the righteous have than the wealth of many wicked.

If you want to be perfect, go, sell your possessions and give to the poor, and you will have treasure in heaven.

No one can serve two masters. Either he will hate the one and love the other, or he will be devoted to the one and despise the other. You cannot serve both God and Money.

If you lend money to one of my people who is needy, do not be like a moneylender: charge him no interest.

For the love of money is a root of all kinds of evil.

Jesus entered the temple area and drove out all who were buying and selling there. He overturned the tables of the money-changers. 'It is written', he said to them, 'my house will be called a house of prayer, but you are making it a den of robbers'.

May your money perish with you, because you thought you could buy the gift of God with money.

You say 'I am rich; I have acquired wealth and do not need a thing'. But you do not realize that you are wretched, pitiful, blind and naked.

Now listen, you rich people, weep and wail because of the misery that is coming upon you. Your wealth has rotted, and moths have eaten your clothes. Your gold and silver are corroded. Their corrosion will testify against you and eat your flesh like fire.[1]

One wonders whether a feeble echo of these biblical precepts and admonishments was still heard by managers and staff of the

---

[1] All quotations are from the 1952 edition of *The Holy Bible* published in London by William Collins Sons & Co.

Vatican Bank (IOR) while they planned and enacted an array of financial offences. In 2015 the 'Bank of God' was charged with tax evasion, money laundering, and a series of illicit manipulations including insider dealing (Nuzzi, 2015; Fittipaldi, 2015). A committee created by Pope Francis was entrusted with the study of the financial and administrative condition of the Vatican and revealed greed and corruption among cardinals, who hijacked money destined for the poor, hid it in tax havens, and ignored money-laundering regulations. Its stocks and shares were found in less than virtuous multinationals such as Exxon, Dow Chemicals, and a number of arms producing companies. Very little of the money donated by Catholics worldwide to assist the poor and those suffering from war, disease, and disaster reached its official destination (Parks, 2016).

From the Good Life to the Just Reward

Biblical narratives of rich men and beggars can be visually intense, as Luke's story of Lazarus, who wishes to be fed the crumbs which fall from the table of a sumptuously clothed gentleman. When stray dogs lick the sores that cover Lazarus' body, the gentleman is not moved and gives him nothing. 'Both die: Lazarus goes to heaven, and the rich man to hell' (Leclercq, 1959: 31).

If a form of radical, divine justice traverses the Scriptures, the Christian world, at least initially, seemed at the same time to inherit the secular notion of the 'good life' from Greek philosophy. Those 'pagans' who spread such philosophy did not have the gift of grace, but achieved wisdom and virtue. Didn't Plato anticipate the concept of the Holy Spirit, which he described as the 'world soul' (Marenbon, 2015)? What Aristotle (1995) termed *eudaimonia*, namely a general feeling of wellbeing compounded by the awareness of living as best one can possibly do, chimed with a state of grace brought by communion with divinity. Echoing Aristotle's repugnance for the art of acquiring property, Mammon was deemed a source of evil: money, which the Greek philosopher regarded as a sham, a convention whose possession does not guarantee spiritual fulfilment, was equated by Christians to the excrements of the devil. Equally, the attitude towards usury reiterated the old repulsion for this activity, the basest example of acquisition for acquisition's sake, 'which makes barren metal breed', a form of unnatural gain pursued at the expense of others which makes 'currency the child of currency'

(Aristotle, 1995: 28). The prophet Ezekiel included usury among the other abominable things such as rape, murder, and robbery and, consistently, the books of Exodus prohibited it.

Similarly, in Dante's Inferno, there is little distinction between hypocrites, cheaters, thieves, fraudsters, and usurers: they are all immersed in the same kind of filth (Manguel, 2015). In Circle VII the poet does not stop to examine usurers, nor does he mention their names, because he does not want them to be remembered. Those who create money through money have no face, no individuality, they only have a purse. Here, his powerful verses convey disgust rather than pity (Dante, 1965). Cupidity is depicted as a she-wolf, who longs for empty things and threatens the entire society: her 'nature is so perverse and vicious that she never satiates her craving appetite, and after feeding, she's hungrier than before' (ibid: 94). The covetous are scattered in the Inferno, and in Circle IX is the greatest among them, Lucifer, who coveted the ultimate power of God himself.

Until the fourteenth century usurers could be excommunicated and denied Christian burial unless they gave back the interests they had charged, but accountants would attempt to avoid penalization by recording loans as investments (Gilchrist, 1969). Although still regarded as a sin, charging moderate interest for loans was slowly accepted, or at least deemed a venial sin, and in Purgatory usurers could atone for their greed. Similarly, merchant-bankers who professed to be good Christians had to justify their wealth and somewhat atone for their professional sin. They had to Christianize their own activity, for instance, by going to mass or giving money to the local parish. The Church, in effect, provided no clear guidelines around their job, although retaining the traditional diffidence towards money: the master of deceptions (Le Goff, 2010). The nascent financial activities made the position of the Church even more uncomfortable, forcing ecclesiasts to establish when earnings were legitimate and to what extent speculation was acceptable. Although engaged in economic activity, the Christian elite continued to officially scorn those whose operations in the market violated Christ's precept of fraternity among humans. These remained sinners, because their earnings relied upon the exploitation of time, their goods and finances being valorized through deferral. This was a sacrilege: time belongs to God. However, despised in the year AD 1000, some traders occupied a high rank during the years of the Renaissance. Usury, for example, was able to move freely in the Christian conscience when the invention of Purgatory made it a venial and redeemable sin (Le Goff, 1987).

Deviating from the precepts of St Chrysostom and St Ambrose, who preached that the sun, the stars, the rivers, and everything else had to be possessed in common, wealth appropriated by the rich slowly ceased to be scandalous. This became apparent between the eleventh and twelfth centuries, when in Europe money achieved some form of legitimacy and, despite the awareness of its danger-ousness, of it being an obstacle on the way to Salvation, found its place in the moral economy. First of all, the activity of those han-dling money was acknowledged as work, although money-lenders became rich while sleeping. The principle of utility also came into play: merchants and their financiers allowed the persistent links between the West and the East. Finally, the wealth accumulated, often, turned into patronage of art and culture, a way of tem-pering the sin of avarice. True, St Bernard scolded bankers but also teachers, the latter because they sold knowledge and science, which again belonged to God. However, the work of both was legitimized and came to be perceived as a useful contribution to humanity, therefore deserving of remuneration. St Paul, while preaching to 'love God and your neighbour', also made an impas-sionate plea to obey civic authorities and respect traders (Badiou, 1997; Welborn, 2015).

To sum up, greedy people knew that they were on the front line among the potential damned, but permanent contrition and repentance, through the practice of charitable acts, would give them hope of forgiveness. Their capital, therefore, was symboli-cally located in Purgatory, a great medieval invention, a place where sinful souls would purge with sorrow while waiting to be received in Paradise. As a definition of 'just' war took shape, a code of the 'just' reward for bankers and merchants was simul-taneously established, until the creative innovation introduced through the Antinomian Heresy rescued the rich. Thanks to this 'heresy', salvation was guaranteed irrespective of the sinful acts committed, because faith in itself would liberate humans from the duty to perform virtuous deeds; righteousness overrode morality and the law (Atwood, 2009). Finally, justification of private prop-erty found a solid base when the propertied were regarded as the only individuals endowed with the resources to potentially help the needy. Private ownership was seen as the best means of plac-ing goods at the disposal of others. On the other hand, echoing the precepts of the Talmud, the impoverished began to be seen not only as incapable of supporting themselves but also of helping others (Simon, 2009). And helping others contributed to the development of accounting, with notes, receipts, and bills recording transactions and donations. Companies started holding books whose front page would contain a religious formula: 'In the name of the Holy Trinity and of all the Saints and Angels of Paradise, or, more fittingly, In the name of God and profit' (Soll, 2014: 18). Something was lacking, however, from this benevolent picture of charitable souls, namely a 'scientific' rationalization of the effects generated by the new economic practices. St Bernardino provided such rationalization.

Saints and Economists

A missionary, reformer, and scholastic economist, St Bernardino of Siena was also the 'Apostle of Italy', born in Tuscany of a noble family. During the great plague that hit Siena in 1400, he helped the sick and then travelled extensively across the country to preach and take care of the needy. He refused to be elevated to Bishop for fear that leading a diocese would 'institutionalize' him and detach his daily life from that of the poor. Bernardino followed but also expanded Aquinas' teaching and wrote an entire work devoted to the 'purging' of economic activity. Composed during the years 1431–3, his *On Contracts and Usury* starts with a preliminary justification of private property to then dissect the ethics of trade, discuss values and prices, and conclude with a lengthy moral analysis of usury. Property provides a vital aliment to an efficient economic order, he stressed, while traders perform the essential function of moving goods from areas of surplus to areas of scarcity. They store and preserve products making them available when consumers require them, and those manufacturing such products transform raw materials into finished commodities. Of course, these activities may be carried out licitly or unlawfully, but all occupations, including that of a bishop, offer occasions for fraud and sin. All economic actors, on the other hand, deserve to gain profits as legitimate returns for their work, the expenses incurred, and the risks taken.

In St Bernardino we find a complete apologia of the entrepreneurial spirit, formed of managerial ability and intuition that deserve large remuneration. A rare combination of effectiveness and creativity, such spirit is fed by diligence, responsibility, labour, and assumption of risks. Producers and merchants show efficiency when they are able to assess the quality of products, establish the right price, and responsibly estimate risks and profit opportunities. Very few, he observed, are capable of doing all that. Prices are determined by the fluctuation of demand and supply, and goods requiring extra labour command higher prices. Governments, in this respect, could not and should not introduce regulations fixing market prices, or levels of wages, as the latter too are determined by the demand and supply of labour. Wage inequalities were justified by this saint-economist through the differences in skills, ability, and training required by specific occupations and the scarcity of those possessing them.

Before violently condemning usury, St Bernardino addressed another form of financial transaction in which hidden interest was charged, namely currency exchange. In this type of transaction, interest fluctuated along with the fluctuation of currencies themselves, thus presumably being more uncertain and risky than usury operations. St Bernardino argued that this specific form of interest was permissible in that currency conversion enabled international trade. However, the vigour that characterized him in the arena of personal morality, where he fought against all forms of 'filth', remained intact when dealing with usury. His benign analysis of the economic process turned into a frenzy, whereby money-lenders were equated to infectious and blasphemous individuals who took advantage of people borrowing for frivolous or vicious purposes. Usury concentrated money in a few hands and would bring the wrath of God, inviting the Four Horsemen of the Apocalypse. Those who 'sell time' commit a sacrilege:

[A]ll the saints and all the angels of paradise cry then against him [the usurer], saying 'To hell, to hell, to hell.' Also the heavens with their stars cry out, saying, 'To the fire, to the fire, to the fire.' The planets also clamor, 'To the depths, to the depths, to the depths' (Monroe, 2014: 134).

In a more nuanced analysis, however, Saint Bernardino appeared to justify the charging of interest in situations in which there was a clear *lucrum cessans*, that is to say when the money borrowed would be invested as productive capital. In his words:

Money then has not only the character of mere money or a mere thing, but also beyond this, a certain seminal character of something profitable, which we commonly call capital. Therefore, not only must its simple value be returned, but a super-added value as well (ibid: 141).

It is wonderful to note how a saint managed to strike a balance between the necessity of a financial doctrine and the perceived Christian immorality of counting money.

Not all saints, however, were economists, although some were well versed in business. St Teresa is shown in a sculpture of Bernini with her flung-back face as if she were asleep, or perhaps as if inebriated by pleasure. Her ecstasy made her a sumptuous icon of the Counter-Reformation, a physically towering figure hinting at the humanity of Christ and the Christians (Kristeva, 2015). After taking the vows, going into seclusion, and punishing herself by wearing prickly and torturous robes, she proved to be a perfect businesswoman. Unlike Catherine of Siena, she did not lick the pus from a cancerous breast but, as a form of sacrificial devotion, Teresa engaged in the fourth degree of prayer, which is rapture: 'This shows how the destitution of the self in the psych-soma begins with the sense of being distant from all things, in an acute state of melancholic loneliness' (ibid: 81). But at the same time she efficiently managed her new, innovative religious institution, thus reasserting the presence of God in business. When her brother returned from Peru, the money he brought back was invested in establishing a new convent in Seville, where nothing was left to chance: staff were employed to manufacture goods and carry out trading activities. And yet, she continued to submit to extravagant mortifications, and while praying she would obliterate her elementary needs until reaching a sensory regression, the exile from the self. The injuries she inflicted on herself were, in a sense, a response of Catholicism to its critics, a way of compensating though personal suffering the vulgar practices of the Church, including those in the financial sphere.

Faith and business observed an unprecedented radical separation in the *Spiritual Exercises*, published in 1548 by Ignatius Loyola. Here, we find that individuals were not required to reject the world and its riches, but to be 'indifferent' towards them, because perfection could be attained irrespective of material condition. Even those who possessed large wealth could live a godly life. 'You can possess riches without being spiritually hurt by them if you merely keep them in your home and purse, and not in your heart' (Strier, 2011: 198).

Afterlife and Wealth

Money also entered the Christian consciousness through the invisible path uniting the living and the dead. The wealthy and those who imitated them gave pious donations in order to reserve a place in heaven for themselves and their loved ones, included the deceased. The living took care of the dead and their efforts had significant social and symbolic repercussions. The other world was inhabited by the souls of the departed but also by the bodies of those still living, both regarded as incomplete creatures in need of one another. Privileged burials were arranged close to the shrines of the martyrs or in exclusive chapels in abbeys, convents, and great churches, shaping a proper economy that incorporated life and death. The money donated was 'the ransom of the soul' (Brown, 2015). It was associated with the price paid by Christ for redeeming humanity and ensured a flow of wealth towards the Christian churches (Brown, 2012). At times the poor would benefit from the generosity of the rich, who nevertheless focused their efforts on funding artists and architects: the acts of donation constituted the transfer of treasure from earth to heaven. Jesus himself had said that those who give away all their possessions will find them stored in Paradise, where they will be safe from moths and thieves.

More than the amounts of money being transferred, the continuity of the transfer was crucial, as almsgiving had to become an everyday habit and the Christian ethic a form of commonsense. Augustine equated trade with charity: the former required taking risks in moving goods across lands and seas without the certainty of profit, the latter, equally, entailed sending value to a distant land. And it was God who wanted Christians to act as merchants of sort, encouraging them to engage in this long-distance deal, this travelling without travelling that ensured the salvation of the soul. Thus wealth, heaven, and the poor were joined, in a blatantly commercial logic whereby placing treasure in heaven corresponded to a kind of advanced purchase. The wealth moved upwards thanks to a hidden device similar to a *machinamentum*, which transformed the movement of a wheel into vertical motion, bringing objects from low to high locations. 'Alms came to embrace three pious causes—care of the poor, support for the clergy, and the building and maintenance of churches' (Brown, 2015: 94).

This distributive system of wealth, however, was controversial, because the existence of wealth itself was subject to denunciation: without wealthy people the poor would not exist! On the other hand, as we have seen, without wealthy people who would be in a position to give relief to the poor? Hence the partial acceptance of accumulation, which among other things provided the financial stability and superiority sought by the Church in a changing economic climate, where a new urban elite was emerging. In a parallel theological development, even sin evoked financial issues. 'Sin was no longer seen as a load that could be lifted only by the heavy rituals of sacrifice associated with an archaic, agrarian society. Sin was a debt' (ibid: 97). Nietzsche (1968) saw this very clearly, when he noted that the Christian logic encapsulated the notion of equivalence, whereby offences against God and Christians could be translated, via an appropriate coefficient, into material value: God was like a debt collector working on behalf of the Church.

The appreciation of money was also forged through the bridging of the sacred and the profane enacted by the practice of gift giving. The worlds of ascetic monks and wealthy merchants could thus be joined thanks to donations which put the sinful market operations conducted by the latter in perspective. Here, the poor were excluded from the exchange, as monks and nuns were their intercessors. The generous donors, in their turn, paid an advance fine for their economic activity and attachment to money. Their power as funders of monasteries and convents turned into freedom in the financial sphere.

The precepts of Christianity, however, could still claim validity. For example, donors engaged in financial activity, through faith, turned what in them was corruptible into incorruption; moreover, having given their soul to God, they had clothed themselves with something that could not decay: the eternal spirit. As Luke said, they could now walk through the fire, and not be burned: the Lord would heal all their diseases, while their acts would enjoy the perpetual reprieve called the 'technique of Jesus'. Finally, as in the Gospel of John, love for God alone led to confidence for the day of judgment.

The Parable of the Debtors

Faith, therefore, conferred immunity, but those who withdrew from the world would never obtain the kingdom of heaven.

Redemption was work and consisted of buying back the world, piece by piece and activity by activity, although this divine purchase entailed the abandonment of everything, beginning with one's egotism (Ellul, 2010). In the *Parable of the Debtors*, Matthew compared heaven with the marketplace, governed by a king who brings his accounts up to date with servants who have borrowed money from him. The king forgives one of his debtors, who instead sends to prison someone else who borrowed money from him. The sovereign, in response, calls the servant he had forgiven and says: 'You evil servant! I forgave you that tremendous debt because you pleaded with me. Should you have mercy on your fellow servant, just as I had mercy on you?' Then the angry king sends the man to prison to be tortured until he has paid his entire debt. But if Matthew was in favour of redeeming debts as a form of rejection of money and its temptation, how did he become the patron saint of accountants, tax collectors, and bankers? In Matthew, in fact, the renunciation of riches was not a moral instruction and the poverty proposed by Jesus was a mere recommendation, which needed not be carried out to achieve salvation (Leclercq, 1959).

A closer analysis shows that Matthew, following St Bernardino, advocated forgiveness only for debts that had been invested in some form of productive or financial venture. In his *Parable of the Talents*, a man gave his servants some golden coins to hold and manage, only to discover, later, that the coins had been buried. His fury was triggered by the realization that those coins had not been invested: the servants should have entrusted them to a banker in order to secure some interest (Soll, 2014).

The economic exchange between the kingdom of heaven and Christians was based on the conception of humanity enslaved by Satan, with God 'buying back this humanity by striking a deal of sorts with Satan by paying him the price of his son' (Ellul, 2010: 171). Augustine had stated this very clearly: Christ was a merchant who bought the rebirth and eternal life of humanity by stretching his arms on the Cross. Redeeming humanity was a form of deal-making, and Satan appeared as an insatiable seller epitomizing the adorers of Mammon, for whom everything had a price and nothing could be given as gift. In this sense, money was the mark of the devil, whereas God, in contrast, gave everything for free: He did not demand a return for the love he gave. This biblical justice seemed far removed from the principles guiding markets, where debts were not forgiven and human affairs followed the rules of greed. The original debt was paid by God so that humans could be given the freedom to forget the debts of others, but could persons aspire to replicate the acts of God? The rule of money, on the other hand, would bring destructive conflicts, to the building of Babylon, the great prostitute where economic and political power resided. Babylon exemplified the loss of trust, faith, and love, now only found in economic exchange. 'The prostitute holds a golden cup in imitation of what God does: the establishment of a communion; but in her sense, it is communion with her corruption' (ibid: 228). Destroying Babylon, therefore, amounted to the annihilation of the logic of money and markets, and what was left was humanity. But again, even this destruction was part of the deal, of the divine buying back what Satan had appropriated.

Economic exchange, ultimately, was embedded in the relationship between sin and intercession, as the impurity of humans required constant offerings, a permanent movement of finances within the community of believers.

Innocence and Idolatry

Mysticism was not the only device put in place as a response to the Protestant Reformation. With the Council of Trento in 1563, the Catholic counterattack included the display of spirituality and devotion in the form of beauty, as if enemies (and even God) could be awed by aesthetic exhibitions of faith. The extraordinary Baroque churches and the unparalleled efflorescence of religious art were part of the publicity campaign to compete with Protestantism (Jameson, 2015b). Painters and architects joined armies and inquisitors to reassert authority and restore an image tarnished by corruption.

In the face of Protestantism, the Church decides to advertise and to launch the first great publicity campaign on behalf of its product. After Luther, religion comes in competing brands; and Rome enters the contest practicing the usual dual strategy of carrot and stick, culture and repressions, painters and architects on the one hand and generals and the Inquisition on the other (ibid: 3).

But the display of such treasures had the unintended consequence of depicting the Catholic elite, yet again, as extravagant idolaters worshiping their own shallow and glamorous religious expressions. In some classics of Protestant literature, not surprisingly, the Catholic power system was described as sinful, a materialistic pestilence spreading through Christianity.

John Bunyan, born in 1628 near Bedford in England, was brought up amid the religious fervour that culminated in the civil war, when Puritanism was sweeping the country in opposition to the papist views of the monarchy. He heard voices 'not of this world', and at the age of ten was already oppressed by religious guilt, whereas at eighteen he denounced himself as a sinner. In 1645 he marched with Cromwell's troops, and his obsessive religiosity absorbed the martial traits needed by preachers and crusaders. The first part of his masterpiece, *The Pilgrim's Progress*, was published in 1678 while the author was serving a prison sentence imposed by the restored monarchic authority. In the book we encounter Mr Great-heart, who guides the pilgrims to the celestial country, and Mr Honest, who warns against street robbers. His appeal is addressed to determined believers who are prepared to fight, 'for a Christian can never be overcome, unless he should yield himself' (Bunyan, 1952: 261). The pilgrims come from the town of Stupidity or the city of Destruction, and escape from greed, vulgarity, and hypocrisy. But this is what they find while their pilgrimage progresses, when they reach the town of Vanity. The town is inhabited by 'bad men', although its residents also include Mr Contrite, Mr Holyman, Mr Love-saints, Mr Dare-not-lie, and Mr Penitent. The daily life of these 'good men' is a struggle against homicidal monsters and the lure of material goods. Outside the town stands the hill of Lucre, where the silver mine exerts its 'attractive virtue upon the foolish eye' (ibid: 295). But not far away there are the Delectable Mountains, where sincere Christians can rest, and Mount Innocence, where Godly-men (Protestants) wear a white garment that remains immaculate when Prejudice and Ill-will (Catholics) throw dirt at them.

Whoever they be that would make such men dirty, they labour all in vain; for God, by that a little time is spent, will cause that their innocence shall break forth as the light, and their righteousness as the noonday (ibid: 302).

The innocence of the chosen stands pure despite the tempta-
tions of vanity which marks its apotheosis in the recurrent fairs.
Here, all sorts of things are sold and bought: honours, titles,
lust, pleasure. Delights of all sorts are offered: whores, bawds,
wives, husbands, children, masters, servants, lives, blood, bodies, souls, silver, gold, pearls, precious stones, and what not.

> And moreover at this fair there are at all times to be seen jugglings, cheats,
> games, plays, fools, apes, knaves and rogues, and that of every kind. Here
> are to be seen too, and that for nothing, thefts, murders, adulteries, false-
> swearers, and that of a blood-red colour (ibid: 98).

Lavish and lascivious, Catholicism was also deemed idolatrous,
its places of worship resembling the vanity fairs just described. In
Paradise Lost, atonement for one's sins is not achieved through
the building of altars, but through the intimate experience of
the presence of God. John Milton (1968) saw in Adam and Eve
primeval examples of idolatry, the former for his worshiping of
objects, the latter for her narcissism, for her placing her faith into
herself. Milton referred to Solomon's temple as *Pandaemonium*,
an artifact that deviates from its original nature as a place of
devotion to become an opulent but shallow object of adoration.
Pandaemonium, however, can also allude to the Basilica of St
Peter and the Pantheon, where Catholics practised their false
faith and where authorities perfected their claim to ruling by
divine right. Milton's epic poem is based on a theological argument which particularly emphasizes free will and human frailty,
along with the danger of pride. The fallen angels are led by Satan,
who gathers his followers to inform them that a new world is
being built and plans his mission to disrupt the project. Satan
possesses a decaying beauty, a splendour obfuscated by sadness
and death: he is majestic though in ruin. But these qualities are
deceptive and serve him solely as weapons to tempt humans as
well as Christ. He offers Jesus, who is not a divine figure but
as exposed to temptation as Milton himself, the possession of
Greece, its art and poetry, but the offer is rejected. Acceptance
would have meant the victory of arrogance over the light of
humble faith and Christian virtue. The true light is not found in
Athens, but in Jerusalem (Praz, 1967).

Paradise Lost is set in an ideal universe, beautiful, simple, and
symmetrical. In the imaginary astronomy constructed by Milton,

the earth is purified and pristine, and its inhabitants value nature and together pursue unflawed beauty (Fowler, 1968). The 'fallen' world, on the other hand, is epitomized by those who 'prevent the best things to worst virtue abuse, or to their meanest use' (Milton, 1968: 203).

While regarding Catholics as spiritually deficient, Milton followed the idealism of Dante and Petrarch, combining it with the principles of liberal Puritanism. He modelled his work on the Italian masterpieces he knew well and provided a magnificent portrait of the enemy that obsessed the English Reformation as a whole, the devil. Against such enemy, he prefigured the establishment of a community of saints, arranged according to the principles of a republican oligarchy, but after the Restoration in 1660 he accepted that his plan to regenerate the country had failed. *Paradise Lost* illuminates the splendid, darkens the gloomy, and aggravates the dreadful; it is one of those books, as Johnson (2009) remarked, that the reader admires and puts down, and forgets to take up again. It is a poem on civil war, where Heaven and Hell fight impious battles and that the author, who applauded his compatriots for the execution of Charles I, wrote in fetters when dealing with angels and at liberty when addressing the devils: 'he was a true poet and of the devil's party without knowing it' (Blake, 1994). Perhaps he was indeed of the devil's party, and yet Shelley (1994) dreamed that Milton's spirit rose and shook all human things built in contempt of humans, shaking thrones and sacrilegious altars.

The Reformation fought against sacrilegious altars, the scourge of Christianity symbolized by the adoration of dead things mistaken for God. In the Book of Knowledge, idolaters rest their hope on works of gold and silver, or on useless stones made by human hands. In Exodus, God is possessive and does not accept the existence of other divinities: those who adore false gods will be punished through three or four generations. Idolatry, however, came in two types: the former addressed to natural phenomena, the latter to idols created by humans, such as money. Against it, God gave the earth, which must be cultivated and attended to, as humans are not required to merely contemplate or worship creation, but inhabit and possess it (Petrosino, 2015). Ultimately, against the 'fall' caused by idolatry, with the Protestant Reformation the principle of possession received a powerful rehabilitation.

Rabelais and the Spirit of Capitalism

Most readers, at this juncture, would expect a timely reference to the work of Max Weber and his association of the Protestant ethic with the spirit of capitalism. But before delivering the due homage to Weber, it might be worth examining the arguments of a Renaissance man, long predating him, on the relationship between religion and money. Rabelais witnessed the fight between the interests of the Catholic and the Protestant oligarchies and proposed a solution that would satisfy both. This 'compromise' was theorized by Panurge in his monologue on lenders and borrowers, where creditors and debtors were urged to create economic harmony like the 'purification process' produces blood in the organism. God never imposed on humans to be debt-free, because lenders and borrowers can contribute to the spread of mutual love and solidarity. For example, creditors are inclined to wish their debtors a long and wealthy life. Therefore, those who lend money are gorgeous and admirable persons, while those who don't are as ugly as demons.

Imagine a universe without creditors and debtors: there would be no rule among the different entities. Jupiter, not recognizing his debt towards Saturn, would deprive it of its orbit. Saturn would ally with Mars and throw all the elements upside down, while Mercury will refuse to provide any service to anybody. Venus would not be venerated because she had not leant anything, while the Moon would be dark: why should the Sun lend her its light? (Rabelais, 1993: 331).

In this eccentric economic philosophy, people must owe something, lest no one feels an elementary feeling of obligation towards the others and the system in which they cohabit. Without debts nobody would help their neighbours and the world would be devoid of faith, hope, and charity, replaced by diffidence, indifference, and rancour. By analogy, an organism rejecting credits and debts would see the brain refusing to guide the eyes, feet, and hands, while the hands would refuse to do anything for the brain. The heart would give up working, the lungs would not lend its services, and the liver would stop functioning, while the bladder, denying its debts, would suppress urine. 'Soon the body would putrefy and the soul, with indignation, would run to meet the devils, chasing money' (ibid: 332).

In the four volumes published by Rabelais between the 1530s and 1540s, Bakhtin (1981) noted that everything of value achieves its full potential, expanding spatially and temporally. Gold and wealth grow because growth is inherent in their nature, and because the laws of the economy, like Rabelais' prose, create surprising logical links, unexpected connections, and unpredictable outcomes. *Gargantua et Pantagruel* depicts the distortion of things brought by economic initiative, the departure of material life from religious tradition, and the official ideology. 'Thus, in Rabelais, the destruction of the old picture of the world and the positive construction of a new picture are indissolubly interwoven with each other' (ibid: 169). His new world brings even the lofty and spiritual things in contact with food and drink, and two whole chapters of his book offer thick lists of dishes and appetizers. The struggle of Catholicism with Protestantism, and particularly with Calvinism, is portrayed as a struggle between King Lent and the Sausages that inhabit Savage Island. Both sides are composed of warrior-cooks armed with iron spits, frying pans, kettles, pots, mortars, and pestles. Rabelais was just realistically describing how the world was evolving, distancing itself from the false asceticism of both Catholics and Protestants, and perhaps suggesting that gluttony and drunkenness had long flourished in monasteries and dioceses.

Gargantua et Pantagruel was banned as was the painting dedicated to its author by Honoré Daumier, where Louis-Philippe is swallowing bags of coins handed over to him by miserable men and women. Daumier pleaded guilty in 1832, was fined and sentenced to six months in prison.

It is ironic that such manifestations of Gargantuan greed were ignored by Max Weber (1948; 1977), who chose to focus on the rationality of emerging economic activity as an extension of the rational restraints simultaneously emerging in the religious realm. In his classical text, Weber scrutinized the absolute values of the Protestant ethics which had a particular elective affinity with the spirit of capitalism. His entrepreneurs were pious and thrifty, a variety that perhaps was mainly found in the English industrial revolution. 'To what church do you belong?' was the question encountered by entrepreneurs establishing themselves in markets and making new social contacts, as if faith could guarantee respect of credit relations. In a personal communication, Weber tells of a salesman who conceded that, although 'everybody may believe or not believe as they please', he would be extremely cautions in dealing with a businessman not belonging to any church. 'I wouldn't trust him with fifty cents. Why pay me, if he doesn't believe in anything?' (Weber, 1948: 303). Admission to a congregation was recognized as a guarantee of the moral qualities required in business matters, and ultimately determined the creditworthiness of acolytes.

The accumulation of money, surely, required an inner-worldly form of asceticism, self-esteem, and self-interest, a conduct inspired by a methodical, rational way of life which, in Weber, paved the way for the spirit of modern capitalism. These values are the foundations of individualism and were 'placed at the service of maintaining and propagating the bourgeois Puritan ethic, with all its ramifications' (ibid: 321). Marx had already seen this connection, when he pointed out that the cult of money was enveloped in its own asceticism, requiring self-denial and self-sacrifice. In the *Grundrisse*, he examined the relationship between the economy and 'frugality, contempt for the mundane, temporal and fleeting pleasures', and concluded by noting the 'connection between English Puritanism or also Dutch Protestantism and money-making' (Marx, 1973: 232).

The values identified by Marx and Weber, on the other hand, entailed a form of hypocrisy and opportunism, as they might turn into operative means which were, as Weber put it, beyond good and evil. Means that were beyond good and evil were not only used by entrepreneurs guided by Weberian substantive rationality, they were also put in place by adventurers who were substantially irrational and untouched by the spirit of 'formalistic impersonality'. Perhaps Weber neglected how charlatans and businessmen possessed similar picaresque characteristics. Along with working, praying, and saving, success also arrives through pleasure, invention, and foolishness, as we shall see in the chapters to come.

Economics and Religion

Catholics and Protestants, while being avariciously attached to money, had the problem of maintaining their religious faith detached from it. Attachment and detachment, on the other hand, could not be achieved through an intermittent movement between the material and the spiritual, but had to be established in a permanent fashion by means of clearly dividing boundaries. A process of separation and differentiation helped divide material greed from ascetic yearning and turned them into two autonomous spheres of human practice and sensitivity. The crucial significance, in this respect, of the Antinomian Heresy has been mentioned earlier. Financial interest and religious belief came to co-exist in a multiple reality composed of relatively isolated domains, each guided by specific principles and values. The creation of distinct academic disciplines was among the outcomes of this process of separation, whereby from the initial magma constituted by theology, they differentiated into subareas of enquiry and knowledge. Philosophy separated itself from theology, and the law and the natural sciences from philosophy (Jameson, 2015). Meanwhile economics claimed its independence from ethics, and at the same time politics got the upper hand on philosophy (Arendt, 2015).

In the analysis of Hannah Arendt, the millenarian conflict between philosophy and politics starts with Socrates' trial. The great philosopher loved talking to his co-citizens in the agora, the place of the market and of public meetings. Socrates, who never wrote anything, stimulated his interlocutors to examine their own convictions, asking ironic questions and asserting counterintuitive truths. He was charged with corrupting the young, as is well known, while in fact he exposed the corrupt in the political and economic spheres. In both spheres, he saw individuals and groups acting out of volition and choice, but claiming their good faith and describing the negative outcomes of their action as unintended consequences. In a dialogue of Socrates with Hippias, the former argues that 'good' people who cause harm voluntarily are worse than 'bad' people, whose actions are not controlled by volition and choice (Plato, 2005). The trial of Socrates, in brief, marked 'the prejudices that the polis had against philosophy [which] are the same that economists have towards religion' (Arendt, 2015: 28). For Socrates, political and economic power as domination could only be countered through the visible manifestation of an ethics, namely the natural outcome of an ethos, a conduct which is deeply rooted in the way of life of individuals.

The separation of economics from religion (and ethics) can also be located within the development of selective interests in social systems described by Luhmann (1985). This process isolates single human spheres into specific settings while limiting and localizing expectations. Selectivity, according to Luhmann, helps reduce the complexity of human life, prompting the adoption of a blasé attitude for discerning among the large amount of stimulations and needs we experience. The separation of the divine from the economic sphere became a necessity for systems to survive and achieve what was thought to be a degree of security, safety, and stability. By the same token, the reduction of complexity led economics to 'invent' its own ethical principles, a process that prompted Max Weber (1978) to argue that markets are antithetic to all other communities, because the latter, not the former presuppose amicable feelings among people. The most striking antithesis between markets and communities, according to Weber, is found less in economic action as such than in 'economically oriented action'. This phrase refers to: a) every action which, though primarily oriented to other ends, takes account of economic considerations; and b) every action which, though primarily oriented to economic ends, makes use of physical force as a means. 'It thus includes all primarily non-economic action and all non-peaceful action which is influenced by economic considerations' (ibid: 64).

Although connected to the spirit of economic development, as Weber indicated, faith nevertheless became essentially noetic, exclusively inhabiting the intellect, an abstraction cultivated within the intimacy of emotions. For this reason, Christianity as a whole, as Arendt (2015) suggested, can be said to offer possibilities of escaping guilt, avoiding responsibility, and neutralizing inner conflicts. Abstract faith buried in the intimacy of thoughts and emotions rendered Christianity a powerful source of conformism, with 'subjectivity structured on the basis of normativity and the lack of critical judgment' (ibid: 104).

Some critical or 'social' Christians may object that this process is far from being accomplished and that the fight between spiritual and material needs is still ongoing. True, religion is like philosophy: it offers the 'pathos of wonder' so that the dogmatism of mere opinion is avoided. Religion, as we have seen, had also an important guiding function in the acceptance or rejection of the changes occurring in the economic sphere. Judaic and Christian faith put salvation as the ultimate goal and the realization of the Kingdom as the supreme achievement. These eschatological faiths were against the notion of cyclical returns that characterized pre-Christian religions. In *The City of God*, Augustine (2003) had no interest in the history of the world: while for the Greeks history was knowledge of the past, for the Christians history was projected onto the future, when its ultimate goals would be achieved. The idea of endless cyclical periods, therefore, was rejected because eternal repetition was judged deleterious for humanity and destructive of hope. The theory of the eternal return of the identical excluded the very possibility of thinking about the definitive grace (happiness) brought by the advent of the Redeemer: thus, time was not repeatable.

The Christian eschatology, revolving around ultimate goals, was transformed by the Enlightenment into the notion of progressive history. Simultaneously, the Church became increasingly involved in economic activity, until the sixteenth-century Reformation enacted the crucial rupture by joining the earthly project of inner growth with individual improvement, collective development, and economic initiative. Christianity became secularized, a fact of personal consciousness, but at the same time also generated a range of collective political and economic rules. The faith in the salvific function of work, sacrifice, and thrift replaced the hope for the advent of the Redeemer; 'hope' was incorporated in voluntarism in the form of 'activity' and faith was subjugated to worldly powers (Carandini, 2012).

Other notions and topoi underwent a similar evolution. Providence, for example, which derives from the Latin word *providentia*, entails notions of imagination and foresight. These notions became intertwined with future progress, while salvation was assimilated to development. This process of secularization produced a conversion of Christian eschatology into a utopian philosophy of history, and more precisely the transformation of the theological concept of the end of time through Christ into the enlightened faith in endless progress. It transformed eschatology into progressive history and the divine project of salvation, which was earlier inscrutable, into a project for a future consistent with the ideology of the rampant economic elite.

The virtue of Prudence, in its turn, was associated with that of Providence. In the past, for instance in Aquinas, prudence was not a form of permanent precaution or spiritual pettiness, but contained precepts relating to *recta ratio agibilium*, appropriate criteria for action. Slowly, prudence was turned into mere obedience to formal rules, while laws, including economic 'laws', were placed above virtues (Zamagni, 2015). Markets became the place of human and civil progress, while prudence denoted behaviour oriented towards self-interest.

Economics was not allowed friendliness, it was only required to describe human motivations as pure and simple and devise models bereft of such things as goodwill and moral sentiments. As Sen (1987: 1–2) argued, it is extraordinary that economic thought evolved in this way, describing human goals in such spectacularly narrow terms, also because 'economics is largely an offshoot of ethics'. The 'laws' of economics, therefore, became a-historical, like those found in the natural sciences or in physics. This naturalization of the economy could take place because the Christian sensibility was receptive of the new 'laws'; economic principles and rules were already part of the affective register that from Augustine to St Bernardino had brought the norms of Christianity closer to those of economics.

Norms act on us from all sides, that is, in multiple and sometimes con-tradictory ways; they act upon a sensibility at the same time that they form it; they lead us to feel in certain ways, and those feelings can enter into our thinking (Butler, 2015: 5).

The relationship between Christianity and economics returned in Hegel (1948) in a singular way. In a fragment on love, his analy-sis focused on the negotiation believers carry out between their individuality and their belonging to a community of faith. As individuals, they are holders of objects, property, and posses-sions, but as believers, they have to renounce them, submit to sacrifice, and negate themselves. The possessions thus abandoned become dead matter, and believers who intend to still maintain a 'living' relation with them have to split their personality into two segments: one bound to spiritual life, the other to dead items. In Hegel, however, participation in a religious community is not an individualistic act but implies communion with other subjects who inhabit the world from which the believer derives. 'For Hegel, the subject discovers that other human beings are part of its own identity, that in relating to others the human subject enacts (or actualizes) some of its own most fundamental capacities' (Butler, 2015: 125). In sum, the personality split theorized by Hegel does not legitimize a *homo economicus* characterized by self-love and self-sufficiency, a solipsistic and self-satisfying individual who deems the world outside the self unnecessary (Ruggiero, 2013). However, his thought is not radical enough to lead him to equate economic success, or love for dead matter, with necrophilia.

Inspired, indeed, by a radical perspective, the anti-Hegelian theology of Kierkegaard (1983a; 1983b) posited that the human and social worlds have to be transcended and that faith requires a perennial practice of infinite inwardness. The intimacy of faith, finally, allows for greed in the material life to be separated and marginalized as trivial, unworthy of ethical assessment. This type of love for the infinite advocated by Kierkegaard does not imply that believers turn their back to gold and leave it alone as, 'the wise leave flowers without plucking them' (Shaw, 2010: 7). Humans will pluck the gold up, toiling underground and over-ground night and day until, having built a Plutonic empire, they think they are masters of the world.

The Triumph of Plutus

The scene is set for the triumph of Plutus, the god despised and adored in Greek mythology and in the Roman imagination, both immersed in the ethical dilemmas faced by consciousness in rela-tion to money. In the Greek mythology Ploutos (or Plutus) refers to wealth, he is blind and lame, indiscriminate, and awkward and clumsy in accumulating riches. In Aristophanes' comedy he is depicted as an old man distributing riches to people whose moral standards would disqualify them from any gift, while elsewhere he appears as a juvenile holding a cornucopia held in the arms of Eirene, the goddess of peace or Tykhe, the goddess of fortune (Kerényi, 2002). A son of Demeter, the goddess of agriculture, he may symbolize the random dynamics whereby wealth is dis-tributed blindly to individuals who have no particular moral or civic merit. Plutus, in effect, lacks judgment and is fearful, being terrified by potential thieves who might appropriate his treasures. He is painted with wings, as he is inclined to retreat swiftly when in danger. Aristophanes juxtaposes his wealth to the poverty of many, suggesting through his character Penia that wealth can be inimical to the arts, science, and virtues, but despite these author-itative warnings, when Plutus recovers his sight in the temple of Aesculapius, the temples of other gods are neglected, and all sac-rifices are offered to him.

The theme of Plutocratic empire returns in Wagner's *Das Rheingold*, where the conflict between devoting oneself to love and other fruitful and creative activities and the desire to single-heartedly gather riches is examined. In the interpretation offered by George Bernard Shaw (2010: 8), the choice is almost inevitable when Plutonic power is such that all higher human needs and impulses are regarded as frivolous or rebellious, 'and even the mere appetites are denied, starved, and insulted when they cannot purchase their satisfaction with gold'. Plutocratic societies are inhabited by greedy individuals with strong bodies and fierce passions, but also with a brutish narrowness of mind and selfishness of imagination: 'too stupid to see that [their] own welfare can only be composed as part of the welfare of the world' (ibid: 9). In Wagner's opera the tempo quickens when greed, servitude, and evil are described, when a bright light illuminates the rocks at the bottom of the Rhine, revealing gold. The strings accompany the Rheinemaidens' joyous hymn to the treasure they guard, while the chorus announces that a ring conferring limitless power can be fashioned from the Rhine gold to those who forswear the power of love. The hunchbacked dwarf Alberich declares his curse on love, 'and wrests the gold away with terrible force. He scrambles off with it, deaf to the lamenting cries of the Rhinemaidens' (Millington, 2006: 517). This world described by Wagner is not inhabited by humans, but by dwarfs, giants, and gods, and the gods are certainly not of a higher order than humans. On the contrary, the world is waiting for humans to redeem it from the lame government of the gods, and 'from the instinctive, predatory, greedy, and the patient, toiling, stupid, respectful, money-worshipping people' (Shaw, 2010: 29).

Plutus appears in paintings and fables, in England as an allegory of political corruption, in France in popular songs and comedies. Among the latter, is *The Triumph of Plutus*, written by Marivaux in 1728, in which Apollo is amused by Plutus' plan to steal his lover: how can an old and ugly god be his rival in love matters? But disguised as a financier, Plutus corrupts the woman's friends and guardians with his riches, and his plan comes to a victorious conclusion. Apollo cannot but accept his loss, which is a sign of the time, when greed rules the hearts, and when the gifts of music, dance, and love are shunned (Marivaux, 2013).

The triumph of Pluto transformed economists into catechists who spread the faith of monetary value that would bring salvation. In the words of Marx (1973: 727), this led to 'faith in money value as the immanent spirit of commodities, faith in the mode of production and its predestined disposition, faith in the individual agents of production as mere personifications of self-valorizing capital'. Later, Benjamin (1997) theorized that capitalism had developed into a religion and economics into theology, formed of unalterable components, ultimate and closed, which cannot be superseded. The economy is a 'cult', he stressed, and it is a permanent one, in the sense that it is celebrated on a daily basis: every day is mass day, and its sacred pageantry is displayed constantly. 'This religious structure of capitalism is not only, as Weber would have it, a formation determined by religion, but a religious phenomenon in itself' (ibid: 84).

We shall see in the next chapter how economics as religious phenomenon replaced sin with crisis.

3

Between Sin and Crisis

The financial crisis known as the 'Dutch tulip mania' led to tulip bulbs being traded for very large sums of money throughout the 1620s and 1630s. The 'mania' resulted in a twenty-fold increase in the average price of bulbs and, ultimately, in the sudden crash of the market. This crisis has long captured the imagination of commentators, who question why groups of individuals were prepared to pay the equivalent of several years' income for a single bulb. In a fictional but realistic reconstruction of those events, Amsterdam is described as awash with capital, populated by frenzy dealers, a place where arts are flourishing, 'fashionable men and women stroll along its streets and the canals mirror back the handsome houses in which they live' (Moggach, 2000: 24). The *Semper Augustus* bulb was sold for six fine horses, a dozen sheep, two dozen silver goblets, and a seascape by celebrated painter van de Velde. True, rare tulip bulbs were mainly traded among wealthy aficionados, but the mania did not only affect collectors of luxury items, it also involved a rampant new class of traders guided by speculative purposes (Bilginsoy, 2015). The sublime flower was of extraordinary beauty, displaying blue, white, and crimson colours and at one point, in monetary terms, was worth more than a Rembrandt. A classic description of *tulipmania* appeared in Clarence Mackay's (2004) *Memoirs of Extraordinary Popular Delusions and the Madness of Crowds*, where the author observed that the ordinary activities of the country were neglected and the population, even to its 'lowest dregs', embarked on the tulip trade.

Although the tulip had previously captivated the Bavarians, the Persians, and rulers of the Ottoman Empire, it was in Holland that the mania found its most fertile ground, reflecting the Golden Age experienced by the country in the early seventeenth century. Resources were poured into commerce and merchants opted for lucrative trade with the East Indies or, at home, appropriated rare bulbs. The price of bulbs grew constantly throughout the 1630s, attracting wave after wave of speculators, including farmers and artisans. A futures market developed, with business spreading in taverns, brothels, and barracks. Bulbs were sold when they were still in the ground, with operations taking the form of contracts for future payment and delivery. Distant echoes of contemporary futures markets could be detected in a trade that seemed to rest on empty promises, entrusted to the changing wind.

Tulip mania reached its peak during the winter of 1636–7, when some bulbs were changing hands ten times in a day. But the crash followed soon afterwards, when debtors became insolvent and in a week the flowers lost 99 per cent of their previous market value (Garber, 1989; 2000; Dash, 1999). When the bubble burst in early February 1637, 'buyers for the most part would not pay, and sellers were left holding the bulbs. An obvious folly came to its apparently deserved end' (Goldgar, 2007: 2).

The waves of fear and greed displayed during the *tulipmania* were also the ingredients of subsequent crises, and eventually irrationality working together with cognitive and emotional biases gave rise to 'neuroeconomic' studies. But long before that, books of wonders published during the seventeenth and eighteenth centuries listed *tulipmania* among earthquakes, storms, fires, comets, plagues, wars, famines, and incredible ways to die, all prodigies equally worthy of mention. However, the tulip craze was not only described as a prodigy, but also as stupid. A Haarlem priest likened it to the plague, a sickness of the head, a tale of idiocy, greed, and madness. 'Novels, plays, even operas have been written about the craze. Stories are told of huge fortunes won and lost, and all focused on the most improbable of objects: the tulip bulb' (ibid: 4).

Critics of the trade pinpointed the unreliability of the flower in contrast with the reliability of God. God, not tulips, would save us; to build one's life on tulips was to build on sand or on sick foundation. If not deemed sinful, the activity of selling and buying bulbs was at least regarded as imprudent, as it was based on rush judgments, on the inability to establish monetary value and to adopt trustworthy conducts. The financial mechanism itself was absolved, while moralists, at most, would single out dishonest traders as responsible for the crisis. The blame was laid at the door of deceitful mediators and criminal florists, collectively engaged in setting up an oligopoly of sorts manipulating most exchanges. The dishonest operators, it was suggested, would force prices up by buying all that was on offer, thus creating an artificial demand, and selling afterwards on a falsely created rising market. The victims of such practices ignored not only the value of tulips but also the moral stature of those trading them.

While in some religious pamphlets the search for profit was still stigmatized, the central preoccupation was the social mobility that the widespread participation in this search was likely to generate. Of course, powerful merchants, landlords, doctors, apothecaries, and even ministers and elders of the Church were chiefly involved in the trading of tulip futures. But the trade was also benefitting a variety of manual workers and artisans, such as weavers, whose involvement in the craze was seen as a prelude to the abandonment of their traditional activity. It is hard to establish whether this fear was provoked by an appreciation of productive manufacture and a simultaneous rejection of financial adventure, or whether it was associated with a threat to social order caused by the upward mobility of the working population. In both cases, however, concerns were epitomized by images of 'weavers leaving or even destroying their looms in hope of something better' (ibid: 267). Without the constraints of the spinning wheel, moreover, men would find the way to the tavern unencumbered. The rapid social advancement of the workers coupled with their discovery of pleasure was, in sum, inappropriate.

Weavers and tailors now apparently rode about on horses or in wagons or *calessen*, small open coaches, and even, in the winter, a sleigh. One author vented his disgust that the florists, who had themselves sprouted from the 'shit wagon', had come to be able to ride around on knightly horses (ibid: 268).

Nice clothes and fine food were acceptable if those enjoying them had earned such pleasures through strenuous sacrifice, in appropriately productive settings where discipline reigned. The tulip trade, however, when involving artisans and other workers, took place at inns, where Bacchus was worshipped and where beer was no longer good enough for a rampant social class.

To summarize, if a form of financial crime was detected in the Dutch tulip mania, this was associated with unscrupulous traders manipulating the market, not with the characteristics of the market itself. When greed was stigmatized, the recipients of the

stigma were mainly ordinary artisans and workers who dangerously subverted the natural order by imitating wealthier people.
For them, not for the wealthier, the point was made that the
financial sphere resembled gambling paired with sinful drinking
and a diversion from honest toil.

A *Satire of Tulip Mania* by Jan Brueghel the Younger (*c.*1640)
depicts speculators as brainless monkeys in contemporary upper-
class clothes: one monkey urinates on the previously valuable
plants, others appear in debtors' court and one is carried to
the grave.

London and Paris Bubbles

Crises and bubbles hit the London markets in the 1690s, 'in
almost every case built around a new joint-stock corporation
formed, in imitation of the East India Company, around some
prospective colonial venture' (Graeber, 2011: 341). Colonialism,
but also the recurring wars in Europe, determined an unprecedented expansion of the financial sector of the economy, thus
creating a situation in which the distinction between military and
financial initiative became blurred. The shares of the East and
West India companies were traded in the stock market, which
therefore subsidized military occupation and, at the same time,
commercial enterprise. In 1717, the East India Company, after
establishing numerous trading posts along the east and west coasts
of India, was exempted from payment of custom duties, and in
1757 turned from a mere commercial venture into a ruling entity
(Mukherjee, 1955). Its members or employees, called 'servants',
were largely rapacious and self-aggrandizing; they conducted
their own private trading activities, thus damaging the overall
profits of the company. Controlling the locals as well as its own
'servants' proved too large a burden and the company's financial collapse seemed imminent. After a series of governmental
loans and bail-outs, the East India Company was not hampered
but encouraged to continue its activities, as it was given greater
autonomy in running business in America.

Responsibility for its financial collapse was imputed to unscrupulous employees; those predatory insiders who created their
own parallel speculative system. The company itself and its financial operations were judged as healthy as any other expression
of the 'civilizing mission' undertaken by colonizers. An advocate

of free trade and an opponent of monopoly, John Stuart Mill, defended this monopolistic company; a theorist of parliamentary democracy, he was willing to countenance commercial forms of despotism (Mill, 1990; Ruggiero, 2013).

The South Sea Bubble occurred in 1720. This large corporation managed to buy a substantial part of the national debt in England and, as its stock market performance escalated, inevitably set the tone for new financial adventures. New firms mushroomed, some of which were short-lived but still able to attract investors. 'Each issued stocks, whether their scheme activity consisted in the production of soap or the insurance of horses' (Graeber, 2011: 347). Financial operations were facilitated by the belief held by investors that they could outsmart their fellow investors or competitors and that other people's gullibility could turn into a fortune for them. Fraud was rife, as in an episode told by Charles MacKay (2004), in which an operator promised revenues to customers without specifying what his business was about and, after a day or so of trading, vanished with the money collected.

If one is to believe MacKay, the entire population of London conceived the simultaneous delusion, not that money could really be manufactured out of nothing, but that other people were foolish enough to believe that it could—and that, by that very fact, they actually could make money out of nothing after all (Graeber, 2011: 348–9).

In the same year, in other European capitals optimism around making easy money grew relentlessly. The debts accumulated during the Spanish Secession War were turned by states into short-term bonds and obligations, attracting myriads of investors. New schemes were created, including some selling insurance against the vagaries of commercial life. Among them, some had a solid financial basis, while others limited themselves to selling mere pieces of paper, triggering excitement that spread more rapidly than the schemes themselves. Satirical prints of the time depicted investors, again, as monkeys eating 'cabbage', or rather pieces of paper with different types of cabbage written on them. 'Certainly it made more sense to spend a thousand guilders for flowers beautiful in color, or scent, than for a piece of paper, a South Sea share certificate' (Goldgar, 2007: 307–8).

The bubbles which occurred almost simultaneously in France and England were caused, at least initially, by the initiative taken by private agents to gain access to government bonds held by the public. For example, bondholders were persuaded to swap their government certificates for the shares of the South Sea Company, which promised higher profits but collapsed in 1720. Optimistic investors thought they could always resell to future optimists. Simultaneously, numerous other joint-stock companies, nick-named 'bubble companies' were founded, and 'there is a definite impression that many, though certainly not all, schemes were fraudulent' (Scheinkman, 2014: 14). Fraudulent or not, financial operations assumed remarkably similar forms. Companies pursued rapid expansion through acquisition of government debt, they then issued shares whose value constantly grew, passing over the risk to the last purchasers of those shares. Bubbles and crashes, on the other hand, were accompanied by innovative, though not necessarily less damaging ways of thinking about the economy and its monetary element, as in the case examined below.

John Law

A Scottish financier, John Law (1671–1729) saw in money a means of exchange rather than the receptacle of value. Money was, in his view, the means to encourage trade, the real purveyor of the wealth of nations. A compulsive, bankrupt gambler and a dandy, he killed a man in a duel, was charged with murder, and sentenced to death. He escaped to Amsterdam and travelled across Europe, until the problematic economic condition of France attracted him to Paris. After the wars waged by Louis XIV, the country experienced a shortage of precious metals and was unable to issue the quantity of coins necessary for economic recovery. When the sovereign died, John Law presented his plan to the Duke of Orleans, Regent to underage Louis XV. He soon became Controller General of Finance and in 1716 set up the Banque Génerale de France with three-quarters of capital based on government bonds and a quarter on customers' liquidity. The new private bank was allowed to issue its own currency supported by the depleting national gold reserves. He then founded the Mississippi Company, which eventually became the Company of the Indies and was funded in the same way as the bank. The wealth and power of the Company later made him the virtual sovereign of Louisiana. Following the Company's success, international trade increased by 60 per cent over two years, while the number of French ships engaged in commerce leaped from sixteen to 300. In brief, John Law managed to stimulate economic initiative by replacing gold with paper credit and reducing the national debt through shares in commercial ventures. If the idea of paper money was ahead of his time, his practice chimed with the prevailing mercantilist philosophy, as he created a monopolistic enterprise thanks to government support. Success made shares balloon to over sixty times their initial value and the inflationary effect forced Law to devalue banknotes and stocks. As people rushed to convert paper money to gold, the sale of the precious metal was temporarily banned but, when it was lifted, the renewed rush led to fifty people being stampeded to death. The Company's shares, ultimately, became worthless and John Law was dismissed and chased by the victims of his visionary exploits (Allen, 1969; Murphy, 1997; Gleeson, 2000).

In the analysis provided by Schumpeter (1954), there was logical economic reasoning in the idea of managing currency, manufacturing money, and making credit a propeller of development. John Law, first, lucidly observed that the use of a commodity (money) as a means of circulation affects its value; second, that the exchange value of money, as a consequence, depends on its productive use; third, that precious metals have no other value than the capacity to buy goods. Hence, such metals could be replaced by cheaper material, or even by something that had no value at all, such as printed money, because 'money is not the value FOR which goods are exchanged, but the value BY which they are exchanged' (ibid: 322). If money has no intrinsic value and its supply is fully manageable, Schumpeter concludes, John Law was right in attempting to control, reform, and lead to new levels the whole of the national economy in France. His gambling, in a deeper and wider sense, constituted a noble effort to manage the economic process.

Crises, not sins, let alone crimes, we have encountered so far.

Luxury, Usury, and Crime

Early criminologists did address financial issues, although they did so less as criminologists than as economists. One has to peruse their economic writings, therefore, and hope to come across some hints regarding financial delinquency. This type of delinquency, moreover, emerges when classical authors dealt with economic initiative in general, namely with conducts that may or may not be connected with delinquent conduct, but may be harmful or beneficial to the economy itself. From this perspective, the damage caused by financial operations, no longer associated with sin, had to be interpreted through novel categories. Let us examine the thoughts of Beccaria and Bentham on the matter.

Cesare Beccaria (1995: 69) repeatedly highlighted how the powerful were protected by their own laws, which manifested the passions of a few men and left 'a gulf between the poor and the rich'.

Who made these laws? Rich and powerful men, who have never condescended to visit the filthy hovels of the poor, who have never broken mouldy bread among the innocent cries of starving children and a wife's tears (ibid).

Both powerless and powerful people were the object of his analysis, the latter including 'noblemen and magistrates', whose criminal acts possessed a 'greater force' and were 'more far-reaching', 'destroying the idea of justice and replacing it with the right of the strongest' (ibid: 73). The crimes of the powerful, in his view, were imitative in nature, as violations bred new violations, spreading illegality across society (Forti and Visconti, 2007).

In his economic writing, more specifically, Beccaria identified crimes committed in the financial sphere when, for example, he discussed currency fraud. He warned that, with gold and silver becoming currency for their universal capacity to mediate economic transactions, 'cupidity and personal interest bring disorder' (Beccaria, 1804: 20). Precious metals attracted the initiative of forgers, who flooded markets with their fake currency and took advantage of the lack of proper regulations. The authorities were therefore urged to control the quantity and quality of 'the precious metal that circulates in commerce and guarantees its validity' (ibid: 21). The solemnity of this guarantee could do little, however, against commercial speculation, which Beccaria described as 'securing information around where a good will be abundant, and therefore cheaper, and where it will be scarce, therefore more expensive, and knowing on time how to move those goods cheaply from one place to another' (ibid: 165).

An ardent advocate of freedom of commerce, Beccaria tried to explain how such freedom could lead to illegitimate conduct. At the basis of his explanation was the distinction between sterile and useful expenses, with the former encouraging unorthodox practices (Wahnbaeck, 2004). Speculation, the result of greed, may be legitimate if it turns into accumulation of wealth which eventually will be invested productively. In this way, Beccaria expressed the classic notion of utility, namely that individual desire should generate collective happiness, and that exorbitant earnings are justified through the beneficial effects they produce for all. Beccaria was aware that financial operations generated exorbitant amounts of wealth and that its distribution was far from fair. Therefore, he found himself in the uncomfortable position of justifying increasing inequality and, at the same time, engaged in denouncing powerful groups and institutions perpetuating such inequality. A way of outflanking this moral and political dilemma, which he followed, was to regard economic initiative, including the related financial activities, as forms of gambling. Another way of evading the dilemma was offered to him by the possibility of focusing on two discrete aspects of economic conduct: luxury and usury. And it is through the analysis of both that he formulated his views on legitimate and illegitimate conduct in the market. Let us see in more detail, first, how Beccaria's argument on luxury can be linked to financial issues.

As a lecturer of political economy at the Palatine School in Milan, he trained future administrators, teaching them concepts of value and the principles of money circulation. In his thought it was consumption (or demand) rather than industry (or supply) which fuelled the engine of economic development. Inevitably, he was then led to focus on the particular forms of consumption that fall in the realm of luxury. His discussion was based on the Epicurean pleasure–pain principle, according to which human action is caused by 'flight from pain and love for pleasure' (Beccaria, 1995: 33). The search for pleasure is a never-ending process, first, because there is uncertainty as to how long it might last, second, because it might cease to satisfy when the possibility for greater pleasures suddenly arises. Constant dissatisfaction, therefore, is shunned through conspicuous consumption, an equally never-ending and expanding process, an innate part of the human natural quest for pleasure. 'Since any pleasure will lose its appeal (turn into pain) in the sight of even greater pleasures to be attained, there is no limit to man's urge to indulge in luxuries' (Wahnbaeck, 2004: 168). At first sight, the Dutch craze around tulips appears to find perfect justification in this pleasure–pain theory, which suggests that the human never-ending search for pleasure is innate. But let us investigate further.

Inadvertently or otherwise, Beccaria's argument complemented Bernard Mandeville's (1989) position expressed about four decades earlier, when luxury was seen in purely relativist terms: because the wants of humans are innumerable, Mandeville stressed, what is luxury for one person is a necessity for another. Wealth is not the outcome of frugality, nor does luxury trigger 'avarice, rapine or corruption', let alone produce 'effeminate or enervated people' (ibid: 141). The production of luxurious goods, in fact, is a factor of economic growth, as it requires the employment of many people. On this, however, Beccaria's economic reasoning was more nuanced.

Financial success, whether legitimate or otherwise, brings luxury consumptions, which like all other consumptions entail 'the acquisition of a good keeping the displeasure of deprivation at bay' (Beccaria, 1804: 102). In classical thought, luxury was deemed 'proportionate to the inequality of fortunes' (Montesquieu, 1989: 225), or regarded, alongside avarice, as the inseparable companion of economic growth, as we have seen in Mandeville. For Rousseau (1993), it brought the dissolution of morals, while for Hume (2011) it could become vicious when pursued at the expense of virtues such as liberality and charity. For Beccaria (1804), luxury caused a type of pleasure that overtook the sheer displeasure of deprivation, lasting well after the 'grief of want' has disappeared. For example, a person who desires a certain kind of food is not only keen to satisfy her hunger, but also to enjoy a specific taste, while 'any nauseating food would satisfy a person who just wants to eat' (ibid: 103). There are, however, two types of luxuries, the first of which, noted Beccaria, does not imply forms of exchange, productivity, or other interactive operations. For example, expenses for luxury goods may only require a sterile service by someone capable of providing them. These are harmful expenses, in that the persons providing the service could be employed instead in productive activity benefitting all. The number of servants and the variety of their liveries, in this sense, are improbable indicators of the general wellbeing. On the other hand, luxury may entail an exchange of things, and can turn into added value enjoyable by all. Beccaria, in brief, marked the boundary between harmful and beneficial market operations, including those of a financial nature, at the point where they become unproductive. Financial crime, therefore, is not an intrinsically illegal conduct, but is merely dysfunctional for its economic consequences. Echoing commentators of the financial crises discussed earlier, Beccaria ended up absolving the financial system per se, to which, as already mentioned, he attributed some characteristics of gambling, while singling out individual wrong-doers in that system. It is impossible to establish whether such characterization was inspired by his knowledge of compulsive gambler John Law and of his private and public deeds.

Legitimate forms of luxury, implying an exchange of things rather than an exchange of things with services, were fed by certain banking operations, which determined the disproportionate wealth of bankers. But such wealth was well deserved due to the important social role they played. Beccaria also contended that, by charging interest to customers, banks did no more than assert the utility of their resources. Money, in other words, possessed its own specific utility, like land, labour, and industry, all measurable with respect to what they brought to the community. The value of money was determined by the activities it made possible and encapsulated the profits that such activities might generate:

Every sum of money represents a portion of land, and the interest to be paid to creditors constitutes the value of the produce delivered by that land ... This is, then, the true and legitimate interest of money, namely the ordinary interest of fairness and justice (ibid: 118).

An eminent associate of Beccaria in campaigns against torture and for penal reform, Pietro Verri (1999), expressed similar views, arguing that without luxury there would be no industry. Luxury accelerates the circulation of money, at the same time providing an incentive for the poor to emulate the rich. It encourages land-owners, manufacturers, and financial operators to innovate, thus leading to growth (Capra, 2002). 'And while the peasants themselves were excluded from conspicuous consumption, they would nevertheless profit from it because it guaranteed both their jobs and their income' (Wahnbaeck, 2004: 157).

While Beccaria and Verri witnessed and contributed to the reassessment of luxury during the eighteenth century, only the former aimed at distinguishing between appropriate and inappropriate financial operations and unravelling the core deviant nature of speculative conduct. Charging interest for lending money is not usury, Beccaria claimed, because interest coincides with the immediate utility of what is lent. Usury, by contrast, is 'the utility of utility', in other words, it is the search for advantages which do not reflect the immediate productivity of what is lent. In Beccaria's formulation, therefore, usury appears as a form of financial delinquency, because it seeks advantages which are not translated into immediate productive performance: the money earned does not coincide with its actual utility in terms of production or value-adding investment. Moreover, the earnings acquired do not correspond to those yielded by a piece of land through its produce, the land being, in Beccaria's view, the only source of wealth. In conclusion, usury in the form of financial delinquency implies a deceitful, unfair distribution of wealth: the money appropriated exceeds its social utility.

From Utility to Happiness

Beccaria's utility turns into the variable 'happiness' in Jeremy Bentham's philosophy, a variable from which the moral value of every act derives. A typical objection to this philosophy is that, as a goal, happiness may be valued irrespective of the morality of the action producing it. Hence,

Suppose a hundred people in a community, with an option between a course of action which will make fifty-one happy and forty-nine utterly miserable; and a course of action which makes the fifty-one somewhat less happy and relieves the forty-nine of their misery. To consult happiness, the first course of action should be pursued; to consult numbers, the second (Laufleur, 1948: xi).

In sum, a preliminary choice is required between happiness of a large mass of people or intense happiness of a few. Choosing the latter, it becomes hard to establish boundaries to conduct. In Bentham's argument, however, happiness was referred to the largest possible number of people and was not a zero-sum good: more given to one person will not entail less given to another. On the contrary, in his view, personal advantage turned into advantage for the public at large, like, for example, exorbitant earnings by some brought earnings for others as well, a circumstance that Bentham described as a 'sanction'. A sanction 'tends to make a man conclude that his own greatest happiness coincides with the greatest happiness of others' (ibid: xiii). Echoes of Beccaria's and Verri's advocacy of luxury return in this formulation. For

Bentham, there are popular, moral, legal or political, and religious sanctions, each specifically according their approval to conduct in general and economic initiative in particular. In the financial sphere, following Bentham's argument, we may conclude that even speculative or illegitimate operations may be legally, politically, morally, and religiously 'sanctioned' if they contribute to the happiness of the general public.

Ambiguous though this deduction may sound, it perfectly reflects the ambiguity of financial delinquency itself and of its appreciation by early criminologists. Bentham's distinction between primary and secondary mischief adds to the ambiguity of his argument while, perhaps, providing a possible solution to the dilemma. Primary mischief, he declared, 'is sustained by an assignable individual, or a multitude of assignable individuals, while secondary mischief, taking its origin from the former, extends itself either over the whole community, or over some other multitude of unassignable individuals' (Bentham, 1948: 153). If a person is attacked and robbed, she will be the primary sufferer of a mischief, while for her creditors and children the mischief will be of a secondary nature, in that they will suffer from that person's changed financial condition. For some crimes, however, it is impossible to identify the victims, because 'they are out of sight and there is nobody whose sufferings you can see': tax evasion is one such crime (ibid: 163). Other crimes occurring in the financial sphere, in Bentham, are 'accidents', while crashes and crises are described as follows:

A groom being on horseback, and riding through a frequented street, turns a corner at a full pace, and rides over a passenger, who happens to be going by ... he has done mischief by his carelessness (ibid: 164).

Bentham was aware that accidents due to carelessness were not the only features of financial conduct, which could be motivated by pure greed. But because those who love money today, he contended, will probably love it, at least in equal degree, tomorrow, and because they 'will find inducement to rob, wherever and whenever there are people to rob', punishing them is ineffective, needless, and unprofitable (ibid: 168). This is why, Bentham concluded, embezzlement and commercial fraud are not usually punished as theft, and in general, anyway, financial acts of delinquency can be assimilated to what the author termed *offences operating through calamity*. As natural events, of course they may be dangerous, danger being 'the chance of pain or loss of pleasure', but calamities do not target specific groups or individuals and are not guided by intentional design to provoke harm. Similarly, harmful financial acts are either involuntary or victimless, again they are crises not sins. But Bentham's argument did not stop here: at times he took pleasure in expressing one view and its opposite. Was this a sign of his intellectual openness or of the ungraspable nature of financial delinquency?

Intentional harmful acts, in his view, may take place in the financial sphere, and when they do they should be regarded as acts of mere delinquency. These include 'offences by falsehood', committed by those who abuse of 'their faculty of discourse', namely 'the faculty of influencing the sentiment of belief in other men ... give other men to understand that things are otherwise than as in reality they are' (ibid: 222). The promise to earn money in financial operations may hide such abuse, and Bentham conceded that this could be detrimental to a country as a whole, as it runs 'against the increase of the national felicity, against the public wealth, against the national population, against the national wealth, against the sovereignty of the state, or against its religion' (ibid: 223).

'Offences by falsehood' are usually accompanied by abuse of trust, a variable that Bentham discussed at length. Those invested with trust, he remarked, are bound to make sure that their behaviour benefits others, and their good faith is measured through the assessment of their capacity to keep promises. But consent by a trustee may not be obtained fairly. 'If not fairly obtained, it is obtained by falsehood, which is termed fraud' (ibid: 251).

The beneficiary of that behaviour, however, may be a non-assignable entity, therefore, again, making it hard to assess the outcomes of the trusted person's acts. Breach of trust consists 'in not doing something that a person ought to do, or in doing something she ought not to do', but when responsibility for the breach is not attributable to a specific, identifiable trustee, 'we name this disturbance of trust' (ibid: 226). Financial crime, within this logic, could be deemed a form of 'disturbance of trust'. But in order to locate more precisely this type of crime in Bentham's analytical framework, we need to return to his classification mentioned earlier. The consequences of mischievous acts can be 'original' or 'derivative', the former affecting a specific victim, the latter victimizing a wider sector of society. Mischievous acts of the second type cause both pain and danger, because they may spread and harm society at large. Derivative consequences, on the other hand, produce a sort of 'pain of apprehension', Bentham argued, and may 'reinforce the tendency to produce acts of the like kind' (Bentham, 1967: 280). We could apply this formula to the cases presented above, which show an imitative impetus resulting in 'acts of the like kind'. We can also expand the interpretation of these acts by referring them to another classification proposed by the author.

For Bentham, there are private, semi-private, self-regarding, and public offences. The first are 'offences that are detrimental, in the first instance, to assignable persons other than the offender'. We have an example of the second when there are persons to whom the act in question may be detrimental, but such persons cannot be individually identified. Offences are therefore semi-public when they victimize a neighbourhood or a limited community. Self-regarding offences are those which are, in the first instance, detrimental to the offenders themselves. Finally, public offences are offences threatening 'an unassignable indefinite multitude', 'the whole number of individuals of which the community is composed, although no particular individual should appear more likely to be a sufferer by them than another' (ibid: 314–15). According to this classification, financial crime produces both original and derivative consequence, it is private, semi-private, and public, but certainly not self-regarding. There is, however, a crucial addition to these categories, relating particularly to semi-private offences: Bentham contended that these types of offences manifest themselves as 'calamities', like pestilence, famine, inundation, or damage caused by 'persons deficient in point of understanding, such as infants, idiots and maniacs' (Bentham, 1948: 245). We are back to the dual explanation presented before: financial crime may be the result of ineluctable, natural causes and crises, or of individual pathology.

Of interest also is Bentham's treatment of offences more specifically falling in the fiscal sphere. Tax evasion, for example, is a mischievous act, because public money is necessary to defend the community against its external as well as its internal enemies: 'It is certain that if all of a sudden the payment of all taxes was to cease, there would no longer be anything effectual done, either for the maintenance of justice, or for the defense of the community against its foreign adversaries' (ibid: 162). But taxing the income

of traders is impracticable due to the difficulties of ascertaining their profits and losses, hence the 'endless source of evasion'
available to them (Bentham, 1952a: 371). On the other hand, if
equity in taxation should be based on the ability of subjects to
pay their dues, some exceptions to this rule must be identified
through 'particular and superior considerations': 'the most opulent and most powerful classes should be spared' in consideration
of the risky nature of their economic activity (ibid: 375).

Among the beneficiaries of tax exemption Bentham included
the holders of government annuities, namely the creditors of the
nation who in his view must be protected in their dealings. In a
telling footnote, he finally referred to the South Sea Company,
arguing that its members, who engaged in dealing with government, if required to pay tax, 'would relinquish the market altogether': 'had these dealers who part with their money not been
protected against diminution in the value of the property they
purchased, they would not have dealt at all' (ibid: 383).

This benevolent attitude was extended to overtly fraudulent
practices in the financial arena, for which Bentham proposed
an apparently simple form of self-regulation. For instance, all
'banking-houses' should keep books where profits and losses
are recorded. Inspectors appointed by the Treasury should check
those books and 'the truth of the contents be verified by oath'.
Employees should be examined *viva voce* in some respectable
judicial office, and if losses were recorded, 'the public should not
be a sharer in the loss … for this is one of the few businesses,
if not the only business, in which no clear loss can take place'
(Bentham, 1952b: 404). Losses in this sector of the economy were
caused by gross negligence or imprudence on the part of a dealer,
'and there is no reason why the public should suffer for the fault
of the individual: and if it did in this way, the inlet to fraud would
be unbounded' (ibid). The practice of bailing-out banks, according to this formulation, creates a criminogenic environment for
those who operate in them.

Unlike traders, bankers should indeed be taxed, in that according to Bentham, bankers do not have a shop, they do not sell
anything: they live upon the interest of money, with the peculiarity that the money upon the interest of which they live is not their
own but other people's. 'A man whose occupation is to use other
people's money can afford to give up a portion of the profit in

support of that government to whose protection he is indebted for the faculty of keeping it' (ibid: 406).

Like for Beccaria, it is when addressing the issue of usury that we find Bentham's allusions, but also explicit reference, to financial delinquency. As we have seen, Beccaria argued that the interest charged by money-lenders corresponds to the value that money could produce if productively invested, while he identified usury with operations taking place in the speculative, unproductive sphere. Bentham moved beyond Beccaria's distinction, attacking the kernel of the theory that money was by nature unproductive and that interest, therefore, amounted to bribery or theft. At that time laws limited the charging of interest, in a sort of moral compromise championed, among others, by Adam Smith. That the arrangement was unpopular was proven by the general acclaim with which Bentham's *Defence of Usury* was received.

Bentham's views on usury were consistent with his opinion that economic activity should be divided into two groups, 'agenda' and 'non-agenda' initiative. The former were typified by state intervention in the control of private enterprise and markets, the latter by the initiative of private individuals. In England, he observed, most useful things were produced by individuals, and wherever a greater degree of opulence was observed, this was the outcome of 'non-agenda' activity (Manning, 1968). Also in money exchange Bentham (1787a: 1) advocated 'the liberty of making one's own terms, a meek and unassuming species of liberty [that] has been suffering much injustice'. The regulation of money-lending was deemed absurd, as would be the regulation of any other market exchange. Why should someone earning as much as they possibly can from the use of their money be labelled with the opprobrious name of a usurer? Those who sell a house trying to maximize their profit are not so called. Money is an ordinary good and, as such, should be subject to the law of the market: demand and supply. For this reason Bentham was against any form of law fixing the interest rate, as he was against taxing money-lenders who would, in response, cease to lend, or burden the borrower with the tax: a prohibition upon borrowing is a denial of relief to those who want to borrow, he said. It is much easier to get goods than money, Bentham contended, and those who deal in goods make a profit that is on average around 10–15 per cent. Money is lent at a statutory 5 per cent.

In the way of trading, then, a man can afford to be at least three times as adventurous as he can in the way of lending, and with equal prudence. So long, then, as a man is looked upon as one who will pay, he can much easier get the goods he wants, than he could the money to buy them with, though he were content to give for it twice, or even thrice the ordinary rate of interest (ibid: 6).

In the eighteenth century the debate on the interest rate revolved, among other issues, around prodigality, in the sense that limiting such rate was seen as a restraint to prodigal borrowers. In Bentham's view, prodigals were not affected by laws fixing the rate of interest, as they would borrow anyway. On the other hand, those who had no collateral would find it hard even to find a friend who was prepared to lend them money, because they were unlikely to pay it back.

In a letter to Adam Smith, Bentham (1787b: 1) felt that, after learning a lot from a 'professor of eminence', he was forced to criticize him. And 'should it be my fortune to gain any advantage over you, it must be with weapons which you have taught me to wield, and with which you yourself have furnished me'. Smith's argument was that if the legal rate of interest were established at a level as high as 10 per cent, a great amount of money would be lent to prodigals, who alone would be willing to pay up such high interest. Sober people, he contended, would not venture into the competition. A great part of the capital of the country would thus be kept out of the hands that were most likely to make a profitable and advantageous use of it, and 'thrown into those which were most likely to waste and destroy it' (ibid: 2). In reply, Bentham contended that prudent and sober people would never venture into any innovative project, thus never contributing to growth and improvement: 'they will pick out old-established trades from all sorts of projects' (ibid: 3). Development has always been based on risk, he claimed: any new manufacture, any new branch of commerce, or any new practice in agriculture, as Smith himself taught him, may present themselves as forms of speculation in which the innovator promises himself and others extraordinary profits. But if the innovation is successful, Bentham continued, the new trades and practices become established, while competition reduces them to the level of other trades and practices. Of course, there will be misconduct and fraud, but these, along with bankruptcies, only account for 'not much more perhaps than one in a thousand'. Ultimately, one has to accept 'dangerous and expensive experiments' and these should be encouraged, even through monopoly. 'A temporary monopoly may be vindicated, upon the same principles upon which a monopoly of a new machine is granted to its inventor, and that of a new book to its author' (ibid: 5).

Regulating the prices of goods, including money, is a difficult task. This was the opinion of Bentham, who argued that legislators attempting it would also have to regulate the quantity of what each consumer was allowed to buy. Such quantity was already regulated, he suggested, by the diligence and prudence of purchasers. You cannot prohibit a contract because one person sells too cheap or buys too dear, Bentham insisted, unless we are faced with fraud or ignorance of the value of what is sold and bought. When this happens, idiocy is the main culprit.

Before reaching the end of the century, it may be useful to summarize the discussion so far. Beccaria was aware that the powerful, including those operating in the financial sphere, were protected by their own laws, and that the inequality exacerbated by financial operations was morally and politically abhorrent. He also attempted to establish to what extent and under which circumstances money operations had to be regarded as socially harmful. In the eighteenth century, currency fraud, speculation, luxury, and usury gave early criminologists large amounts of material to probe their theories, with Beccaria distinguishing between productive and sterile financial conduct and Bentham attributing to idiocy, calamity, and abuse of trust the occurrence of irregularities. The former described forms of financial criminality based on the false claim of the value of stocks irrespective of economic performance, a description provided by contemporary analysts with respect to a chain of similar scandals (see following chapters). Few criminologists, today, would impute financial delinquency to accidents or calamities, although many would focus on single cases and pathological financial agents just like Beccaria and Bentham did on ignorance, isolated wrongdoers, and predatory insiders. Perhaps both Beccaria and Bentham should have given more attention to the social outcomes of market optimism, when unfettered crazes attracted all sorts of fraudulent operators (Galbraith, 1987). Contemporary criminologists, on the other hand, may want to take more seriously the implications of development and its potential encouragement of unorthodox practices, thus following Bentham's intuition that the economy needs 'dangerous and expensive' experiments if it is to grow.

Fin de Siècle

In the political sphere, Beccaria's work was prescient with respect to future violent events: state savagery provided examples of barbarianism and was replicated by rebels and revolutionary executioners. In France, the ruling classes became the target of the very violence characterizing their rule. In the economic sphere, his concerns around currency fraud, speculation, and the 'gambling spirit' of banking operations found concrete manifestations when immediately after the French Revolution the National Assembly decided to create a national paper currency, the *assignat*. Slowly and timidly the notes started to circulate, their value being supported by the land confiscated from the aristocracy and the Church. Due to their original purpose, namely the purchase of seized properties, the assignats were only issued in large denomination, a circumstance that made them useless for the majority of day-to-day transactions. The sale of what were now state properties helped reduce the national debt, and as Michelet (1981: 197) complained, 'the Republic had to court the rich, unable as it was to survive without money'. Public goods became the objects of financial speculation, recreating a new landed aristocracy while the old one was being suppressed. 'The communal goods, a patrimony belonging to the people, were sold out' (ibid). The coins of the old regime were not abolished, nor was it established that they could be exchanged on a par with the new currency, with the result that even the National Assembly had to pay a high commission (which reached a 20 per cent peak in 1791) to change large denomination assignats for small change.

In response to the emergency situation, public authorities started to issue smaller denomination paper money, followed by manufacturers, artisans, and swindlers, all apparently motivated by patriotic feelings in the mission of rescuing the national economy. Forgers and counter-revolutionaries were described as accomplices in undermining the Republic, and even when incarcerated the 'traitors' were chased by people storming into prisons. The Belgian, the Swiss, and particularly the English were accused of counterfeiting the new French currency. When in a London basement in Sloane Square anti-revolutionaries were caught producing false assignats, they claimed they were doing noth-ing wrong, because the assignats themselves were illegal, having replaced the old currency. The paper money of rebels and regicides was fake by definition, they argued, as it was introduced through violence and violation of property: if assignats were illegitimate, then their imitations were perfectly legitimate (Spang, 2015).

The 'patriotic bills' did help to address the severe shortage of small change, but the disparity between the new and the old cur-rency meant that ordinary people paid exorbitant costs in daily transactions still conducted in old regime coins. A demonization of paper money ensued, involving foreigners and French alike. Edmund Burke (1969) commented that, despite the millions of assignats forced on people, the state deficit remained unaccep-table, prompting the authorities to issue more and more paper money. The only disagreement among politicians in revolution-ary France, in his opinion, was around 'the greater or the lesser quantity of assignats to be imposed on the public sufferance' (ibid: 360). The authorities were all 'professors of assignats', and all experience of their inefficacy did not discourage them. If they were depreciated, what was the remedy: issue more of them! The French, in brief, 'have no more notes in their song than the cuckow; though, far from the softness of that harbinger of sum-mer and plenty, their voice is as harsh and ominous as that of the raven (ibid). Burke's invective, of course, was based on his rejec-tion of the revolutionary process as a whole, of that desperate adventure in philosophy and finance that hoped to build wealth with confiscated property. Revolutionaries were likened to blind-folded bulls pushing their slaves by the point of the bayonets into swallowing paper pills, unaware that their action lacked the subtle dexterity of ingenious fraud. While plundering citizens and subjugating them to the state, the authorities were just encourag-ing other entities to follow suit, with the result that thousands of fraudsters circulated in the streets. Forgers, exchange agents, and employers were all involved, the latter paying wages in depreci-ated paper. According to Burke, John Law was more honest than this new ruling class, in that he at least, while being a speculator, established trading routes leading to India and Africa: his was, in comparison, a form of generous delusion. Moreover, his fraud was not complemented by force: 'this was reserved to our time, to quench the little glimmerings of reason which might break in upon the solid darkness of this enlightened age' (ibid: 369).

Perceiving darkness in his enlightened age, Burke denounced a French scheme introduced with great pomp which consisted of producing coins from the bells of suppressed churches: the scheme, in his view, was a folly that baffled argument, went beyond ridicule and excited no feeling but disgust. The darkness of his own thought, however, emerged when he lamented that issuing paper money was an act of subversion, akin to the reversal of the old regime, and the overturning of laws and tribunals. The principles of natural subordination could not be rooted out, he insisted: people had to be obedient and respect the property that they did not possess. They had to labour to obtain what they could obtain and if this was disproportioned to their efforts, 'they must be taught their consolation in the final proportions of eternal justice' (ibid: 372). Citizens, however, could not wait for eternal justice to restore fairness of proportions and, along with punishing counterfeiters, they marched with assignats in their hand demanding change, went on strike, threatened to plunder shops, and stopped shipments of money. They were unwilling to express their patriotism by accepting assignats at face value, knowing that trade and exchange mechanisms played against them. Moreover, paper was light, flimsy, perishable, it blew away in the wind. Theirs became an overt hostility against the trade of money, in a period that saw the decriminalization of usury and the liberalization of markets: the law, according to the authorities, protected all types of commerce and there was no need to provide extra protection for the commerce of money, a merchandise among others. Not law, but nature, made money to be bought and sold: 'setting a fixed price for the exchange of coins and assignats was no more plausible than converting lead into gold' (Spang, 2015: 161).

The eighteenth century came to an end, and assignats and other paper money issued during the Revolution became collectors' items. During the following century, as we shall see, there was no need to create new currency for financial crime to prosper.

4

Bankers and Robber Barons

We are now in the century of railways and robber barons, of iron, steel, empire, deadly wars, and financial distress. Innovation and development are accompanied by speculation, periodical crises, bubbles, and bankruptcies.

In response to the damage caused by financial adventure, particularly the South Sea Bubble, in the UK the Bubble Act 1720 attempted to regulate practices and prevent manias. When it was repealed in 1825 the British economy had undergone sensational change, positioning the country at the pinnacle of industrial development. Heavily centred on the construction of railways, such development entailed new financing systems and growing collective participation in projects which were privately led. It is hard to say whether the scandals that occurred in the nineteenth century were the result of lack of regulation in this crucial sector of the economy, or conversely whether they could have been avoided had the Bubble Act still been in place (Evans, 1968; 1970; Taylor, 2006). The cases discussed in this chapter leave the question unanswered, describing a situation where the enormous power of those involved may have merely neutralized the restraining effect of any Acts or regulations. Another unanswered question is whether the institutional responses to such scandals were merely confined to exemplary punishment of the most socially harmful and outrageously brigandish conducts.

Railways and Crooks

In the UK as well as in the US major financial operations fostered by the development of railroads saw the involvement of British capital. In the 1850s, British investors occupied relevant positions in the New York Stock Exchange, and by 1870 growth in the UK was achieved thanks to the reinvestment of capital produced abroad. 'Unsound businessmen' and 'shady promoters', as labelled by Hobsbawm (1968: 118), were able to raise capital not only from potential partners or other informed investors, 'but from a mass of quite uninformed ones looking for a return on their capital anywhere in the golden world economy'.

New legislation which made joint stock companies with limited liability possible encouraged more adventurous investment, for if such a company went bankrupt the shareholders lost only their investment but not, as they had been liable to, their entire fortune (ibid).

These developments were reflected in the mid-Victorian economy in the growth of a class of *rentiers* who lived on the profits and savings of the previous two or three generations: by 1871 Britain contained 170,000 persons of rank and property without visible occupation. 'The comfortable avenues of Kensington, the villas and spas and the growing seaside resorts of the middle class, and the environs of Swiss mountains and Tuscan cities welcomed them' (ibid: 119). The cases presented below may offer a picture of some exemplary outcomes of the new business climate.

The Royal British Bank

The trial of the directors of the Royal British Bank started on 13 February 1856, when the first witness, secretary and solicitor of the bank Mr Paddison, was called for examination. Among the issues discussed were the debts of some of the original founders of the bank: Mr Gwyne, Mr Mullins, and Mr Brown, who was also a defendant. The bank was proven to lack sufficient assets to continue its lending and trading activities. Mr MacGregor, the first Governor of the bank, had deposited a large amount of securities of considerable nominal value, so that the debts in question appeared to be 'covered' by sufficient reserves. In fact, the securities were worthless, therefore the assets to counterbalance the debts were also valueless. The Court demonstrated that: 'The report and balance-sheet submitted at the end of the year 1855 to the shareholders by the directors misrepresented the affairs of the bank; and then in the case of each of the directors separately, that there was evidence of a conscious representation in that misrepresentation' (Perth Gazette, 21 May 1858). Lord Cambell summed up on 27 February the nature of the charge: the defendants were accused of having 'conspired together to represent falsely and fraudulently that the Royal British Bank and its affairs had been during the year ending 31st December 1855 in a sound prosperous condition, producing profits divisible among the shareholders'.

The conspiracy revolved around the promise that shares would bring a 6 per cent dividend and was practically enacted by the directors buying the shares of their own institution in order to keep up their prices. There was, therefore, 'a manifest common design, an acting in concert to do that which was wrong, making the inference that a conspiracy had been formed reasonable' (ibid). The bank was in a state of insolvency at the end of 1855 and the behaviour of its directors was not judged merely 'improper or improvident, but utterly conspiratorial' (ibid). After meeting for two hours, the jury returned a guilty verdict and the defendants were sentenced to twelve months' imprisonment.

The Tipperary Bank

The bank collapsed in February 1856, making old men weep in the streets and women kneeling to ask God not to turn them into beggars for ever. The bank was founded in 1838 by John Sadleir, a 24-year-old man who 'saw the opportunity to tap the humble hoards of the farming classes in his native Tipperary' (Fahey, 2015: 1). Branches were open across Ireland, issuing notes, paying good interest on deposits and high dividends on investments, making John's career prosper. In 1846, he moved to London and became a parliamentary lobbyist for a number of railways companies, and afterwards a Liberal MP in England. Returning to Ireland, he was elected in Sligo and proved successful in investing in railways, sugar, tallow, and land. His reputation began to falter when a London bank refused to cash a draft drawn on his Tipperary bank. He had withdrawn £200,000 and was insolvent, and after writing a number of regretful letters to his relatives and his victims he swallowed prussic acid. The closure of the bank a few days later caused major losses to the Bank of Ireland and individual investors and customers, including a priest who lost £2,000 he had collected to build a church, a Poor Law Union that provided dinners for the poor, and some 800 people holding savings of less than £50. A farmer who blamed his wife for depositing £350 in the bank beat her to death.

Expressed in figures, the collapse showed a level of liabilities more than ten times that of the assets available. John had forged share certificates and all sorts of bills and used the bank as his private wallet. Described as a national calamity, efforts to untangle his dealings continued until the 1880s, and there were even rumours that he had forged his own death certificate.

Popular fiction mirrored these events. For example, Charles Dickens (2012: 134) immortalized John Sadleir in *Little Dorrit* as Mr Merdle, a master financier who turns everything he touches into metaphorical gold, a ruthless operator whose spectacular crash victimizes whoever has the misfortune to deal with him. Immensely rich, Merdle is a man of 'prodigious enterprise', in the banking as well as in the building sector. And of course, he is in Parliament and, necessarily, in the City, and he is also 'Chairman of this, Trustee of that, President of the other'. At dinner parties, Dickens puts him against walls or behind doors, hardly enjoying himself, a loner perhaps plotting the next adventurous financial move.

Legendary Tycoons

Industrial development in the US created a number of legendary tycoons, whose designation as robber barons was due to the alleged murky fashion in which their fortune was accumulated. The term, originally applied in the Middle Ages to feudal warlords, traversed the centuries to designate unethical businessmen engaged in monopolistic practices and corruption (Josephson, 1962). Crucial industries, due to little regulation, were left to the domination of a small number of individuals, who capitalized on the extensive natural resources available, the mass of potential workers migrating to the country, and the general acceleration of business in the years following the civil war. Railroad builders bought political influence through lobbying or bribes, promoting a doctrine of laissez-faire or market freedom while in fact ensuring state intervention in their support. Notable examples were Cornelius Vanderbilt (owner of steamships and railroads), Andrew Carnegie (steel manufacturer), J. P. Morgan (financier and banker), John D. Rockefeller (founder of Standard Oil), Russell Sage (financier), and Jay Gould and Jim Fisk (Wall Street traders).

Allegations of misconduct were also due to the inability of government to check the veracity of financial reports in which entrepreneurs listed losses and profits: the reports were deemed 'inaccessible and indecipherable' (Soll, 2014: 170). Uninformed investors, as a consequence, could be deceived, as they could not fully understand the workings of the financial operations in which they engaged, nor could they assess, when investing in the railway business, to what extent their shares depreciated as a consequence of tracks and steam engines becoming obsolete. Depreciation account statements were the remit of large investors, who could hardly be challenged, even by the most zealous of auditors. Cases of insider trading, false balance sheets, and monopoly creation multiplied, which led Mark Twain to suggest that 'a railroad is like a lie—you have to keep building it to make it stand' (ibid: 171).

Mark Twain and Charles Dudley Warner (1873), in a co-authored novel, used the expression 'the gilded age' with painful sarcasm, describing life in eastern American cities as bare survival for most, and luxury for a few. Garish wealth and bruising poverty touched elbows in the palatial mansions lining Fifth Avenue and the slums filled with migrants. 'And showy displays of wealth were not limited to the cities. One of the trademarks of the wealthy during the Gilded Age were country estates and sprawling mansions in resorts such as Newport and Rhode Island' (McNamara, 2013: 3). Twain and Warner's fictional speculators advise young men on how to forget bread and butter or mere livelihood, and aim at something else. 'I will put you in a way to make more money than you'll ever know what to do with'. Speculators always have some 'prodigious operations on foot' but keep quiet, lest competitors find out about the 'little game'. There is, for example, an operation in corn that looks promising. The temptation is to buy all the 'growing crops and just boss the market when they mature—ah, I tell you it's a great thing'. Speculators, therefore, keep quiet and have quiet men working for them: investing amounts to furtive betting on 'a horse to put up money on! There's whole Atlantic oceans of cash in it' (Twain and Warner, 1873: 183).

Sometimes portrayed as self-made men, job providers, and builders of the nation, robber barons simultaneously attracted popular antipathy for the ruthlessness shown to employees in industrial disputes and the persistent, unashamed display of their wealth. The following are exemplary biographies of robber barons.

Jay Gould

After making a considerable fortune through unscrupulous trading in Wall Street during the civil war, Gould gained the reputation of a pure manipulator. Regarded as a perfect villain, he was portrayed in satirical cartoons as a thief running with bags of cash in his hands. In 1867 he was co-opted by Daniel Drew and Jim Fisk on the board of Erie Railroads and together they attempted to put out of business the richest man in America, the legendary Cornelius Vanderbilt. Politicians were bribed in Albany, New York, the state capital. An agreement was, nevertheless, worked out so that Vanderbilt too, at least indirectly, benefited from the unlawful deal (Renehan, 2005).

After thoroughly studying the odd fluctuations of the gold market, Gould devised a strategy to corner it. Feelings of omnipotence persuaded him that he could essentially control the gold supply in the US, putting him in a position to influence the entire national economy. The strategy could only work if the government abstained from selling gold reserves, thus leaving the market in thrall to private monopolies. Jay Gould bribed officials and succeeded in bringing the price of gold to such a level that panic ensued on Wall Street. However, on the day which would become known as 'Black Friday' (24 September 1869), the federal government was forced to intervene to drive the price down, and despite the proven unorthodox manipulation, the culprit was allowed to walk away with a profit estimated in millions of dollars.

Gould and his partner Fisk ran the Erie Railroad until 1872, when the latter was assassinated in a Manhattan hotel. At the funeral, the network of interests became visible, with entrepreneurs, law enforcers, judges, and representatives of the political machine sharing their grief for the loss of a friend. Jay Gould remained active in the railroad business, buying and selling stocks, and in the 1880s was attracted to the New York City transportation system, then bought the American Union Telegraph Company, and by the end of the decade he dominated much of the transportation and communication infrastructure of the US. When he died in 1892, his wealth was estimated at more than $100 million.

Cornelius Vanderbilt

Known as the 'commodore', Vanderbilt started working with his father at the age of eleven and at sixteen he bought a small ferry-boat with a $100 loan. Described as a tough guy and a cutthroat entrepreneur, he moved from sailboat to steamships, always undercutting and ultimately defeating competition. After creating the largest shipping empire in the world, he sold all his patrimony to invest in the railway sector. At the age of seventy-two, significantly past the average life expectancy for the period, he managed to tackle competitors who thought he was too weak to fight. As the owner of the only rail bridge giving access to New York, he controlled the gateway to the largest and busiest port in the US, a weapon that at one point he decided to use. Closing the bridge he blockaded the cargoes of rival railroads companies, causing a dramatic crisis in their stocks. He then bought the cheap shares of those he victimized, creating the largest single railroad company in America. In a move described today as a hostile takeover, he also bought several other firms and opened the Grand Central Depot, the biggest train station in the country, reaching his symbolic apotheosis. Realizing that profit would soon shift from the building of new lines to the transportation of new cargo, he directed his finances toward the kerosene business, predicting its central role in the indus-trialization of the country. Among his famous statements was a bellicose warning thrown at his business rivals: 'Gentlemen, you have undertaken to cheat me. I won't sue you, for the law is too slow. I will ruin you. Yours truly, Cornelius Vanderbilt' (Stiles, 2010: 37).

John D. Rockefeller

From a humble social background, Rockefeller reached the pin-nacle of the late nineteenth-century oil industry. His Standard Oil Company, by 1880, refined 90 per cent of the oil produced in the US. Largely regarded as a villain engaged in unfair business prac-tices, only in the late part of his life did he manage to establish a reputation as a generous philanthropist. By the end of his life he had donated more than $500 million, and his foundation con-tinues to the present day. His fortune was based on monopolistic tactics, routing rivals, and dictating prices.

He started working at the age of sixteen and at nineteen, with a friend, he founded a distribution company dealing with grain, meat, and other foodstuff. Meticulous organization and book-keeping led to success, fostering ambition to access new mar-kets. Oil had been discovered in Western Pennsylvania in 1859 and Rockefeller saw its unlimited potential. In the new sector his business acumen and fanatical eye for detail proved effective and by the end of the civil war he had bought out his partners and was busily borrowing money to expand. With new partner Henry Flagler, he concentrated on and controlled all aspects of oil production and refinement, building barrels and creating a small fleet of boats for transportation. The two also pioneered the use of railroad tank cars. His business came to public attention when Rockefeller started what he regarded as a strategy to reduce the chaotic condition of the oil market. He eliminated small operators and quickly established monopolistic conditions. In 1882 Standard Oil created a trust, bringing together all other firms in the sector, which then acquired the control of the market as a whole. This is when he was accused of ruthless business practices and unfair competition. By now portrayed as an evil robber baron, he was targeted by the Sherman Anti-Trust Act 1890 (Chemow, 2013).

Deviant Benefactors

Accumulating money and then giving some of it in charity follows a long tradition. We have seen that Christianity superseded its reluctance in accepting rich people when these began to be seen as potential benefactors. In secular thought, charity is a form of private welfare entrusted to the patronizing and arbitrary good heart of the wealthy. Like Rockefeller, Andrew Carnegie (1900) stopped his entrepreneurial activities announcing, all of a sudden, that he was going to cease his struggle for more money. In his autobiography, we read, 'I resolved to stop accumulating and begin the infinitely more serious and difficult task of wise distribution' (Carnegie, 1920: 255). His profits had reached $40 million per year and the prospect of increased earnings was astonishing. 'Had our company continued in business and adhered to our plans of extension, we figured that seventy million per year might have been earned' (ibid). He was aware that fraud and other crimes were rife in the business world, but was never tempted to resort to illegality in order to gain more money for his philanthropic deeds.

There had been much deception by speculators buying old iron and steel mills and foisting them upon innocent purchasers at inflated values—hundred-dollar shares in some cases selling for a trifle—that I declined to take anything from the common stock. Had I done so it would have given me just about one hundred million more of five per cent bonds ... but I had enough to keep me busier than ever before, trying to distribute it (ibid: 256).

Railroads contributed to the nineteenth-century industrial development but also 'helped make a number of crooks spectacularly rich' (Woodiwiss, 2001: 108). The early battles for control of the railroads were brutally competitive and engaged individuals from diverse backgrounds, in a period that witnessed remarkable examples of organized lawlessness. Nineteenth-century financial crime is commonly explained with lack of reforms and regulations, with companies and operators refusing to release reports and information or open their accounts, and with operations being suppressed of falsified. 'J. P. Morgan—whose holding company owned the Titanic—complained that President Theodore Roosevelt's trust-busting reforms would make it so that we'd all do business with glass pockets' (Soll, 2014: 175). Resistance against transparency made it difficult for the criminal justice system to intervene, and law itself incorporated a notion of market self-regulation, therefore establishing few obstacles to financial operators. 'Throughout much of this period, cultural perceptions of criminality remained focused on the "dangerous classes" while elite misconduct was seen as a relatively minor social ill' (Robb, 1992: 147).

Smaller operators or petty embezzlers were targeted, while leading businessmen were condoned. For the latter, shame and social disgrace were deemed sufficiently punitive, although those shamed could continue with their practices and, in fact, showed no loss of status. Paradoxically, there was reluctance to intervene in business for fear of hampering the market mechanism and the process of competition, although criminal practices themselves were obvious obstacles to market freedom and competition. It was like condoning unprincipled conduct in the name of conserving principles. The blame for financial criminality was therefore shifted towards its victims, namely imprudent and greedy investors who engaged in what were blatantly fraudulent initiatives. Investors deceived and defrauded were held ultimately responsible for their losses and reprimanded for failing to detect the dangers associated with financial activity: legislation, it was argued, could not protect fools from their folly. Regulation, on the other hand, would create an avalanche of norms of conduct which would end up confusing uninformed investors even more, therefore creating further opportunities for fraud. Private vigilance was preferable, it was stated, albeit the ability to exert it was far from being equally distributed. In the UK, successive parliamentary committees detailing a chain of fraudulent cases did not result in new legislation. 'Despite an alarming incidence of fraud, legislators feared alienating the business community or hindering trade through the imposition of tougher company law' (ibid: 150).

Criminologists, however, may not be content with explanations of crime based on lack of institutional responses to it, and it is interesting to examine whether and how their theoretical production took robber barons into consideration.

Statistical and Logical Impossibility

The application of statistical reasoning to social phenomena opened this century, which along with robber barons brought positivist criminology. Adolphe Quetelet's work, in this respect, was extremely influential, based as it was on his mathematical skills acquired at the universities of Ghent and Brussels. In the 1830s, after abandoning the fields of astronomy and meteorology, he addressed society adopting the principles of measurement, prediction, chance, and error guiding the examination of the physical world. Gathering 'facts of life' and determining the average intellectual features of a population, Quetelet established the existence of a 'normal' social being, whose conduct could be predicted as conforming to the majority. Behavioural regularity, however, was contrasted with the irregularity of abnormal conduct, and in a bell-shaped curve the incidence of deviance was made graphically visible. Thus, both normal and abnormal conducts became, in his view, predictable and were mapped on the basis of moral and social characteristics of individuals in what he termed social mechanics. The influence of probability over human affairs was discussed in his *Treatise on Man and the Development of His Faculties* (1835), where we find a description of average physical and mental qualities, namely of 'normal' individuals who are assumed to constitute the goal of evolutionary processes. Lack of normality in individuals, as a consequence, had to be deemed a social or biological error.

Quetelet devoted his efforts to the measurement of the height of French conscripts and the chest circumference of Scottish soldiers, reaching the conclusion that all populations could be screened both physically and intellectually. When he moved to studying the numerical consistency of crimes, he kindled the nineteenth-century discussions around free will and social determinism. Even Marx (1853) became somewhat fascinated by such 'scientific' measurements, when he totally endorsed Quetelet's (1835) observation that the same crimes repeat themselves every year with the same frequency and provoke the same punishment in the same ratios.

There is an account paid with a terrifying regularity; that of the prisons, the galleys, and the scaffolds. And every year the numbers have confirmed my prevision in a way that I can even say: there is a tribute man pays more regularly than those owed to nature or to the Treasury; the tribute paid to crime! (Marx, 1953: 157).

Marx echoed Quetelet when, pondering on the sad condition of society, he remarked that we can tell beforehand how many people will stain their hands with the blood of their fellow creatures, how many will be forgers, how many prisoners, almost as one can foretell the annual number of births and deaths. Social determinism identified the germs of all crimes and the variety and direction of their development in the specific living conditions of offenders, which prepared the ground for their acts. However, the range of criminals regarded as mere instruments of social dysfunctions, it would appear, did not include powerful individuals and groups, let alone financial criminals. Addressing the rich, Marx limited himself to reminding them that 'a few francs more or less paid to the treasury are equivalent to a few heads more or less submitted to the axe of the executioner' (ibid).

Criminal maps showed that offences were precisely localized in certain areas and among certain segments of the population (Amatrudo, 2009). The poor were significantly more prone to offending, particularly if young, male, unemployed, and uneducated (Stigler, 1986; Beirne, 1993). Surprisingly, however, crime was also found to be rife in wealthy areas, and more precisely in areas where wealth and poverty cohabited, which was interpreted by Quetelet as an effect of the large opportunities emerging from the display of inequality. Also, the impoverished, more than the poor, were proven to be prolific offenders, due to their reluctance to accept a decline in their standard of living.

Looking for a narrow opening in Quetelet's theory, we can hypothesize that his argument relating to 'impoverished' offenders applies also to the financial world, where rapidly changing market conditions provoke sudden ruin for some and material success for others. Impoverishment and simultaneous accumulation of wealth are encountered in turbulent financial periods, when traders compete and, as we have seen above, robber barons aim at the annihilation of rivals. Moreover, as Quetelet observed, in such situations lack of education loses its specific negative influence, impoverished offenders often being sufficiently educated. Financial delinquents, who are also sufficiently educated, may therefore be included in Quetelet's theorizing, also because the author's etiology of crime is based not only on the social status of offenders but also on their moral character. But, in this respect, there is a counterargument in Quetelet's analysis that invites caution: following Aristotle, the author identified virtue with moderation and rationality, and associated temperate habits and regulated passions with investments in saving banks and other institutions that encourage foresight. We are told, in brief, that the financial world contains less the germs of crime than those of its prevention. That those operating in the financial sphere may be characterized by intemperance, irrationality, and deregulated passion was implicitly excluded from Quetelet's analysis. Although he did pinpoint that crime statistics do not tally with the reality of delinquency, and that many crimes will never attract the attention of statisticians, financial crime, excluded from the statistics, was a logical impossibility, due to the 'calming' effect participation in finance generates. Ultimately, he insisted that moral defectiveness prevailed among the marginalized population and constituted a biological trait.

Old and New Crimes

The study of biological and physiognomic characteristics of offenders was expanded by the Positive School of criminology, whose scientific production may have a more or less direct application to the world of finances and the crimes occurring in it.

Following Lombroso's (1876) classification, the powerful, including financial operators, may be regarded as 'occasional criminals', when they are propelled to crime by circumstances and opportunities, or as 'criminals of passion', whose delinquency is due to feelings of love or anger: love for themselves, anger for competitors. In the work of Raffaele Garofalo (1914), we find a distinction between conduct which is criminalized through institutional reactions and conduct which is socially harmful but does not trigger institutional responses. The allusion to the crimes of the powerful here is quite obvious, although specific mention of financial crime is not made. Garofalo (2012: 129) also highlighted offences to the 'sentiment of probity', and referred to 'attacks upon property unaccompanied by violence, but involving breach of trust; obtaining money by false pretenses; embezzlement; voluntary insolvency towards creditors; bankruptcy occurring though negligence or fraud'.

For Enrico Ferri (1967), crime is the result of multiple causes, including cultural, anthropological, and social factors, and we may interpret financial delinquency through his concept of imitation, whereby criminal practices spread like collective conscience, which is formed simultaneously in the individuals composing a group and within the group itself faced with specific conditions of social existence. 'It is not an idea born in the brain of an individual and then propagating itself like the waves of a pond when a stone is thrown into it (ibid: 86). The conditions of the environment are crucial for criminal behaviour. Also, it is to the powerful that Ferri addressed his plea for penal leniency: the powerful were told to respect the laws, to set a good example by abstaining from crime, if they wanted the excluded to behave lawfully.

Financial crime, interpreted through Ferri's thought, would prove that people are neither good nor bad: there are gentlemen and brigands among all social groups, he stated. Delinquency in the financial sphere, therefore, is not determined by the philosophical–political ideas one professes or the occupational role one occupies, but by the 'moral constitution' of the offender which is forged by the surrounding environment. Human beings, according to Ferri, may adopt honest or dishonest moral conducts, but there is an intermediate moral zone inhabited by a class of individuals who are neither solidly honest nor dishonest. This class of individuals straddles vice and virtue, and leans towards one or the other due to internal or external pressures orienting their acts. By the same token, financial operators who hold on to an already atrophied moral sense will find it extremely easy to cross the border and engage in criminal activity. Hence, the incessant emphasis on making money through money will turn into pressure to engage in crime, particularly in 'narrow minds' which are receptive of dominant motives.

In 1879, Pietro Ellero wrote about what he termed 'bourgeois tyranny', which causes crime and monopolizes its definition. He named four passions associated with crime, among which he included 'criminal ambition'.

This is not a noble and dignified sentiment driving individuals to great achievements, nor is it akin to vanity or pride, rather it is a vice of the soul that leads to excessive love and appreciation of oneself and one's authority, and to yearning for yet more authority and domination (Ellero, 1978: 104).

Financial crime could be the result of similar yearning, a type of offending that Lombroso (1902), seven years before his death, described as 'new crimes', namely those committed by powerful people.

Defenders of robber barons tend to depict them as innovators, successful entrepreneurs who attract envy for their business acumen and are held in a sort of disoriented awe due to their genius (Folsom and Robinson, 2010). The 'man of genius' featured among the scientific interests of criminological positivism: Raphael, Michelangelo, and Mozart were not normal people, wrote Lombroso (1971), they were not born solely to work and eat. The list of contents of his *L'uomo di genio* includes Dante, Peter the Great, Mill, Hugo, Rossini, but also characters of great professional interest for alienists: Comte, Baudelaire, Hampère, Newton, Rousseau, Schopenhauer. These, argued Lombroso, are not only persons of high mental development whose genius signals superiority, excellence, or outstanding human capacities, they are also sufferers of neurosis and psychosis. The genius links together ideas that were previously disjointed, this is why the resulting ideas come across as odd or abnormal. But so do 'mad people', who display the most original association of ideas in sudden flashes, disclose incomprehensible digressions which at times appear ridiculous and at times ingenuous, but are always unexpected. Lombroso's depiction of Don Quixote applies in a curious fashion to financial brokers, the ardent innovators who think ahead of those surrounding them, mistake fantasy for truth and, 'with a dose of practical spirit, would reform humanity' (ibid: 25). Those who follow them are honest Sancho Panzas lacking an inventive brain, who try to instil a sense of reality in their masters, but are incapable of resisting or opposing their plans. Large hordes of followers, Lombroso suggested, make the genius a megalomaniac and a demented holder of unlimited power. Mad people and geniuses have made history, and the destiny of peoples is often in their hands. A central role among them is played by 'calculators', who are anomalous for their being prodigious, like those who can calculate mentally the logarithm of a number with eight figures and find it difficult to explain how. Financial delinquents could, finally, be likened to 'criminaloids', who do not show the physical traits of criminals and commit offences which are not treated as such or are carefully disguised as licit endeavours: among them, Lombroso included merchants and professionals.

Positivist criminologists who did not confine their analysis to individual offenders offered unwitting descriptions of financial crazes and manias. They focused on collective 'moral infections', on masses hypnotized and deprived of their will (Sighele, 1985). These collective phenomena, they remarked, grow due to complicity and imitation, producing associative forms of harmful acts, like 'hurricanes, avalanches, overflowing rivers or—more often—beastly hordes' (Gallini, 1985). Society was seen as a large infirm body, in which Gabriel Tarde (1893) detected acne, eruptive fevers, and moral epidemics. Akin to Gustav Le Bon's (2008) analysis of organized crowds who lose a 'conscious personality' and become dangerous multitudes, positivist analysis, however, focused on the variable wealth, the 'unlimited property' held by some who control the destiny of many (Gori, 1968; 2011).

Criminological positivism, in brief, did address some forms of white collar crime and the crimes of the powerful, although it failed to specifically analyse financial delinquency. We can only conjecture, therefore, that their views lend themselves to an extension embracing the type of delinquency concerning us here. Aware of the ability of powerful offenders to conceal their criminality or to decriminalize their conduct, positivists looked at power in general, at social arrangements causing dysfunctions, misery, and illegality. In this way, they reiterated an attitude towards criminality which belonged to the socialist thought inspiring them: capitalism was seen as criminal per se, a circumstance that rendered the analysis of its specific expressions of delinquency redundant. In this context, Gabriel Tarde, mentioned earlier, followed a more promising trajectory.

Passionate Interests

When discussing 'the brigandage of the nobility', Tarde
(2012: 178) did not imply that there was a time, even during
the most barbarous period, when murder, theft, rape, and arson
were the monopoly of the higher ranks of society. He meant that,
'when a man of the lower ranks was found to be a murderer, a
thief, a "stuprator", an incendiary, he stood out by reason of the
terror which he inspired, ennobled himself to a certain extent,
and broke into government circles'. Criminal careers, in his view,
could easily lead to business and politics, and vice-versa. Let us
examine his thought in some detail.

Suspicious of any miraculous providence producing harmony,
Tarde (1902) proposed a complete reversal of mental habits: nothing in the economy is objective, all is subjective, he maintained
(Latour and Lépinay, 2009). Hence his focus on psychological
phenomena, treated less as personal or interior issues than as
what is most social in us: these phenomena he termed 'inter-
psychological'. Individuals and society are not, in Tarde, distinct
or opposing entities, rather, they are 'temporary aggregates, partial stabilizations, nodes in networks that are completely free
of the concepts contained in ordinary sociology' (ibid: 9). The
terms 'social', 'psychological', 'subjective', and 'inter-subjective'
are, thus, essentially equivalent. All these different dimensions
relate to one another thanks to a principle of contagion, through
a series of 'imitative rays' crossing them all simultaneously. It is
worth probing whether these concepts of contagion and imitation
may help us in the analysis of delinquency.

According to Tarde, the notion of value can be applied in three
fields: namely, truth, utility, and beauty. Political economy chooses
to concentrate on utility, making it the only field worthy of attention. It is political economy, in this way, that shapes economic
behaviour, not the reverse. Economic thought, therefore, does not
reveal the anthropological essence of the true nature of humanity,
it just makes the field of utility the only realm in which the notion
of value is significant. And if truth and beauty are sacrificed, economic activity per se may veer towards falsehood and ugliness.
Financial operators exemplify these negative qualities, as they
conceal feelings under abstractions such as interest and revenues,
making them measurable: the economic 'science' is thus equated
to physics or chemistry. Gabriel Tarde remarked that money is

only a sign, it is nothing, absolutely nothing, if not a combination of things, of beliefs and desires, of ideas and volitions. The ups and downs of the stock market, in his view, unlike the oscillation of a barometer, cannot even remotely be explained without considering their psychological causes: 'fits of hope or discouragement in the public, propagation of good or bad sensational stories in the minds of speculators'. True, he conceded, economists have not entirely ignored the subjective aspect of transactions, but they have done so while paying partial or exclusive attention to eternal variables:

Even when they directly envisage the psychological side of the phenomena they investigate, they conceive of a human heart so simplified and so schematic; so to speak, a human soul so mutilated that minimum of indispensable psychology has the air of a mere postulate fated to support the geometric unfolding of their deductions (Tarde, 1902: 22).

Economics is therefore a science of passionate interests, and how can such a science claim that it is disinterested when it is entirely based on the defence of interests? The financial world is where 'prodigious ambitions of conquest' prevail and where billionaires are inebriated with the hope of winning, with the pride of life, and the thirst for power' (ibid: 24). Financial criminals, in this analytical framework, are perfect incarnations of homo economicus, namely individuals with 'nothing human in their heart' (ibid: 25). Invention and innovation are their key weapons, which establish new practices and guide the initiatives that are then repeated. Difference and repetition are crucial, the former caused by invention, the latter allowing for its diffusion. Conflict, however, is inevitable, while harmony is hard to achieve, and innovations have to be constantly generated: these, 'by repeating themselves, will produce other differences, and the cycle will begin again' (Latour and Lépinay, 2009: 39). The economy, including the financial sphere, cannot be imagined to become wise at last, with individuals inhabiting it in a rational and reasonable fashion, ruled by effective governance: 'it is like imagining an ecological system with no animals, plants, viruses, or earthworms' (ibid: 42).

In Tarde's analysis, crime is inscribed in the innovation-repetition dynamic, it is an imitative phenomenon; like language, markets, and governments are constituted by imitative networks

(Tonkonoff, 2013; 2014). Imitation pertains to beliefs and desires, whereby societies structure themselves in terms of values and goals through 'flows' and 'rays' that interweave in constant interactions (Tarde, 1903). Financial crime, like other crimes, emerges from these flows and rays, 'from the magma of opinions, feelings and interests that constitute the fabric of social life' (ibid: 65). It can be innovative in a technical sense as well as in its motivational dimension, or in both. The delinquent financiers and robber barons described in the preceding pages, if we adopt Tarde's views, cannot be deemed closed monads, but individuals who imitate conduct within a specific cultural context, individuals therefore who do not lack socialization or internalization of values, but, on the contrary, possess exceeding doses of them. Similarly, all financial delinquents can be said to have brought the prevailing values to their natural consequences, manifesting the common passions and convictions in a pure, new form. Echoing Lombroso, geniuses and criminals are regarded by Tarde (1893) as companions and expressions of the same social system. The genius of entrepreneurs, for example, cannot be denied, particularly because the examples they give to others are highly imitable due to their higher status. Financial crime, in this view, follows a 'cascade principle': 'As strange as it seems, there are reasons to assert that the vices and crimes located today in the last ranks of the population have fallen there from on high' (Tarde, 1890: 53). Criminality so conceived, namely as a phenomenon of imitative diffusion, establishes cultural patterns and repetitive practices, becoming a tradition. Hyper-socialized individuals, financial delinquents are therefore 'magnetizers' or even catalysts of social energy (Tonkonoff, 2014). Finally, they adhere to a very particular morality: on the one hand, remarked Tarde (1898), they see as legitimate all their dishonest manoeuvres to inflate or deflate the value of stocks, while on the other they are obsessively honest in executing the injunctions of *la Bourse* that they have directly shaped.

Charlatans and Thieves

It is against *la Bourse* that Proudhon (1857) had published before Tarde a manual for speculators, in which he detected charlatans and thieves operating under the appearance of free and regulated transactions. And it is against fraud and failure that

in 1831 the British Parliament passed the Bankruptcy Act, giving accountants a leading role as Official Assignees in managing
bankruptcies, auctions, liquidations, and debt trials. The Joint
Stock Companies Act came into force in 1844, an ambitious
piece of legislation aimed at regulating the financial dealings of
hundreds of companies. However, the newly trained accountants
found it extremely difficult to audit companies that refused to
comply and the ineffectiveness of their regulatory function soon
became evident (Soll, 2014). The Limited Liability Act 1855 (see
earlier) aimed to protect individual investors from bankruptcies,
as they became liable solely for the capital they engaged, not for
the failure of the institution in which they invested. The apparent protection of individual interests went hand in hand with
the appreciation of financial operations as instrumental for the
national interests. Hence, supposedly, the simultaneous growth
in official circles of concerns around the harm caused by financial
crime. The lexicon of financial crime entered the public domain
and prosecutors were asked 'to ensure that crimes particularly
held to touch on the public interest would be regularly prosecuted
instead of depending on the will or ability of individual victims'
(Wilson, 2014: 129).

Limited liability was, however, severely criticized by those
who saw in the new legislation, on the one hand, encouragement
for savings and investments, and on the other, an individualist
philosophy leading to possible abuse and fraud. According to traditional beliefs, shareholders had a responsibility to look after
their own investments, and even when victimized by fraudulent companies, they remained the only effective regulators of
financial behaviour. Consequently, the only legitimate response
to financial crises had to derive from their regulatory duties.
State-imposed safeguards would merely make shareholders less
vigilant. Moreover, limited liability had been intended to make
it more difficult for companies to obtain loans, but this had not
happened, 'due in part to the emergence of limited companies
happy to lend to other limited companies in return for high rates
of interest' (Taylor, 2006: 177).

The profits to be made in financing attracted more companies, whose
shareholders saw the chance of an easy 15 or 20 per cent. Competition
between these finance companies did not drive down the high rates of
interest charged; instead, it drove down the quality of securities accepted
by the companies in return for loans ... Shareholders held more shares

than they could afford, so if calls were made, there was a rush to offload the shares and the share price plummeted (ibid: 179).

The need to regulate financial activity, on the other hand, found obstacles in the very appreciation of its importance for the national economy (Taylor, 2013). Schemes continued to cause manias by promising attractive dividends and, when not fraudulent, they could still victimize investors who did not have the same knowledge and information held by those who were financially empowered. Directors still engaged in illegal trafficking in shares and price fixing. 'Alongside this were widely reported boardroom tactics of delay and the strategic releasing of allotments of shares in order to capture maximum share interest' (Wilson, 2014: 112).

George Hudson

An example of what Tarde saw as imitation turning into tradition is offered by the adventurous life of George Hudson, who can be admired by visitors of the National Portrait Gallery in London. Born in York in 1800, after working as an apprentice in a firm of drapers, he came into possession of a large sum of money, £30,000, which he claimed was a legacy from a great uncle and which he invested in his Nicholson and Hudson company, founded with his wife. He then joined the Tory Party and was elected Lord Mayor in 1837–8, an event that he celebrated with a lavish party. To mark the coronation of Queen Victoria he treated poor parishioners to a succulent breakfast and, at the same time, started his business career in railways. In 1837 an Act of Parliament made him the chairman of the York & North Midland Railway Company, and by 1844 he controlled over 1,000 miles of railway, gaining the name of Railway King. The peak of his career was reached when he drafted plans for projects costing around £10 million and became Tory MP for Sunderland. His firms by now controlled a quarter of the railways built in England. In 1848, however, his business practices began to be exposed: he paid dividends out of the company capital, mixing its reserves with his personal finances, and his shares fell dramatically. He was forced to resign from the several positions he occupied in his business empire and to repay the large sums of money misappropriated. When he was expelled from the official political arena, his wax statue at Madame Tussauds was melted

down. He fled his creditors and hid in France, and upon returning to England in 1865 he was arrested and imprisoned. When
released, he went to live in London, and friends and admirers
raised enough money to offer him a decent yearly income. When
he died, his coffin was returned, by the very railway he had built,
to York, where George Hudson Street was renamed Railway
Street, and only a century after his death was it given back its
original name (Vaughan, 1997; Beaumont, 2003).

Infinite Aspiration and Habit

Tarde was almost contemporaneous with Durkheim, who at first
sight did exactly what the former saw as a mistake to be avoided.
Tarde asked: How can sociologist treat social facts as things,
aping physicists and biologists? In Durkheim's *The Rules of
Sociological Me*thod, originally published in 1895, we find that
social facts consist of ways of acting, thinking, and feeling, external to the individual, and endowed with a power of coercion, by
reason of which the individual is controlled.

These ways of thinking could not be confused with biological
phenomena, since they consist of representations and of actions, nor
with psychological phenomena, which exist only in the individual consciousness and through it (Durkheim, 1938: 3).

A social fact, recognized by the power of external coercion which
is exercised over individuals, is accompanied by the existence
of specific sanctions against every individual effort to violate it.
'One can however, define it also by its diffusion within the group,
provided that one takes care to add a second and essential characteristic that its own existence is independent of the individual
forms it assumes in its diffusion' (ibid: 10). On the contrary, as
we have seen in Tarde, collective beliefs and desires, along with
the individual forms they assume, are not independent form one
another. Moreover, where in Tarde crime can be seen as a form of
innovation that encapsulates common beliefs and emerges from
the magma of opinions, feelings, and interests that constitute the
fabric of social life, in Durkheim it is a symptom of 'the malady of
infinite aspiration'. In transitional periods, in his view, when new
social and economic configurations take shape and the division
of labour intensifies, needs and desires are freed from moral con-
strains. As a consequence, aspirations become unmoderated. 'The

quest to make more and more money is unlimited and therefore unrealizable; however successful individuals are in accumulating wealth they may still feel unfulfilled' (Giddens, 1978: 48).

Durkheim's idea of the 'normality of crime' is well known, as is his prediction of an increase in deviant behaviour as a result of growing social differentiation and individualism. His views, therefore, set him apart from Tarde when he argued that limited amounts of criminality are functional to social conservation as they reinforce collective feelings and solidarity among law-abiding individuals. By repelling crimes and criminals, he maintained, societies attempt to identify their own collective norms of morality and legality. Durkheim, however, also expressed intense alarm towards high rates of serious crime, which he deemed a manifestation of 'morbid effervescence', therefore profoundly dysfunctional to social conservation. On the contrary, for Tarde crimes and criminals do nothing more than *express* collective norms.

Tarde's intuitions relating to imitation and interweaving social values found appropriate development in the work of Max Weber (1978: 311), who posited that practices in the economic arena turn into 'habituation and custom', and although illicit, they determine 'unreflective conducts morally approved by the surrounding environment'. This process is propelled by imitation:

Adherence to what has become customary is such a strong component of all conduct and, consequently, of all social action, that legal coercion, where it opposes custom, frequently fails in the attempt to influence actual conduct (ibid: 320).

We ignore whether notions such as morbid effervescence, imitation, and habit were inspired by cases similar to the one presented below.

The Vienna Stock Exchange crash

The crash occurred in May 1873, when many 'Ringstrasse Barons' went bankrupt, ending a period of economic expansion that seemed limitless. The case showed how the victims of financial delinquency may be varied and how the indignation against it depends on the status of those being victimized. The crisis reached the Court, affected army Generals, led entrepreneurs to suicide. Bankers and confidants of the Emperor were shattered, the entire imperial family was affected; Archduke Ludwig Viktor, Franz Joseph's brother, was ruined after following the 'tips' of speculators. Baron Gablenz, a highly paid commander of the army, lost large amounts of money and, when his plea to the Emperor for financial support was unheeded, he killed himself.

The economic boom preceding the crash had been triggered by the initiatives of banking and railway businesses, with the monarchy one of several financial actors involved. Joint-stock companies prospered on the enthusiasm kindled by the construction of the Ringstrasse in Vienna, which was part of a tumultuous building programme, and by the prospect of a World Exhibition. The frenzy led to the foundation of banks and companies which existed only on paper. On May 1873 the Vienna Stock Exchange plummeted, spreading panic among shareholders. The National Bank, short of reserves, could not intervene (Edelbacker, Kratcoski, and Theil, 2012; Linsboth, 2015).

Scrooge or Faust?

The century of corrupt bankers and robber barons was also the century of 'scientific' examination of crime and criminals. As we have seen, in Quetelet we find only a narrow opening through which financial delinquents can enter his system of thought: all criminals, in his view, possess an abysmal moral character, but mainly belong to the marginalized classes. Crime is not the exclusive reserve of uneducated people, and can be committed not only by the poor but also by the impoverished. Financial operators who commit crime because suddenly impoverished, however, may not be included in Quetelet's reasoning, as the financial world, in his view, trains people in moderation and self-control. The Positive School offers more, and the categories and concepts elaborated by Lombroso, Garofalo, Ferri, and Gori find application in the financial sphere, where criminals can be equated to 'criminaloids', 'occasional criminals', 'geniuses', 'mad people', or simply representatives of capitalism. Tarde described crime as the mechanism whereby conduct innovates beliefs and principles to then crystallize them into behavioural patterns and ultimately tradition. Financial criminals, from this perspective, express values and convictions that they share with society at large. A similar appreciation of tradition in the analysis of conduct is found in Weber, while Durkheim's work locates financial crime among those forms of 'morbid effervescence' which are dysfunctional rather than functional.

Much has been written about white-collar crime in the nineteenth century. This type of crime may have flourished because of the organizational changes in companies which made dishonesty easier, or because of the growing impersonality of relationships between managers, shareholders, and the general public. There were many rogues among company owners and directors but also, at a lower level of infamy, 'dishonest stockbrokers and embezzling clerks had a place in economic demonology' (Robb, 1992: 3-4). From railway mania onwards, investors became familiar with ingenious forms of crime, sometimes as victims, sometimes perpetrators (Perkin, 1971). A classical account of nineteenth-century life in London highlighted the greater threat posed by white-collar crime when compared to the harm caused by crimes such as theft, burglary, shoplifting, and pickpocketing (Mayhew, 1968). Financial crime became similar to traditional games of chance and fortune telling, ironically confirming that the word 'speculation' originally referred to the fantasies of divination (Fabian, 1990). Dickens' description of speculators, misers, and dishonest financial operators was noted earlier, but for a deeper characterization we have to turn to the writing of Goethe in 1808, when in *Faust* he equated the creation of value to alchemy (Soros, 1987; Goethe, 1999; Binswanger, 1994). Turning little into more, and more into more still, is the elementary principle of economic growth, as turning base metals into gold was the purpose of alchemic experiments, and while alchemy failed, economics can only succeed as alchemy.

5

Black Tuesday and Beasts of Prey

In the first half hour of 29 October 1929, later to be known as Black Tuesday, 3.5 million shares were traded in New York City, as large investors sold in a frenzy, after small investors, the previous week, had already lost everything. More than $14 billion evaporated, a figure almost five times larger than the entire US federal government budget. 'The atmosphere on Black Tuesday and the days immediately following was one of panic' (Lange, 2007: 37). Thousands gathered on Wall Street in the afternoon and police on horseback were mobilized: in a matter of days the stock exchange was closed down, the first time since the start of the First World War in 1914. What was to become the Great Depression caused considerable social harm: the national income was cut by half, 30 per cent of the population lost their jobs, malnutrition and diseases spread, schools shut down, homelessness became a major problem, and suicides rocketed. Contemporary observers reported that in the cities 'families slept in tarpaper shacks and tin-lined caves and scavenged like dogs for food in the city dump' (Schlesinger, 1957: 3), while others trudged the urban streets on hunger marches. Rural America was in similar disarray: mobs chased bankers and intimidated judges. Many feared that the country was on the verge of revolution and thought of running away with as much cash as they could carry.

Banking dominance grew under Wilson's administration during the First World War and lasted until Roosevelt took office in 1933. Calvin Coolidge, the most pro-business president during this period, was quoted as saying that America, being a business country, needed a strictly business government (Bombasaro-Brady, 2010).

Much has been written about the 1929 crash and the following economic slump, in an attempt to pinpoint causes, responsibilities, and dynamics, and with the hope of identifying the weaknesses in the financial system so that future crashes might be thwarted (Minsky, 1982; Bierman, 1998; Kindleberger, 2002; Parker, 2008; Ahamed, 2009; Galbraith, 2009).

According to Galbraith (2009: 187), the collapse in the stock market in the autumn of 1929 was a natural outcome of the previous period of speculation and euphoric mood, and the only question concerning that speculation was how long it would last. Sooner or later, confidence in the short-term increase in stock values weakens and, as a consequence, investors begin to sell and prices to fall. There follows a rush to 'unload' and the speculative orgy ends. 'This was how past speculative orgies had ended. It was the way the end came in 1929. It is the way speculation will end in the future.' The euphoric mood, moreover, was also felt outside Wall Street, for example in Florida, where a real estate boom saw purchasers betting on the doubling of their property, only to find out that no further purchasers were available when the market showed embryonic signs of collapse (Galbraith, 2009).

Keynesians would argue that the lower aggregate expenditure at that time, exacerbated by the reluctance of the Federal Reserve (the Fed) to intervene and sustain demand, brought the economic system down, creating unemployment and, consequently, driving the economy further down. This vicious circle, according to other commentators, was due instead to the rapid expansion of credit in the 1920s, namely 'over-banking', with the state providing too many licences for the establishment of financial institutions at state level. Capital requirements and deposit safety nets were set at low levels, allowing incompetent and fraudulent bankers to enter financial markets. The system was fragmented and undercapitalized, it was argued, and the risk of failure was compounded by imprudent lending policies. Monetarists, on the other hand, would suggest that the stock market crash of 1929, although causing a recession, would not have turned into a depression, had the government quickly injected money into the system. According to this view, agents and investors began to panic and banks, already dealing with insolvent borrowers, were allowed to fail. The refusal by the Fed to make emergency liquidity available is seen by some as a moral choice, in that it made the weaker financial institutions collapse and the fittest survive, in this way purportedly instilling a dose of prudence in investors. The crisis, from this perspective, had morally beneficial consequences. Others would just remark that economic cycles are principally the outcome of human activities and choices, which cannot be predicted within binding and universal statistical or empirical frameworks (Norton, 2012).

Another explanatory variable is mood. Speculation, it is explained, is boosted by widespread confidence, an optimistic feeling that everybody can get rich. It is also fostered by faith in the honesty and benevolence of others, whose market conduct will be essential for one's getting rich. Economic booms thrive on such optimism and faith, while speculative enthusiasm may only be restrained by caution, suspicion, and mistrust.

Easy availability of credit caused by rapid growth in savings lured investors into risking some funds with the prospect of greatly enhanced profits.

'Speculation, accordingly, is most likely to break out after a substantial period of prosperity, rather than in the early phases of recovery from a depression' (Galbraith, 2009: 188). From a criminological perspective, this is an important statement, as it attributes to 'abundance' rather than 'want' the source of dysfunctional conduct in markets. We shall discuss this point later, when outlining the debates around white-collar crime; first, we will turn to the criminal aspects of the 1929 crash.

Fraudulent Schemes

Many forms of crime emerged during the financial crisis, including theft, misrepresentation, fraud, diversion of funds from their stated use to another, dealing in company stock on inside knowledge, selling securities without full disclosure of relevant information, and forging account books (Kindleberger, 2002). Among the victims of these types of delinquency were investors wealthy enough to risk part of their money in all sorts of schemes, be they honest or fraudulent. The following is one among many major perpetrators.

Ivar Kreuger

Unlike common speculators who, on close examination, display juvenile, poor, or pathetic skills, Ivar Kreuger deployed aristocratic qualities in dealing with his clientele, despite being 'the biggest thief in the long history of larceny—a man who could think of embezzlement in terms of hundreds of millions'

(Galbraith, 1959: 9). It is a characteristic of the financial community that a big thief can be mistaken for a noble operator,
because in that community 'there is the tendency to confuse good
manners, good tailoring and, above all, an impressive bearing
and speech with integrity and intelligence' (ibid: 10). Kreuger
was extraordinarily competent, a quiet operator who won the
respect and confidence of the many people he exploited. Hyper-
rational in his moves, he applied his skills as a former engineer to
the precise calculation of the costs and benefits of his ventures,
involving informed as well as uninformed actors, all charmed by
his elegant lack of loquacity. In one of the rare interviews he gave,
he was remarkably candid on this point. 'Whatever success I have
had may perhaps be attributable to three things: one is silence,
the second is more silence, while the third is still more silence'
(Galbraith, 2009: 115). Kreuger's rise and fall spanned the years
of boom and depression between 1922 and 1932.

In August 1900, 20-year-old Ivar Kreuger arrived in New York
aboard a small ship from his native Sweden. He tried to find
work with a number of different construction firms. Some three
decades later, at the age of fifty-two, he had become a multimillionaire, established a virtual international monopoly in the
manufacture and sale of matches, and gained control of a chain
of other valuable industrial enterprises. He kept thousands of
investors satisfied with consistently high dividends, selling in ten
years stocks worth a quarter of a billion dollars to the American
public alone. His amazing career was brought to a sudden end
when, with engineering precision, he shot himself in his Paris
apartment in March 1932. His stocks plummeted to record lows,
but his reputation still remained intact. Still regarded as a genius,
he was likened to the hero of a Greek tragedy, a bold, intelligent,
immortal planner paying with his life for the fortune he brought
to himself and many others.

Soon after his death, however, a number of bankers and brokers in Stockholm and New York, along with some of his closest
associates, began to suggest that, due to recent insurmountable
difficulties, he had been forced to dangerously cut corners in his
business. Three and half weeks after Kreuger's fatal shooting, the
accountants of Price, Waterhouse, Ltd, who had been hired by
the Swedish authorities to conduct a preliminary examination of
his multiple and tangled affairs, revealed that he had perpetrated
gross fraud. He had deliberately listed assets that were 'greatly in

excess of the items they purported to represent, entirely fictitious, or duplicative of assets belonging to and appearing on the books of associated companies' (Shaplen, 1959: 20). The great financier, once described as the 'Puritan of Finance', had also ordered and supervised the counterfeiting of $142 million worth of Italian government securities, and had personally forged the signatures of the appropriate Italian officials on them. But this was only the beginning. After five years of investigation of the financier's 400 companies around the world by batteries of accountants and lawyers, 'the final rendering showed that Kreuger, between 1917 and 1932, had inflated earning on the books of his various real and unreal companies by more than a quarter of a billion dollars' (ibid: 22). A substantial portion of the missing millions had been given as bribes to officials across the world who had helped him in his career.

Although he was found out as a fabulous falsifier, for years he was also perceived as a brilliant business organizer, a fiduciary alchemist endowed with the art of making gold. The mystique endured even when a number of the bonds and other assets he listed turned out to be nothing but fabricated collateral for loans or deals he never made. The appreciation of his ability was perhaps due to the fact that his culpability, in the eyes of many, had to be shared with those he brought along in his entrepreneurial forays, those who helped to shape his skills, those 'who nourished him so ardently with their own ambition and avarice, and who saw reflected in his tremendous success their own image of wealth and glory' (Shaplen, 1959: 18–24).

A Flood of Corporate Larceny

Accompanied by prosperity and greed, the crash was also caused by what Galbraith lists as a number of weaknesses. Among these, first, was the poor distribution of income, which meant that the economy relied on exorbitant but 'niche' investments aimed at high-spending consumers of luxury goods. Second, an inadequate corporate structure which in the 1920s (like today?) was vulnerable to the penetration of grafters, swindlers, and impostors. 'This, in the long history of such activities, was a kind of flood tide of corporate larceny' (Galbraith, 2009: 195). Third, the most important corporate weakness was inherent in the vast constellation of holding companies and investment trusts which controlled large segments of the utility, railroad, and entertainment business. For such companies the temptation to curtail productive investment and turn to financial speculation was too strong. These weaknesses found an original synthesis in the character presented below.

Richard Whitney

Born in 1888 in Boston, Richard was son of George Whitney, the president of the North National Union Bank. He was educated at Harvard University and, when he moved to New York in 1910, he founded a bond brokerage firm with his brother. His uncle had been a partner in J. P. Morgan & Co., where his brother also held a position. This helped his business take off and gain entry to the New York Stock Exchange. His father-in-law had served as president of the powerful Union League Club and Richard was therefore able to enter the exclusive elite of New York City, soon becoming treasurer of the New York Yacht Club. Elected to the board of governors of the New York Stock Exchange in 1919, he reached its presidential position not long thereafter. On Black Thursday (24 October 1929) he agreed to act on behalf of several colleagues representing Morgan Bank, Chase National, National City, and other institutions, buying shares in prominent US corporations, including US Steel, at rates significantly higher than their market value. The move was meant to slow down the slide, as a similar move had calmed a financial panic which erupted in 1907. The market did recover slightly, but a sudden relapse followed on Black Tuesday (29 October 1929).

His reputation as a financial genius crumbled when information about his speculative investments and considerable losses began to circulate. He had responded to setbacks by borrowing heavily from relatives and friends, and his success in remaining afloat increasingly relied on sums of money he embezzled. He stole from the New York Exchange Gratuity Fund and the New York Yacht Club, while from his father-in-law he took $800,000 worth of bonds. In March 1938 evidence emerged of his fraudulent activities and his company was declared insolvent. When arrested, he pleaded guilty and was sentenced to a term of between five and ten years in Sing Sing prison: when escorted in handcuffs by armed guards, thousands of people turned up at Grand Central Station in New York to witness his fall from grace. His brother eventually returned the money owed by Richard who, having behaved as a model prisoner, was released on parole after serving three years and four months. He returned to business supervising a dairy farm and twenty-five cows, before becoming president of a textile company in Florida. Banned for life from the financial world, he lived a quiet life until 1974 (Brooks, 1999; Mackay, 2013).

Swindlers and Greed

The crash contributed to the ensuing depression which, in turn, extended the period of low stock prices. This was deemed by some as evidence that the previous prices had been too high. The blame for such high prices was laid on speculators, who were seen as responsible for having driven the rate of interest to unprecedented levels. In the *New York Evening Post* of 25 October 1929, John Maynard Keynes talked of 'the extraordinary speculation on Wall Street', while many commentators who filled the pages of the *Economist* shared his opinion. Among other causes for the crash, the Bank of England's discount rise from 5.5 per cent to 6.5 per cent was also singled out, as the new rate overtook the dividend offered by the stock exchange in New York. Therefore, as English investors shifted their money back to London, Wall Street was weakened. Keynes delayed in shifting his own money, thus losing a remarkable portion of his investment (Bierman, 1998). Deflating the balloon of American stock values became an international task, a form of protective interventionism that since 1926 Keynes had already advocated when declaring the end of laissez-faire. In 1930, he started his series of essays on 'one of the greatest economic catastrophes of modern history', which threw the system into a 'colossal muddle', showing how easy it was, in his view, to lose control of a 'delicate machine, the working of which we do not understand' (Keynes, 1972: 127). His explanation of the big crisis revolved around the attitude of lenders and borrowers, with the former distrusting the efficacy of the latter, therefore requiring high interest rates, and the latter growing increasingly reluctant to borrow money for fear that the sale of the goods produced, with the fall in prices, would not bring sufficient returns over costs. The well-known Keynesian proposals logically followed his argument, namely that 'consumption goods can only be restored by the public spending larger proportion of their incomes on such goods' (ibid: 131). Activity, doing things, spending, setting great enterprises afoot; these were the solutions proposed, not the government's 'foolish programme' to reduce its expenditure which had disastrous effects on employment (Ruggiero, 2013).

Financial distress during the crisis led to fraud, a strategy to dump the burden of losses on others and, using indeed a Keynesian argument whereby demand fosters its own supply, we can suggest that swindling was demand-determined. Economic booms build up fortunes and spread greed, and swindlers come forward to exploit that greed. Professional cheats are then joined by amateurs who are pushed 'over the line into fraud, embezzlement, defalcation, and similar misfeasance' (Kindleberger, 2002: 77). Swindling also increases as a result of a taut credit system and declining prices, and when it manifestly spreads, distress grows along with mistrust, often precipitating crash and panic.

While Keynes saw in the financial system of the time a colossal muddle, a delicate machine the workings of which we do not understand, the efficient markets hypothesis preached that the system, on the contrary, incorporated all relevant information about future events. 'The study of corporate structure, malfeasance and fraud disappeared from the agenda—competition and reputation would take care of that' (Galbraith, 2009: viii). It is in this climate that the character presented below took shape.

Charles Ponzi

The details of Ponzi's biography are difficult to verify. He is described as a migrant who moved from Italy to the US after graduating from the University of Rome. He arrived in Boston in 1903, at the age of twenty-one, and later he confessed that during the journey he had lost all his money gambling. In an interview published in the *New York Times*, he boasted: 'I landed in this country with $2.50 in cash and £1 million in hopes, and those hopes never left me' (Zuckoff, 2005: 48). After a series of humble jobs, he moved to Montreal, where he managed to find work at Carossi Bank servicing the local Italian population. When the bank collapsed as a result of the high interest rates it practised, Ponzi, temporarily unemployed, used his uncertain knowledge of the financial system in the forging of cheques. These early scams landed him in prison, although while incarcerated, he wrote letters to his mother telling her that he was working in the institution rather than serving a sentence there. When he was released, his charisma and confidence intact, he got involved in the smuggling of migrants between Canada and the US. This new activity led to a second sentence, this time served in a prison in Atlanta.

After returning to Boston, he married in 1918 and moved from one job to the next, including a tedious position in his father-in-law's grocery. This is when he hatched the scheme that would be forever associated with his name. After receiving a letter from a company based in Spain that contained an 'international reply coupon', he realized he could exchange such coupons with a number of priority stamps from other countries. Buying the stamps in one country and redeeming them for US postage stamps became a way for him to make money. He structured his business in the following way: he sent money to partners operating abroad, who would buy foreign currencies at depreciated market value; he then used the foreign currencies to buy international postal union coupons and exchanged them with the more expensive stamps in the US. It is estimated that sales brought more than 400 per cent profit on investments. The next move was to involve investors in such a profitable scheme, promising returns as high as 50 per cent in forty-five days. Ponzi paid new investors not with his actual profit but with the money he had received from previous ones, and was soon able to buy a mansion in Lexington. At this time, he earned a reputed $250,000 a day. His downfall began in August 1920, when investors panicked, encouraging a thorough investigation. He was arrested and found guilty of eighty-six counts of fraud. He spent fourteen years in prison, was divorced by his wife, and died penniless in Rio de Janeiro in January 1949 (Dunn, 2004; Zuckoff, 2005; Kindleberger and Aliber, 2005; Frankel, 2012).

The Return of Criminaloids

That criminals inhabited the business arena was clear long before the 1929 crisis, as we have seen when traversing the robber barons era. Early in the twentieth century, some thought that America's barbarians came from above, as writers and investigative journalists described the consortia between business, politics, and crime at the local level (Woodiwiss, 2001). Social activists and reformers expressed concern about predatory wealth and detected the existence of a class of people adept at manipulating, corrupting, and destroying the foundations of the social order. This class was the 'shame of the cities' (Steffens, 1904). An academic researcher and theoretician, Ross (1907) identified what he termed 'social vulnerabilities' which were being exploited by a new group of individuals that he labelled, echoing Lombroso, *criminaloid* (Schrager and Short, 1980). The hallmark of criminaloid practices was that, even though they were technically illegal, they had 'not come under the effective ban of public opinion' (Ross, 1907: 48). Approaching an *ante litteram* definition of white-collar crime, Ross remarked that perpetrators did not deem themselves culpable, nor did they appear such in the eyes of the public, hence they did not perceive their actions to be criminal.

Their behaviour therefore took place in a perilously ambiguous realm— frequently quite harmful in its effects on individuals and on the social order, yet unrecognized as such by the public (Schrager and Short, 1980: 15).

Ross lamented this indifference and advanced a number of reasons for it, including the high social status of perpetrators, their respectability, and the impersonality of their relationships with those they victimized. His findings prompted the need for a redefinition of crime and a re-conceptualization of its aetiology. The destructive practices adopted by the elite, in his view, were more dangerous than those of their low-brow cousins such as street offenders. The latter caused limited damage, while the new class of offenders, sporting the livery of virtue, were 'beasts of prey' and could 'pick a thousand pockets', poison and pollute thousands of minds, and imperil numerous lives (Ross, 1907: 30). Big business criminaloids rob and kill on a grand scale, he intimated, but manage to escape punishment and ignominy while repelling the criminal label.

   Soon afterwards, the prolific representatives of the Chicago School of sociology addressed the dysfunctional outcomes of rapid urbanization and migratory flows, locating deviance and crime within specific natural areas. When Park (1925) analysed the decisive factors instigating the movements of crowds, he drew a parallel with the fluctuations of markets, both in his view determined by psychological dynamics. The disorderly crowd reflected a condition of instability found in markets, a condition he did not hesitate to define as 'crisis'. Commercial and financial exchange, like crowds, inhabited a space which was always critical, that is a space where 'the tensions are such that a slight cause may precipitate an enormous effect' (ibid: 22). Labour agitators and political leaders were equated to stock-exchange speculators, for their respective ability to control and manipulate the public. Crowds as well as markets were characterized by contingency and impersonality, in a constant climate of unstable equilibrium. Both were animated by casual and mobile aggregations, a perpetual agitation caused by unpredictable alarms or inscrutable collective conduct.

To what extent are mob violence, strikes, and radical political movements the results of the same general conditions that provoke financial panics, real estate booms, and mass movements in the population generally? To what extent are the existing unstable equilibrium and social ferment due to the extent and speed of economic changes as reflected in the stock exchange? (ibid: 22).

Park's 'critical condition' was twinned with what he identified as psychological moments. These, he contended, arise with high frequency within societies that have acquired a high state of mobility. Let us see how 'psychological moments' were addressed from another perspective.

Anality and Learning Processes

In the early twentieth century, psychoanalysis connected money to anality and the unconscious. Ferenczi (1914: 321) linked attitudes towards money and financial affairs to excrements held back, the first form of 'saving' of the growing human being, a bodily activity turning into 'mental striving that has anything to do with collecting, hoarding and saving'. Coprophilia then turns into interest for small solid objects: glass marbles, buttons, fruit pips are eagerly collected, not for their intrinsic value, but as measures of value, as primitive coins, in an imitative allusion to money exchange. With Melanie Klein (1923) the relationship with money, rather than described as being instinctive, was examined as the result of a cultural process, in which children are taught that they cannot have all the objects surrounding them. The instinctual drive to amass wealth was then linked by Freud (1927) to the civilization process, understood as the building up of knowledge about the extraction of useful things from nature. This process is threatened by individuals and groups who are frustrated, because their desires are left unsatisfied, and are incapable of respecting prohibitions, as they find it hard to accept privation, namely internal self-coercion. Surely, the 1929 financial crash signalled the existence of widespread frustration and collective intolerance to privation, and following Freud we may suggest that in the absence of effective self-coercion the survival of society and civilization required open, external coercive measures. Freud was aware that such measures might not work when addressed to neurotic individuals, although he also argued that non-neurotics might develop hostility and reject privation, therefore feeling alienated from the very process of civilization. The greatest impediment to civilization, in Freud, derives from instinctual aggressive inclinations and the major metaphor he used, in this argument, was of an economic nature. Happiness, in his view, is a problem of *the economics of the individual's libido.* 'If the loss of instinctual satisfaction is not compensated for economically, one can be certain that serious disorder will ensue' (Freud, 1930: 34).

Following the Wall Street crash, in Vienna, where Freud lived and practised, the Credit Anstalt Bank collapsed through the sudden depreciation of its assets. It failed despite support from the Bank of England, precipitating a crisis in German banks. It is curious that Freud did not interpret this event as an example of aggressive inclinations or as a threat to the civilization process. We can only conjecture that the event and the financial crisis in general were manifestation of 'the economics of collective libido'.

Klein, on the other hand, attributed to learning processes a central role in the shaping of conducts, while Freud suggested that all social groups and individuals, irrespective of their social rank, associate happiness and desires with economic satisfaction.

Edwin Sutherland, to whose pioneering work we now turn, developed his own version of learning processes and economic satisfaction.

Differential Association

The 1929 crash proved that social interdependence can at times be troublesome or even disastrous. Honest operators and investors became committed to crooks and, before clearly realizing the nature of their commitments, found it necessary to defend them in order to defend themselves. They became part of a subculture, an enclave that was forced by the events to adopt specific techniques and rationalizations to perpetuate themselves and their acts. The echo of what is known in criminology as differential association can be heard in this formulation.

Enacting a revolutionary turn in the history of criminology, Sutherland (1940) warned that sources such as 'case histories' and 'criminal statistics derived from the agencies of criminal justice' were bound to lead scholars to conclude that crime is caused by poverty and the individual and collective characteristics associated with it. Such sources neglected the vast areas of criminal behaviour by businesses and professionals. The robber barons of the previous century, he noted, were white-collar criminals, as proven by Vanderbilt's statement: 'You don't suppose you can run a railroad in accordance with the statutes, do you?' (ibid: 2). Sutherland also mentioned Krueger, Whitney (see earlier in the chapter), and many other 'merchant princes and captains of finance', concluding that 'more important crime news may be found on the financial pages of newspapers than on the front pages' (ibid). Among the several types of white-collar crimes which concern us here, he included misrepresentation in corporate financial statements, manipulation of stock exchange, embezzlement and misapplication of funds, tax frauds, and misapplication of funds in receiverships and bankruptcies, namely all conducts that Al Capone called the legitimate rackets.

Referring specifically to the financial world, Sutherland focused on violations of trust, which he divided into two categories: misrepresentation of asset values and duplicity in the manipulation of power. We have seen examples falling in the first category, while conduct of the second type is exemplified by company directors buying and selling for profit something that belongs to their own companies. The offenders, in such cases, hold two antagonistic positions, like for instance a football coach who is permitted to referee a game in which his own team is playing. Data provided by Sutherland indicated that 75 per cent of the banks examined by the Comptroller of Currency had violated the law, that 20 per cent of lie detector tests of employees in Chicago banks showed they had stolen funds, and that 80 per cent of financial statements of corporations were misleading. 'The financial cost of white-collar crime is probably several times as great as the financial cost of all the crimes which are customarily regarded as the crime problem' (ibid: 4–5). While burglaries and robberies secured around $120,000 in a year, the sum stolen by Krueger was nearly 2,000 times as much. Of greater importance than the sums stolen, Sutherland explained, is the damage white-collar criminals cause to social relations, as their behaviour creates distrust, lowers the collective morale, and produces social disorganization on a large scale.

On the impunity of white-collar criminals, the argument was made that criminologists would not hesitate to accept as data a verified case study of an offender who had never been convicted. By the same token, white-collar criminals who have never been convicted should be included within the scope of criminology, provided reliable evidence is available. Evidence regarding such criminals may not appear in criminal courts because the injured parties are more interested in recovering money than in culprits being punished, therefore it is only in civil tribunals that relevant material for study can be found. Moreover, certain conduct has to be deemed criminal even when conviction is avoided through pressure which is brought to bear on courts or other entities and subjects. For instance, gangsters and racketeers manage to avoid punishment due to the pressure they exercise on witnesses, victims, and public officials. Similarly, 'white-collar criminals are relatively immune because of the class bias of the courts and the power of their class to influence the implementation and administration of the law' (ibid: 7). Sutherland continued the comparative examination of conventional and white-collar crime by focusing on 'persons who are accessory to crime'. In a case of kidnapping, prosecution is not confined to the offender who forcefully takes away the victim, but extends to the various persons who identified her, studied her movements, provided logistic help, enacted custodial duties, negotiated the ransom money, and, finally, put the money into circulation. On the contrary, the prosecution of white-collar criminals frequently focuses on one precisely identifiable perpetrator. Thus, political corruption, bribe taking, and embezzlement, which require the participation of a range of actors, are regarded as crimes committed by individual, solitary offenders.

Financial crime, according to Sutherland, shows that 'law is like a cobweb; it's made for flies and the smaller kinds of insects, so to speak, but lets the big bumblebees break through' (ibid: 9). And as the most powerful group in medieval society secured relative immunity by 'benefit of clergy', contemporary powerful groups do likewise by 'benefit of business or profession'. In contrast to the power of financial criminals is the weakness of their victims. Investors and stock-holders are disorganized, Sutherland argued, they lack technical knowledge and are unable to protect themselves. Financiers who managed to take large sums of money from Vanderbilt soon realized that it had been a mistake to target such a powerful client and that in the future they would confine their efforts to customers scattered all over the country, who would be unable to organize and fight back. In brief, 'White-collar criminality flourishes at points where powerful business and professional men come in contact with persons who are weak. In this respect, it is similar to stealing candy from a baby' (ibid: 9).

Revealing an appreciation of the variable 'mood' as expressed earlier in the economic analysis of the 1929 crash, Sutherland reiterated that poverty, in the form of stress afflicting business in periods of depression, could not be positively correlated to white-collar crime. On the contrary, crime in the financial arena was seen as a by-product of the optimism characterizing periods of economic boom. The 'mood' was translated by Sutherland into a process whereby behaviour is learned in direct or indirect association with those who already enact it, so that 'those who learn this criminal behaviour are segregated from frequent and intimate contacts with law-abiding behaviour' (ibid: 11). Whether a person becomes a criminal or not is determined largely by the comparative frequency and intimacy of their contacts with others who violate the law. This is what he called the process of differential association. From Sutherland's theory we may deduce that financial criminals start their careers in good neighbourhoods, graduate from prestigious colleges, and access particular business situations in which criminality is rife, where they learn the techniques and the rationalizations to perpetuate that type of criminality.

In the uncut version of *White-Collar Crime* finally published in 1983, the chapter 'Financial Manipulations' opens with the description of the practices of corporations or their executives involved in fraud or violation of trust. The initial outline of such practices include:

embezzlement, extortionate salaries and bonuses, and other misapplications of corporate funds in the interest of executives or of the holders of certain securities; public misrepresentation in the form of stock market manipulations, fraud in sale of securities, enormous inflation of capital, inadequate and misleading financial reports, and other manipulations (Sutherland, 1983: 153).

Sutherland noted that in the previous decade at least fifty-nine of the seventy largest corporations had engaged in financial manipulation, and that 150 charges had been brought against them by official investigating committees and public authorities. The chapter is an analysis of those 150 charges, a florilegium of criminal conduct that preceded, accompanied, and followed the Wall Street crash and the ensuing Great Depression.

Executives and directors of a corporation are trustees and their managerial skills should be devoted to the interests of the corporation as a unit. However, they also have personal, multiple, and often conflicting interests. The long anthology compiled by Sutherland starts with violations of trust in the interest of particular executives, small groups of executives, specific groups of security holders, investment banks, and other corporations with which these executives are connected. A prominent case in which a director used corporate funds for his personal affairs was that of Mr Seiberling, 'the organiser and practical dictator of the Goodyear Rubber Company'. He stole around $4 million and explained that he regarded the corporation he managed as his own: he used personal funds for corporate purposes on many occasions, just as he used corporate funds for personal purposes on other occasions.

Closely related to embezzlement by individuals are cases of officers abusing their position in order to make a profit at the expense of the corporation. For example, the president of the American Sugar Refining Company purchased huge quantities of sugar with his own funds, and knowing that the introduction of a new tax would bring the price up, held the sugar and later sold it at a considerable profit to the corporation. Similar cases occurred in the steel industry, where executives owned personal companies and offered services to the corporation employing them. In other words, they acted as both buyers and sellers of the services provided. In other cases, executives were employed by a company which was owned by a corporation they controlled through ownership of shares, a situation making manipulation in their own financial interest possible.

Another type of violation of trust consists in causing damage to a subsidiary company and its shareholders. For example, the Inland Steel Company owned 80 per cent of the stock of the Inland Steamship Company. The directors sold the assets of the latter to the former company, therefore acting as buyers and sellers at the same time. 'Minority stockholders of the Inland Steamship Company charged in a suit that the price paid was insufficient and that they had been illegally deprived of their property' (ibid: 156). Similarly, the Radio Corporation of America established a partnership with General Electric and Westinghouse Electric in 1919, and only in 1932 was the nature of the partnership revealed. The Radio Corporation had given free shares to its two partners in return for the right to manufacture, sell, and distribute radio apparatus controlled by the two corporations.

Sutherland's classification continues with violations of trust in the form of favouritism of one group of security holders at the expense of another. Thus, the stockholders of the American Tobacco Company drew a reorganization plan following the suggestions made by the executives of the corporation. Later they discovered that the reorganization was very favourable to certain securities held principally by the executives themselves. Other violations of trust are perpetrated by investment bankers, who sit on many boards and control financial policies. An instance of this type saw the US Steel Corporation entrusting bankers with a reorganization plan. The plan devised turned $200 million of stocks into 5 per cent bonds. 'This proposal appeared economical, but it concealed a profit of $10 million which the promoters [the bankers] expected to make from the conversion' (ibid: 158). Some analogy can be found in the Goodyear Rubber Company case, in which the company director, Clarence Dillon, bought the services of a firm known as Kennedy & Co that he owned.

The appropriation of enormous salaries and bonuses by executives constitutes another area of fraud. Sutherland provided details of a number of such illegal appropriations by officers who were in a position to manage the corporation in their own interest. The defence made by executives echoed contemporary arguments: the number of persons qualified for executive positions is small, therefore large rewards are necessary as incentives to secure efficiency and, consequently, to benefit the corporation in the long run. Huge salaries and bonuses, on the other hand, may be given surreptitiously by subsidiaries or parent companies, a practice that continues even when the corporation's profits decline and shareholders lose part of their money. Cases involving this type of illegal appropriation by executives occurred at Bethlehem Steel, Union Carbide, Warner Brothers, and Loew's.

Among the seventy corporations studied by Sutherland, forty were found to engage in public misrepresentation of their finances. One type of public misrepresentation is termed 'stock watering', which consists of deliberately overvaluing stocks in relation to the corporation's tangible assets and performance. The practice of stock watering is common in corporate mergers, when the actual wealth of the parties involved is hard to ascertain. Companies, however, can also increase their capital and issue new stocks without any change in their material assets, like General Motors did in 1916 and Goodyear in 1920. The latter company became unable to meet its obligations to shareholders and was charged with fraud, because 'the officers knew early in 1920 that it was on the verge of bankruptcy and misrepresented the financial condition of the corporation in the hope of securing additional funds' (ibid: 166).

Sutherland equated the use of inside information by directors to robbery, like in cases in which shares were bought and sold according to the planned change in dividends. For example, James R. Keene, an executive of the US Steel Corporation, became famous for his ability as a market manipulator: he was put in charge of the sale of securities and 'by judicious buying and selling at the same time he forced the price upward' (ibid: 168). Forcing the prices of shares up amounts to 'creating a market', a practice that, as Sutherland explained, can also take the form of gifts given to influential persons, who receive free shares with the justification that they are, for the corporation, equivalent to advertising expenditure.

Public misrepresentation in the annual reports of corporations may conceal their actual financial operations. Failure to provide adequate information to shareholders and the general public became widespread during the early years of the Great Depression, when reports showed fictitious earnings and hid losses. Union Carbide reported a net income of $18 million in 1931 and only around £6 million in 1932. 'One of the devices of some corporations is to invest in their own stock, pay themselves dividend on these stocks, and record the dividends as income' (ibid: 170). Conversely, in periods of prosperity, reports can conceal parts of the profits. In a final list of miscellaneous manipulations, Sutherland mentioned coercion to buy or sell securities, illustrated by the case of the Firestone Rubber Company. During the 1920s the company attempted to develop a rubber plantation in Liberia and started to buy land in that country. With the cooperation of President Herbert Hoover, it gave a loan to the Liberian government under conditions that gave Firestone control of the financial policies of the country. After objecting strenuously to the conditions imposed, the Liberian government caved in, and its fears were fully justified when, years later, the League of Nations stepped in to stop the exploitation: 'the money expended since the Firestone loan had been squandered as a result of the deplorable advice of the American financial advisers in Liberia' (ibid: 173).

Sutherland's prose may appear to some readers as the outcome of a fixation, its hectic rhythm the reflection of an obsessive mind. It is time, therefore, to turn to calmer, more reflective contributions.

Theft and Cupidity

A key thinker in the criminology of the turn of the century, Willem Bonger (1916; 1936) focused on the influence of economic conditions on criminality, rejecting biological and psychological explanations which were mainly addressed at pathological minorities. Analysing the relationship between modes of production, social contexts, and crime, he concluded that inequality was to be seen as the major causative variable. The classification of a conduct as criminal, rather than simply immoral or anti-social, was determined, in his view, by the degree of challenge against the dominant social order it incorporated. Crime was the manifestation of the weakening of altruism, caused by the prevailing economic arrangements which undermined 'the moral strength of people and [made] it more likely that criminal ideas will be converted into criminal acts' (Hebberecht, 2010: 60). After contesting the assumption that religious belief acted as a crime prevention force and criticizing the criminalization of homosexuality, he also dismantled the thesis linking race to crime. Egoism, which in the subaltern classes was stigmatized and punished, among the dominant classes was condoned and rewarded.

Among the class of people manifesting egoism, Bonger included 'greedy bankers', who in the late 1920s 'continued to sell the bonds of several Latin American countries after they had been told that the countries had stopped paying interest' (Kindleberger and Aliber, 2005: 147). In sum, he did not limit his work to the examination of 'thefts committed from poverty' and the role of relative and absolute deprivation, he also discussed 'theft committed from cupidity'. Echoing Edwin Sutherland, he warned that observing exclusively prisoners and known offenders yielded a distorted view of crime, and that if we compare conventional criminals with those who never steal but commit all sorts of reprehensible acts, 'the comparison is not to the advantage of the latter' (Bonger, 1916: 113). Their trickery and their pitiless egoism, he claimed, often make them more dangerous to society than others, which is one of the reasons for criminology not to build its knowledge system solely through the investigation of conventional delinquency.

Thieves driven by cupidity, he remarked, earn enough to satisfy their more pressing needs, and 'they steal only when the occasion presents itself in order to satisfy their desire for luxury' (Bonger, 1916: 108). Such needs are spawned by a competitive environment and the never-ending desire to accumulate wealth, with the result that incessant greed creates increasingly new needs.

In a society where some are rich, who have more income than is needed to supply the fundamental necessities, and who create other needs for themselves, in such a society the cupidity of those who have not similar incomes at their disposal will be awakened (ibid).

Conventional crime, from this perspective, seems to constitute imitative behaviour adopted by the disadvantaged, who express the same desires as their wealthy counterparts. Luxury attracts those who witness the spectacle of other people enjoying it, and the greater the gap between the rich and the poor, the stronger the attraction. The misdeeds of the wealthy, therefore, are more serious than the crimes of the excluded, in that they spread egoism and infinite material hunger: 'If one has much, the other, an imitator, wants the same' (ibid).

Bonger reiterated this point in a number of ways, for example arguing that people whose work brings them in touch with money most tempted to appropriate it, legally or otherwise. In this respect, he did mention the financial world, of course, but extended his analysis to cover those business areas were the circulation of money is constant and conspicuous: hence 'the large number of economic crimes committed by workers occupied in commerce' (ibid: 108). Servants were also included in the list, for their hidden or manifest desire to attain the status of those they serve. However, when addressing the thefts of large sums of money, Bonger did not hesitate to single out financial operators who, 'from the nature of their work, have the opportunity to appropriate other people's money'.

When we investigate the reasons for their committing their misdeeds, we shall see that nine times out of ten the criminal is a speculator who has lost, or perhaps an individual who visits prostitutes, and hence has great need for money (ibid: 109).

We do not know how many speculators during the 1929 crisis visited prostitutes, we only know, as Bonger underlined, that the danger for them of being found out was not great, while the number of their offences was enormous.

Money and Genius

There are some common denominators in speculative episodes, the first of which is the extreme brevity of financial memory. Past disasters are rapidly forgotten and the features of crises and the nature of crashes are deemed new. Simultaneously, financial operators tend to believe that their moves on markets are innovative, the outcome of unprecedented discoveries. Every generation of financiers, in brief, feels that theirs is a novel, brilliant way of arranging and re-inventing the market in which they operate. 'There can be few fields of human endeavour in which history counts for so little as in the world of finance' (Galbraith, 1993: 12).

Another common aspect revolves around the experience of seeing one's wealth increase. Those fortunate enough to live through such an experience will never recognize that they are fortunate, nor that their wealth is undeserved. Rather, they will be likely to believe that enrichment is generated by insight, intuition, and a good dose of adventurous spirit. Money, thus, becomes the reflection of the acts and minds of those who accumulate it, mirroring their unique intelligence. Possession of large amounts of money indicates genius. In fact, financial operations do not lend themselves to substantial innovation, and if operators feel that their intelligence places them above ordinary individuals it is because they are oblivious of those, intelligent or not, who preceded them.

All financial innovation involves, in one form or another, the creation of debt secured in greater or lesser adequacy by real assets. This was true in one of the earliest seeming marvels: when banks discovered that they could print bank notes and issue them to borrowers in a volume in excess of the hard-money deposits in the bank's strong rooms ... The depositors could be counted upon, it was believed or hoped, not to come all at once for their money (ibid: 19–20).

Explanations rejecting human error, ruthlessness, in-built dynamics, or ignorance of such dynamics were also advanced. The 1929 crisis might have been caused by the devastating hurricane blowing from the Caribbean in the autumn of 1926 and hitting the financially diligent population of the US, when thousands lost their homes and possessions. God and the vicious weather were then responsible for the debacle, not human liability to financial delusion.

Explanations provided by criminologists, by contrast, were based around the existence of criminaloids, whose practices escaped stigmatisation and repelled culpability (Ross, 1907). 'The shame of the cities' did not perceive their actions to be criminal thanks to their social status, respectability, and the invisibility or abstract nature of their relationships with their victims. These 'beasts of prey' were the object of unprecedented criminological analysis, suggesting that the financial cost they caused was several times greater than that caused by conventional offenders. The damage they produced was also visible in social relations, where it spread distrust and lowered collective morale. Financial delinquency, we were told, is 'learned' through constant association with those who already practise it, in a process in which both the techniques and the rationalizations are slowly acquired by delinquents (Sutherland, 1940; 1983). Differential association proposed by Sutherland enjoyed a good reception in the work of Bonger (1916; 1936), who argued that the classification of a conduct as criminal depends on the degree to which it challenges the established social order. Financial crime does not pose such a challenge; for Bonger, it is one of the automatic outcomes of a social order inspired by egoism, a value that, when expressed by the dominant classes, is condoned and rewarded.

If we share Bonger's views, we can conclude that greedy bankers and cupidity are aided by a competitive environment and the never-ending desire to accumulate wealth.

When in 1933 the Glass-Steagall Act was introduced in the US, many believed that this was the ideal measure to respond to the crash, as it constrained operators into one of the two spheres: investment or commercial banking. The clear separation of the two spheres was meant to protect customers from risky operations. Regulation was also enacted by the Roosevelt administration through the creation of the Securities and Exchange Commission in 1934. Roosevelt himself, however, did not believe that he could stop fraud, he only hoped that the Commission could 'prevent malicious misinformation being given to stockholders, limit insider trading, and ban the preferred stock lists that had helped destabilize the market' (Soll, 2014: 192). The financial world reacted by arguing that regulation stifles markets and hampers innovation. A similar reaction was to be repeated after the crises that occurred in subsequent periods, as we shall see in the following chapters.

6

Incompetent Muddlers and Organization Men

After Roosevelt, in his inaugural speech of 1933, biblically promised to throw the money dealers out of the temple, one may have
expected that, fearing divine wrath, financial delinquents would
assuage their sinful passions. After the Great Crisis, there seems
to be a gap in the history of financial crime, as if all of a sudden
conventional criminals had become the only actors on the scene.
Historians report a sharp increase in street robberies, interpersonal
violence, and theft during and immediately after the Second World
War. In England and Wales, for example, the police recorded an
average of 90,000 indictable offences each year during the first two
decades of the twentieth century, a figure that reached 500,000
during the 1950s. The crime rate quadrupled from 250 per 100,000
inhabitants in 1930 to 1,000 by 1950. A sharper rise was recorded
during the 1960s and 1970s (UK Parliament, 2015). We have seen
in previous chapters how financial crimes flourished in a climate
of unfettered economic initiative and lack of state intervention.
One might assume that, on the contrary, with Keynesian measures
aimed at controlling the economy, barriers were naturally erected
which would hamper this type of criminality. We shall see how
this assumption is not substantiated by events.

In reality, one of the causes of the declining attention devoted to
financial crime in the public domain may have been the growing
direct and indirect influence of the media. Lazerfield and Merton
(1970) noted the increasing concentration of media ownership
characterizing the period, a process which reduced the opportunity to scrutinize the workings of the economic system while
sponsoring its unquestioned acceptance.

Since the mass media are supported by great business concerns geared
into the current social and economic system, the media contribute to the

maintenance of that system. This contribution is not found merely in the effective advertisement of the sponsor's product. It arises, rather, from the typical presence in magazine stories, radio programs and newspaper columns of some element of confirmation, some element of approval of the present structure of society. And the continuing reaffirmation underscores the duty to accept (ibid: 505–6).

By the Second World War, therefore, large business was able to select the social issues deserving of attention, the individuals and groups meritorious of praise, and the norms worthy of compliance. The powerful owners of the media could hardly describe themselves as criminal. 'There were of course, criminal businessmen, but these were seen as exceptional and deviant individuals in a fundamentally sound system' (Woodiwiss, 2001: 165).

Research focused on the war period, however, uncovered the pervasiveness of business crime, particularly in the wholesale food industry, portraying commercial activities as forms of organized criminality (Hartung, 1950). In the US, criminological enquiry also addressed violations of the rules established by Office of Price Administration. Clinard (1952) remarked that all wars witness profiteering by some businesses and the securing of unfair advantages by many civilians, all attempts to circumvent economic controls set up by governments to guarantee more adequate distribution of certain essential goods and to prevent inflation. In general, these controls concern the allocation of scarce industrial materials, the regulation of prices and rents, and the distribution by rationing of vital commodities in scarce supply. Economic stabilization is as essential to success in war as are the production of arms and the efficacy of armed forces. Clinard showed how the compulsory controls imposed for the first time on the US economy triggered the development of widespread noncompliance with rules. As soon as norms came into effect violations began to occur, particularly in the areas of price, rent and, later, rationing controls. Commentators, initially, associated those involved in illicit business with bootleggers, professional criminals, or organized groups, namely the underworld entrepreneurs who had accumulated wealth through the smuggling of alcohol during the Prohibition Era. Later, however, the very definition of 'black market' proved inadequate, as it implicitly excluded businesspeople from the range of racketeers and organized gangs normally engaged in such a market. The illicit economy unveiled

by Clinard showed that sales were made over the officially established ceiling price and transactions of rationed products took
place without 'rationing currency' changing hands. A wide range
of activities were covered, from heavy industrial materials to
items such as clothing, gasoline, shoes, sugar, potatoes, onions,
cigarettes, and alcoholic beverages. Violators were mainly manufacturers, wholesalers, and retailers, while rationing violations
included the theft and counterfeiting of ration currency, false
record-keeping, and 'cash-on-the-side' payments.

Take some suppliers for instance. They do everything on the surface
legally. They deliver beef to the wholesaler and sign for at the ceiling
price. About half an hour later an inconspicuous fellow comes along
and is handed an envelope that contains money. There is no record and
no one is any wiser (ibid: 18).

Of course, the rationing of a large number of essential commodities among millions of people was a serious administrative
problem, with the mass printing of coupons and their distribution
among all consumers and dealers. Coupons acquired the function
of money and counterfeiting of ration currency became a lucrative business: in 1939, $487,019 worth of coupons was detected.
Among the other violations falling in the arena of financial
criminality, were: failure to keep records, falsification of books,
fraudulent of inventories, or their concealment.

Frequently, business criminals claim that the laws they break
are unjust or unnecessary and that government interference damages producers, traders, and consumers. Laissez-faire, in other
words, is said to possess its own laws that make statutes and
institutionally imposed codes of conduct inappropriate and
redundant. Such justifications formed the system of belief also
found by Clinard among illegal dealers, who saw themselves as
benefactors rather than criminals. 'The big manufacturers and
suppliers gained most from wartime violations than any racket-
eer' (Woodiwiss, 2001: 168).

After the war, while corporations acquired the status of benevolent entities and managers gained the reputation of responsible
actors, the delinquency of the powerful, including financial crime,
became almost invisible. This process was accompanied by the
economic boom normally associated with the post-war period,
when financiers, supposedly, could do extremely well without
resorting to crime.

From the New Deal to the Marshall Plan

If the Great Crisis is still regarded as a turning point in economic and social history, it is because it led to a revision of liberal orthodoxy (Landes, 1969). It persuaded governments to accept the principle that the visible hand of the state could help rather than obstruct economic growth. Following the teachings of Keynes, interventionism was also seen as a key tool for the establishment of social harmony and the neutralization of conflict. Economic interpretations of the new policies vary, although paradoxically they converge in some respects.

The views of two major analysts of the post-war period need to be accounted for in order to provide the theoretical background needed in this chapter: Polanyi, a socialist, and Schumpeter, a conservative liberalist (Trigilia, 1998). Both attempted to explain the decline of unbound market freedom and the birth of state regulation of the economy. According to Polanyi's (1944) argument, this shift saw the space of enterprise being reduced and the economy brought back into the womb of society. With this formulation Polanyi meant to underline that economic initiative is not the result of an innate drive and, with Aristotle, to suggest that humans are social not economic beings. The great transformation as described by Polanyi consisted in the apparent superseding of liberal capitalism, when market forces seemed to be destined to lose part of their purchase on development. This transformation, conversely, was interpreted by Schumpeter (1958) as the result less of the decline of a system than of the specific class of entrepreneurs causing, through their incompetence, the economic crisis. In his view, this class was increasingly incapable of producing innovation, a key variable of growth, and unable to respond to anti-market measures and cultures. A weakening bourgeoisie was singled out as one of the major causes of decline, with the growing predominance of large bureaucratized firms undermining the vivacity of smaller enterprises. This weakened class seemed reluctant to adhere to its own values and showed a lack of political vigour in defending itself from the surrounding hostile forces: the state, labour organizations, and disaffected intellectuals. Anti-capitalist policies, particularly of a redistributive nature, were therefore deemed responsible for the decline of liberalism. Both Polanyi and Schumpeter, although from different angles, suggested that these developments would bring some form of socialism, hailed by the former as a liberating system and by the latter as an unfortunate, if inevitable, fate. This chapter proves that they were both wrong.

The New Deal policies were aimed at assisting sectors of the US economy and repair the damaged financial world, but were soon translated into international measures aimed at reconstructing Europe. Ultimately, such policies created a climate favourable to the crimes of the powerful in general and financial crime in particular.

The Marshall Plan, officially known as the European Recovery Program, offered Western European countries the total amount of $13 billion (approximately $130 billion in current dollar value) as aid to help them rebuild national economies. The plan came into operation in April 1947 and its declared economic goals were the modernization of industry, the removal of trade barriers, and the pursuit of prosperity (Craft and Toniolo, 1996; Schain, 2001). Critics, however, argued that economic growth would not take place by virtue of generous donations (Hazlitt, 1947), but through entrepreneurship, socially oriented investments, full-employment policies, strategies for the improvement of infrastructures, the training and education of the work force, and the rise of the purchasing power of consumers. As Keynes taught, the emphasis had to be placed on demand. Donations, on the contrary, could easily return to the donors, in transactions between purchasing European governments and US industrial producers. France and the Netherlands, for example, received sums of money equivalent to those they spent in military action against their colonies, and parts of those sums served to buy American military equipment. The Plan, in sum, directly and indirectly contributed to the building up of European markets for American exports.

Economic aid rarely comes without political prescriptions. Part of the money given to Europe had to be invested in devising strategies for the fight against the spread of communism. In a speech delivered after the decision to bomb Korea in 1950, President Truman announced that the bombing was consistent with the philosophy of the Marshall Plan, which was meant to bring democratic countries together. The ideological goal of the Plan, therefore, was never in doubt (Gaddis, 2005), as proven by the overt funding of political parties competing, in their respective countries, with domestic parties of the left (Chomsky and Ruggiero, 2002). In this way, the official movement of money aimed at helping the economy was supplemented by a clandestine flow of finances destined for covert political operations: financial crime became politicized.

The US in Italy

Italy was among the beneficiaries of the Marshall Plan but, together with the economic boom experienced by the country in the 1950s and 1960s, a process began that was destined to make its elite profoundly corrupt. It is impossible to establish how much of the money received by the country was privately appropriated by political representatives and illegally exported. Nor are there credible estimates of the portion of funds, officially destined to ameliorate the infrastructures, that were in fact shared among the political parties faithful to the US government. The fact that the government never formulated a precise plan for economic recovery or a specific investment programme may be symptomatic of the interests at play in the period. The authorities preferred to spend American funds for short-term political purposes, such as unemployment relief, public works, and housing projects. This helped defuse social conflict and, at the same time, opened up possibilities for illegitimately dispersing the funds received.

Unofficial or furtive money, however, also reached Italy, with slush funds meant to support the rivals of the Communist Party. The fight against communism made the US and the western world in general tolerate the financial irregularities and the unorthodox state practices adopted by the Italian elite. Corruption spreading in Italy, in other words, was deemed an acceptable price to pay in order to keep the country out of Soviet influence. The fraudulent 1948 elections were covertly financed through the Plan, although significant portions of money ended up in speculative financial and military circles. Other funds were given to the Central Intelligence Agency (CIA) for their covert operations, a circumstance that should not surprise, given that the CIA was founded by bankers, namely by experts in moving money around, legitimately or otherwise. As Scott (2007) has reminded us, the initial advisory group which was instrumental in establishing the CIA was formed of Wall Street lawyers and financiers, and their meetings were held in the board rooms of J. H. Whitney, another Wall Street investment firm. Widespread fears of the communist electoral victory led to the feeling that secret counteraction was vital: the Marshall Plan and CIA activity became part of an interlocking grand strategy against Stalin. An example of counteraction was the creation of a right-wing 'stay-behind' group in Italy and other European countries, including the UK. The group was entrusted with the training of counter-insurgency troops and the accumulation and hiding of arms, and its existence as well as the sources funding it were kept secret for decades. 'The CIA-linked agencies developed a strategy of tension in which a series of lethal terrorist bombings, falsely presented as left-wing, were used to drive Italy further to the right' (ibid: 14). In brief, the apparent generosity of the Marshall Plan, designed to help economic and financial stabilization in the country, ended up at the same time promoting financial and state crime. Perhaps it is in that period that, in Italy, the most criminal elite of the western world was gestated.

Eurodollars

The impasse initially experienced across the world during the reconstruction period hampered the circulation of liquidity and the expansion of industry and trade. The fear of communism found an appropriate ally in an invention that could break the impasse. This invention, according to Arrighi (1994), was the Cold War. 'What cost–benefit calculations could not and did not achieve, fear did' (ibid: 296). President Truman terrified American and European people, magnifying the bellicose intentions of the USSR and turning 'Roosevelt's vision of a global New deal to a very shoddy reality indeed, but at least made it workable' (ibid: 297). Economic expansion and European integration required more than the liquidity provided by the Marshall Plan, it needed the mass investments in the military industry that transcended the Plan, the largest ever experienced in peace time. The liquidity problem was initially solved during and after the Korean War, and rearmament continued until 1973 in the form of US military expenditures abroad. The production of weapons, however, was simultaneous with the growth of the financial sector, which followed its own logic and absorbed increasing portions of surplus capital. The dysfunctional effects of financial accumulation became manifest around 1968, when the deposits in Eurodollars could be observed at an unprecedented level after twenty years of unstoppable growth. This was also when the system of fixed parities between the main world currencies and the US dollar and between the US dollar and gold, which had been in place throughout the phase of material expansion, was abandoned in favour of the system of flexible or floating exchange rates (Kindleberger, 1984). Soon the world liquidity and the operations financiers could conduct with it escaped all governmental controls: speculation was encouraged by the floating currency exchange rates and profits became increasingly untraceable. 'Continuous changes in exchange rates among the main currencies and in rate interest differentials multiplied the opportunities for capital held in offshore money markets to expand through trade and speculation in currencies' (ibid: 299). In 1973 the US Federal Reserve and associated central banks had to acknowledge defeat in their struggle to stem the tide of mounting speculation, while the expansion of financial grey areas in the world betrayed the optimistic expectations pinned on the Marshall Plan. The pursuit of economic integration, prosperity, and national security against aggressive communists had created its own enemy, namely the accumulation of furtive money in offshore locations and tax havens (Frieden, 1987). By the mid-1970s the volume of financial transactions carried out in offshore banks exceeded by many times the value of world trade in commodities. An immense volume of liquid funds and markets—the world of Eurodollar finance—was now outside the regulatory authority of any country or agency. The following case explains the links between the Eurodollar market and offshore banking.

Treasure Islands

Wall Street bankers, constrained by regulations introduced after the Great Depression, became increasingly attracted to the City of London, where banks seemed to get away with new unorthodox practices. Midland Bank, for example, in 1955 started accepting US deposits, violating UK rules around currency exchange and offering higher interests than those allowed by regulations. Midland's executives were gently warned by an official of the Bank of England that their practices were unbecoming. Violations in the City of London were solved over tea, with a handshake, and the emphasis in those years was as much on self-regulation as it is today. In 1957 the UK government raised interest rates and introduced stricter norms on overseas lending but, following in the footsteps of Midland Bank, other financial institutions ignored the rules and started using US dollars in their international operations. The Bank of England chose not to intervene and regulate the market, but decided to regard those transactions as beyond its regulatory power, the transactions taking place abroad.

Banks in London began keeping two sets of books—one for their onshore operations, where at least one party to the transaction was British, which was regulated, and one for their offshore operation, were neither party was British (Shaxson, 2011: 66).

The newly born offshore market became known as the Eurodollar market or the Euromarket, and was the result of a simple accounting innovation, although it was destined to play a crucial role in the development of financial delinquency. Wall Street and the City of London were in this way united in an unregulated realm hosting furtive money from all over the world, including the Soviet Union.

  In 1959 the Euromarket of London held deposits for $200 million and by 1960 it reached a billion, before spreading soon to Switzerland, the Caribbean, and beyond. When President Kennedy, in 1963, introduced a new tax on profits from foreign securities, Wall Street operators moved en masse to the offshore tax-free Euromarkets. Finally, the birth of Eurobonds accelerated the move even further, delocalizing financial markets and attracting syndicates made up of many firms and banks in several financial centres, including offshore havens. The creation of these unregulated 'bearer bonds' or anonymous certificates became very appealing to all tax evaders. In a Bank of England memo from 1963 it was stated very clearly that international bankers, however much they disliked 'hot' money, were bound to accept it (ibid). In chapters 9 and 10 more recent developments occurring in offshore markets will be discussed.

Drifting and Rationalizing

Financial offenders can always claim that their criminal behaviour is necessary in order to survive or to achieve vital economic goals. Many employees, for example, appeal to necessity to explain why they go along with illegal activities expected by their employers. In a case cited by Sutherland (1983), an idealistic young college graduate had lost two previous jobs after refusing to become involved in unethical activities. When he landed his third job, he finally came to realize that shady business practices were ubiquitous, but swallowed his disgust and resisted the temptation to quit: the game was rotten, but it had to be played (Coleman, 2006). Employers, in turn, appear to believe that their colleagues and competitors are prone to engage in unethical acts and for this reason they must be beaten on their own terrain: it is difficult to abandon the race to the bottom.

The analysis of financial crime between the 1950s and 1970s offered numerous causal strands. Motivation and opportunity were addressed, and the point was made that the two had to coincide in order for a crime to occur. This coincidence, according to Edwin Sutherland, was not determined by the particular psychological makeup of offenders: in his view, the criminal behaviour of financiers could not be explained by their feeblemindedness or emotional instability, nor could we think that a bank had an inferiority complex or revealed a frustration–aggression syndrome. That white-collar crime was not dependent on the personality structure of individuals seemed to be proven by the fact that corporations continued to offend even when their staff continued to change.

Distancing themselves from Sutherland's teachings, some psychologists did study white-collar criminals and, among the research projects conducted, two of them, carried out in the 1950s and 1960s, are worthy of specific reference. Walter Bromberg (1953) studied the offenders he encountered in his work at Bellevue Psychiatric Hospital, where successful bankers and other operators convicted of various financial violations displayed practical, uncompromising personalities. They came across as intellectually independent rather than mentally obtuse, and most could not see in what way they could be described as reckless. However, they also showed a high degree of egocentrism and unconscious feeling of omnipotence.

Spencer (1965) focused on thirty sentenced offenders held in the open prison at Leyhill in the UK. They had committed fraud in its various forms, were latecomers to crime, and their sentences ranged from three to eight years. Spencer noted that they had experienced a high degree of upward mobility, which could explain their criminality as typical of the parvenus, although he stressed that they were not the typical adventurous or ruthless gambler type. They were mainly 'muddlers' and 'drifters' who had resorted to crime due to sheer incompetence. Most offenders claimed that they had two lives, guided by two sets of norms and principles respectively: one set ruling their professional activities, the other their private existence. Expressing a common rationalization, most claimed that everybody in the same position as theirs acted as they had.

Cressey (1950) produced a key book which was intrinsically polemical with Sutherland's views. First, he studied embezzlement, a crime that the founder of white-collar studies excluded from his interests because it victimizes employers, not government or the public. Second, the subtitle of Cressey's *Other People's Money* was *The Social Psychology of Embezzlement*, which ran against Sutherland's notion that environments, and not the psychology of those inhabiting them, were the main causes of offending. Cressey, however, implied that his embezzlers possessed similar characteristics belonging to most fraudsters, namely individuals who commit criminal violations of trust. He studied 133 male inmates in three prison institutions, adopting a research philosophy known as analytic induction, with initial postulates being continually readjusted on the basis of the data collected. He found that persons become trust violators when they feel that their problem is 'non-shareable', when they are convinced that the problem can be resolved through illicit conduct, and when such conduct does not alter the conception they hold of themselves. This three-pronged situation was termed the 'fraud triangle' and Cressey argued that, whenever all three elements were present, a trust violation would occur. Individuals who interpret their problem as non-shareable are normally reluctant to seek the help of others due to their pride and fear of losing status. Problems, in their turn, could be associated with personal failure, business reversal, or demoralization in the occupational arena, whereas knowledge that the problem can be resolved through acting illegally is based on technical expertise to do so. Echoing Sutherland's differential association, such knowledge was linked with the training received, the surrounding occupational culture, and the daily routine experiences. Finally, rationalizations entailed the belief that violators were only borrowing the sums they had appropriated or that the money taken belonged to them, as a form of compensation for unrewarded work. Embezzlers, on the other hand, also claimed that all successful businesspeople start their career thanks to the use of other people's money. In conclusion, Cressey stated that his research provided at least partial corroboration of Sutherland's views, in that the rationalizations elaborated by the offenders he studied were part of the ideology of their groups and resulted from definitions favourable to law violations through contacts with peers.

In their study of young offenders Sykes and Matza (1957) renamed Cressey's justifications with the term 'techniques of neutralization', and their celebrated contribution has been extensively used for the analysis of white-collar, corporate, and state crime. Such techniques were employed by young offenders to resolve the problem of guilt, and helped ease the commission and the aftermath of their offences. Financial offenders, similarly, can claim that their behaviour does not cause damage to the public, that they are forced by managers to adopt that behaviour, that they are being condemned by individuals and groups who commit more crime than they do, and finally that their acts express loyalty to their own occupational circle.

Gambling as Swindling

Before the end of the 1950s a significant criminological contribution to the study of financial crime focused on what was described as the 'fraud stage of development'. Schur (1957) approached fraud from a sociological perspective, assuming that all its forms contain a kernel of the confidence game procedure. This consists of the creation, by one means or another, of a relation of confidence, through which a swindle is effected. The game is played by a 'swindler' and a 'mark', where the former proposes to the latter a scheme by which they can both make money. The marks give the swindlers their money, which they will never see again. Note how from Beccaria's metaphor of the economy as gambling (in a previous chapter) we are shifting to a notion of financial operators as swindlers. The fact that swindlers are difficult to prosecute, Schur suggested, is due to the general rule whereby a false pretence or representation, to be indictable, must be an untrue statement regarding the past or the present. Swindlers, instead, make false representations with respect to the future. However, even with simplified legislation, authorities would be reluctant to prosecute for fear of obstructing, along with the activity of swindlers, entire segments of business initiative. When sanctions are imposed in swindling cases, they are rarely stringent, and in general the 'con game' is particularly untouchable because of the victim's equivocal position. The victim, in many cases, is as greedy as the swindler, sharing the prospect of easy enrichment, a circumstance that makes certain forms of financial crime akin to victimless crime. A confidence game cannot work 'unless the sucker has got larceny in his soul' (ibid: 299). This gives swindlers an elite position in the criminal arena, also because their activities do not involve violence, although they grant power to the perpetrator and symbolically nullify the persons being deceived.

The victim in some financial crimes, therefore, plays an active role, and the agent, like a swindler, has to convince a second party that together they can harm a third one. A triad is thus formed with the victim establishing a spurious coalition with the offender against an imaginary third party: here is a perfect example of what economists mean by externalities. In financial bankruptcies and crashes, the party that has been cheated and harmed is often the public, an entity extraneous to the damaging transactions that have taken place, who will be charged with the costs of rescue and bail-out operations.

In general terms, most research conducted between the 1950s and 1970s depicted financial crime less as an offshoot of individual relaxed morality or fading personal integrity than as a problem of structural immorality (Wright Mills, 1956). A phenomenon of imitative propagation, financial crime was said to spread through example, at times motivated by what was perceived as business, or even political necessity.

There is however a supplementary trait distinguishing financial crime, a trait that should be linked to the notion of salesmanship: financial operators sell more than mere material commodities, and a premium is placed on their ability to sell anything, particularly new mysterious goods. Their capacity to sell anything is proportionate with their successful personality, which in turn is measured through their propensity to take risks.

A phrase used by Edwin Schur (1972) encapsulates a variety of these characteristics, namely imitation, necessity, risk-taking, successful personality, and ability to sell, the phrase is 'capitalism with a vengeance' and may be fit to provide the backdrop for the following case.

Equity funding

A Los Angeles-based financial conglomerate, Equity Funding Corporation, started marketing mutual fund shares and life insurance to private investors in the early 1960s. The 'funding' concept was designed to attract ordinary customers who, on buying shares would use them as collateral to receive a loan, which in turn was supposed to buy a life insurance policy. Investors were given the prospect of paying back the loan and, after about ten years, making large profits on the mutual fund shares they had acquired. This optimistic strategy was based on the assumption that the value of shares would constantly rise, which was a common feeling in times when economic crisis seemed utterly unlikely. During the initial five years, the shares of Equity observed more than a ten-fold increase, whereas over the following five-year period they became virtually worthless. When the Corporation started losing money, its director falsified the accounts, depicting a healthy situation in order to increase the value of its stocks and attract yet more investors and bankers' loans. Only in 1973 did the case come to public attention, when an ex-employee blew the whistle revealing huge accounting fraud. Information provided to investigators also unveiled the creation of fictitious insurance policies and detailed the role played by many company employees in the deception of investors, including auditors and regulatory authorities. Insider trading charges were also made (Dirks and Gross, 1974; Soble and Dallos, 1975). More than 130 executives participated in or knew about the fraud, therefore they were all found guilty, although in different measure, of having issued 56,000 bogus insurance policies, created $120 million in false assets, and 'even [having] "killed" some of its phony insured in order to collect on their policies' (Coleman, 2006: 32). A federal judge later gave Equity's president, Stanley Goldblum, an eight-year sentence for his role in the case, while numerous other conspirators received shorter terms.

Top executives exert profound influence on the corporations they manage, setting the moral tone for those surrounding them. Conduct and values are shaped through example and followed out of fear, consent, or indolence. Equity's president Stanley Goldblum was punished more severely than his subordinates, causing one to wonder whether the judge sentencing him endorsed the notion of financial operators as swindlers and was familiar with the concept of 'organization man' (Whyte, 1956). This concept earned purchase throughout the 1960s, when it was suggested that a collectivist ethic within organizations was sterile, as it fostered risk-averse individuals incapable of introducing innovative practices. Effectual organization men, on the contrary, were expected to adopt a spirit of rugged individualism and to redraw behavioural boundaries. An extremely influential book on management, *The Organization Man* was to be followed by numerous contributions that may help in the analysis of financial crime.

Corporate Functionaries

Between the 1950s and 1960s a number of surveys showed that around half the US population admitted committing some form of tax evasion. Violations were found to be most common among middle and upper income groups, especially businesspeople and lawyers. It became evident, during those years, that big businesses had the power to obtain specific, industry-by-industry tax breaks and to benefit from loopholes that made corporate tax avoidance completely legal. As a result, the tax burden shouldered by big corporations steadily declined for the following four decades. It is against this background that managers and corporate functionaries became the object of several studies.

These 'new kind of men' servicing organizations were depicted as morally unbound: inspired by a military ethic of sort, like good soldiers, they limited themselves to taking orders and executing them. In Weberian terms, they were dispensable individuals who could be replaced without the organization losing its purpose and established practical routine. Rights and duties were spelled out in formal rules, but they could be redrafted, as they frequently are in all evolving organisms. Due to the possible co-existence of different ethical standards among organization members, the role of managers was seen as crucial in spreading conformity and, in a mediatory fashion, establishing a sort of compromise in the form of amoral pragmatism. This type of pragmatism had to possess a binding force linking together the diverse attitudes and values of employees.

Reaching a form of amoral pragmatism can be seen as an ideal process, a way of achieving an acceptable equilibrium making rational choices possible. Critics of this approach posited that, in concrete situations, the process is indeed only 'ideal' as problems often evade clear and rational solutions (March and Simon, 1958). The issue is that in organizational life it is hard to adopt alternative ways of operating, thus making the choice of optimal conduct almost impossible. There are, in other words, cognitive limits to rationality and organizational members may measure the degree of rationality of their behaviour only when their specific goal is precisely set. So, goal attainment remains the task of organizational men, but goals themselves may vary among the units of the organization and may be seen as series of sub-goals. Members occupying the highest levels in an organization establish its general goals and attempt to incorporate within them all the sub-goals of other members. This will be possible if specialization and fragmentation of organizational tasks make all members interdependent, forcing the mid- and low-level members to adhere to the overall strategy of the organization and actively pursue its goals. The financial world is fragmented and the individual firms operating in it show a high degree of specialization among employees. Following this analysis, we will have to conclude that the judge sentencing the Equity's president was totally aware of how the defendant was the instigator of the crimes committed by the company. First, he had provided inadequate alternatives or none at all. Second, he had subdivided tasks so that the different agents knew only a limited segment of the overall purpose of their action.

Organizations reaching a form of amoral pragmatism establish conducts on the basis of contingent situations, but simultaneously create contingencies so that no other alternative conducts are available. As March and Simon (ibid) contended, top managers have to study the different modes of influencing individual motivation in organizational behaviour. Task specialization helps in this process, as it entails repetition and shapes practices whose ethical content becomes, over time, inscrutable. But organizations do more than merely dull ethical sensibilities. They define the situations employees face in their job, indicate what needs to be done, allocate roles, and establish expected outcomes. Employees are therefore provided with a repertoires of actions to put in place in given situations and are taught to prioritize certain aspects of their job while neglecting others.

Among the multiple responsibilities of executives, Drucker (1966) mentioned the pursuit of 'escalating goals'. By this he meant the discovery of new goals achieved through ways that no one has considered before. A learning process that could be included in Sutherland's differential association theory will make executives focus on results rather than modalities, aim for something that will make a difference, rather than something that is safe and easy to do. Decisions will have to achieve the 'right' outcome, not just an 'acceptable' one. Experimentation is key and executives have the duty to identify the 'boundary conditions' in which decisions are made while being prepared to change those boundaries. Like monks in a monastery, they will end up sharing values within their insulated, parochial enclave and become impervious to the disapproval that may originate from the outside world. The case presented below provides a concrete example of how effectual executives operate.

A Christmas card list

Several top managers of the General Electric Corporation and the Westinghouse Electric Corporation, the two largest US suppliers of heavy electrical equipment, stood trial in a Philadelphia court in February 1961. Journalists described them as 'middle-class men in Ivy League suits, typical businessmen in appearance, men who would never be taken for lawbreakers' (Geis, 2007: 103). The defendants were held in high esteem in their respective communities and in the churches they regularly attended. Their defence lawyers labelled the court's demand for a prison sentence a coldblooded vendetta against their clients, these fine men who would suffer enormously behind bars surrounded by common convicted criminals. Involved in a price-fixing conspiracy, the men violated the letter and the spirit of the Sherman Antitrust Act of 1890, which forbade price-fixing arrangements as conduct harmful to freedom of enterprise. The investigation had started in 1959 and resulted in twenty indictments involving forty-five individual defendants and twenty-nine corporations. The sentence established a total fine of $1,924,500 against the defendants and imposed jail terms of thirty days on seven of them, four of whom were vice presidents, two division managers, and one a sales manager.

The defendants sentenced to jail were handled essentially the same as other offenders with similar dispositions. They were handcuffed in pairs in the back seat of an automobile on their way to the Montgomery County Jail in Norristown, Pennsylvania, fingerprinted on entry, and dressed in the standard blue denim uniforms (ibid: 105).

During their stay they gained the reputation of 'model' and 'intelligent' prisoners, while their companies only suffered negligible damage from the fines: for General Electric, for example, a half-million dollar loss was no more unsettling than a three-dollar parking fine would be to a person with a medium income.

The conspirators used coded names and camouflaged their activities, calling the list of those attending their meetings the 'Christmas card list', the meetings themselves 'choir practice', and the rotating system designating which corporation was to gain a contract 'the phases of the moon'. Among the justifications put forward by the corporations were that they had served the worthwhile purpose of stabilizing prices, that they had only recovered costs, that they had adopted an 'illegal' but not a 'criminal' conduct, and had acted for the benefit of their employers rather than out of personal greed. Confirming Sutherland's argument around the learning process leading to white-collar crime, they invariably testified that the techniques and the rationalizations of price-fixing were common place within the company employing them and that they were taken, soon after accepting their job, to 'price meetings' attended by competitors. 'Every supervisor that I had directed me to meet with competition … It had become so common and gone on for so many years that I think we lost sight of the fact that it was illegal' (ibid: 109). While Westinghouse complained that the punishment suffered had been too harsh and claimed that the individual defendants were unlikely to repeat their offences, General Electric stigmatized its employees for having violated not only the law but also the basic principles and policies of the company.

According to Geis (2007) , looking at this case, not all of Sutherland's ideas concerning corporate offenders were substantiated. Sutherland's emphasis on learning patterns generating illegality did find support, while his argument that the judiciary is reluctant to prosecute while-collar criminals did not. Geis (ibid: 117) concluded that the incidence of white-collar crime had to be located within the relationship between extrinsic conditions and illegal acts. In other words, with satisfactory market conditions corporations would normally desist from committing offences, whereas in conditions perceived as deteriorating they would not hesitate to do so. Later, it will be worth ascertaining the validity of this supposed general law.

Exchange of Financial Services

Financial delinquency can be linked with secretive political projects, as we have seen in the case of Italy. In such cases, conspiracies are based on an exchange of services between official representatives and criminal entrepreneurs. One sensational case which occurred in this period is associated with the name of Richard Nixon. Before the well-known Watergate scandal in which he used covert intelligence and wiretapping to spy on his political enemies and discredit them (Bernstein and Woodward, 2006; The Washington Post, 2013), he was known, since the 1950s, as a politician who highly appreciated friendly relationships with 'finance men', whose generosity could determine the outcome of electoral campaigns. In his re-election of 1972 he received substantial funds from Associated Milk Producers, the US largest dairy cooperative, and as a form of gratitude he approved a substantial increase in dairy prices. He was also offered funds by Gulf Oil and International Telephone and Telegraph at the same time as investigations were underway as to whether the corporations had violated anti-trust laws. 'The Gulf Corporation was revealed as having a systematic, enduring, and illegal system of political "slush" funds, of which a $100,000 contribution to Nixon's 1972 campaign was just one of many' (Woodiwiss, 2001: 279).

Exchange of financial services, however, also occurred between other actors. We have seen earlier that crimes hastily attributed to conventional criminal organizations may be incorporated among business practices. Marshall Clinard's findings, for example, compelled him to assimilate businesspeople in the range of racketeers and organized gangs normally engaged in black markets and illicit economies. In the period under consideration, organized criminal groups performed an ancillary role with respect to sectors of the official economy. They provided a variety of services to, and acted as a supplementary infrastructure for, the legal economy. In a sense, they constituted a parallel clandestine 'tertiary' sector which helped step up the circulation of commodities or the development of political careers (Ruggiero, 1996).

There is a long tradition of study examining the interface between organized criminals and white-collar offenders and the common financial exploits they shared. John Landesco's (1929) research, in this respect, was a landmark, as it showed how organized crime constituted the strong arm of businesspeople and politicians, and how violence intertwined with illegitimate commerce and political campaigning. The alliance of sectors of the official world with organized crime rested on the mutuality of their services: the former offered protection for illicit activities and investment opportunities for illegal profits, while the latter supported, also financially, the candidates protecting them. The partnerships involved traders, falsifiers, lawyers, financiers, fences, smugglers, contract killers, police officers, and political representatives (Moley, 1926).

Between the 1950s and 1970s financial exchange took place between criminal groups and the New York police department, with gamblers putting officers on their payroll (The Knapp Commission, 1972). In Chicago, Mr Gilbert was described as the world's richest cop: he presided over the political–criminal–business consortia, was a campaigner for the Democratic party, owned slot machines, and protected prostitution (Demaris, 1971). The criminological literature of the period did address white-collar crime but only rarely did it get to grips with the relationship between this type of delinquency and conventional forms of organized crime, or with the financial implications of this relationship.

Many contributions took part in the terminological dispute to which Sutherland's formulation had given rise. For example, Aubert (1952) saw in the ambiguity of the concept of white-collar crime the very ambiguity of its nature, proposing to utilize the controversial definitions of what constitutes crime in general to better understand cultural and material conflicts. In the financial domain, such an exercise would lead to an understanding of competing appreciations of economic activity, investments and profits. Edelhertz (1970) regarded the original definition as too restrictive, in that white-collar crime could be committed by a bank clerk as well as by the bank director. In his view, a distinction had to be drawn, for instance, between crimes by persons within an organization operating on an individual basis, crimes boosting business operations, and crimes as the central activity of a business. Perhaps financial crime, in its diverse manifestations we have seen in this chapter, would cover all three types identified in this classification. Pepinsky (1974) argued that, if anything, Sutherland's definition was not broad enough, as it did not include all the acts of exploitation that should be dealt with in criminological reasoning. Exploitation, in his view, 'should supersede the idea of white-collar crime because the concept of exploitation allegedly was socioeconomically unbiased and conceptually unitary' (Geis, 2016: 106). Adapting this formulation to the financial world, we can assume that any definition of crime in this domain is also far from being broad enough. Here, we are in Brecht's ideological territory, according to which founding a bank is more criminal than robbing it.

Definitional debates continued throughout the 1970s, when some authors felt that white-collar offences entail diverse combinations of Sutherland's variables: respectability, social status, and occupation. Breaking down the original definition, therefore, the following sub-categories were suggested: elite deviance, official deviance, and corporate deviance (Ermann and Lundman, 1978; Douglas and Johnson, 1977); also: corporate crime, business crime, political crime, and government crime (Roebuck and Weeber, 1978; Conklin, 1977; Clinard and Yeager, 1980). But all these types of behaviour were not solely identified on the basis of coded prohibitions, because the law failed to prohibit them clearly and strictly. For this reason some authors suggested different conceptualizations based on deviance rather than criminality. Quinney (1970), for instance, considered the correspondence between deviant and criminal behaviour as crucial for the study of white-collar crime. The question he posed was whether or not the conduct defined as criminal was also a deviation from the normative structure of the occupation: 'If it can be established that the behaviours are regarded as deviant, as well as criminal, by the occupational members, the criminal violations can truly be studied as deviations from occupational norms' (ibid: 33). Unfortunately, this formulation, when applied to the financial arena, may find a muddled context in which the very notion of deviance is vague, constantly changing, and is often the result of power contests and negotiations with external forces.

In a subsequent definitional distinction, the two areas of 'crime in business' and 'the business of crime' were delineated. The former type included embezzlement, misrepresentation in advertising, restraint of trade, and a variety of financial crimes such as illegitimate appropriation of public funds, tax evasion, and fraudulent banking operations. The latter type included activities organized for the explicit purpose of achieving economic gain through crime: extortion rackets, illegal gambling, drug trafficking, prostitution. Despite the general statement that the emphasis on money and success had created a way of life that could make criminals of us all, a rigid distinction was maintained between crime in business, defined as occupational crime, and the business of crime, identified as organized crime.

From another perspective, financial crime was assimilated to the illegal acts performed within a legitimate organization and in accordance with the organization goals, which victimize employees, customers, or the general public (Schrager and Short, 1977). When committed by corporate actors, such acts found contexts characterized by complex sets of structured relationships between boards of directors, executives, and managers on the one hand, and parent corporation, corporate divisions, and subsidiaries on the other. Opinion surveys conducted during the 1970s provided evidence that corporate executives believed unethical and illegal practices to be common (Clinard, 1979). The socio-cultural environment in which corporations operated was deemed conducive to these practices, with lawbreaking becoming a normative pattern. A list of defences offered by perpetrators included the inadequacy of government measures and regulations, regarded as costly and incomprehensible, but also the necessity for corporations to commit crime due to economic factors.

At times, critical contributions to the analysis of financial crime were hampered by the prevailing etiology they embraced. Personal circumstances of poverty and disadvantage formed prominent themes of most criminological analysis, so that the growth of crime came to be associated to growing relative deprivation. Financial crime, in this paradigm, found no hospitality. Most critical criminologists ended up focusing on conventional offenders as the marginalized position occupied by these offenders boosted their oppositional identity, in intellectual as well as in political terms. In most key books published between the 1960s and 1970s, the heyday of critical criminology, the words 'bank' and 'financial crime' did not even appear in the detailed final indexes. There were exceptions, however. Some radical publications analysed the nature and extent of anti-trust violations and the entrepreneurs' willingness to act illegally when necessary. In a key book of the period, corporations were said to provide the most vivid examples of organized crime (Pearce, 1976). In the Marxist criminology of the 1970s, ruling class crime and illegal business activities, political illegalities, and police malpractices were regarded as endemic in capitalist societies. 'A central problematic for a Marxist theory of the state is: why are rulemakers the most extravagant rulebreakers?' (Young, 1976). Ideas of 'service exchange' between criminal groups and business were also highlighted, particularly in areas such as the control of unions, industrial espionage, and the support and financing of electoral campaigns. As Al Capone boasted, the biggest bankers, businessmen, politicians, and professionals looked for him to keep the system going. Financial delinquency, therefore, had to be traced in the interactions between conventional criminal groups and representatives of the official world, who exchanged favours and performed a form of mutual promotion. In this respect, Geis' observation that satisfactory economic conditions lead to desistence from white-collar offending has to be revised: the period under consideration was characterized by extremely favourable conditions, and perhaps exactly for this reason, amid optimistic dreams of social ascent and material growth, witnessed a general race towards 'success', however this might be achieved.

In further work, a more precise link was established between organized crime and a wide range of activities carried out within market economies. These activities, along with the illegal fashion in which they were performed, displayed a distinctive entrepreneurial character. 'When viewed apart from traditional assumptions about lower-class and immigrant groups, the events described as "organized crime" become part of a much wider problem that includes major segments of white-collar crime as well' (Smith and Alba, 1979: 37). Illicit entrepreneurs could be bankers, wholesalers, retailers, and power brokers, although the names by which they were defined were respectively loan sharks, smugglers, fences, and bribe takers. Smith and Alba argued that the analysis of both corporate and organized crime should focus on entrepreneurship rather than criminality, a shift that might better describe behaviour patterns as products of marketplace dynamics. In drawing a number of common traits shared by the two types of crime, the authors also mentioned how illicit entrepreneurs avoided the imposition of regulatory power through corruption, a device which paralleled the legitimate entrepreneurs' use of lobbies and other political tools which, indeed, included corruption. More specifically, once organized crime was understood to be rooted in the marketplace, similarities among a wide range of events, which are commonly seen as distinct, could be recognized. Many events described as corporate crime, it was argued, possess an entrepreneurial character similar to typical organized crimes such as bookmaking, smuggling, and loan sharking. 'They reveal a degree of organized, concerted action among a large number of individuals engaged in illicit endeavor similar, in behavioural terms, to that of traditional organized crime' (ibid: 38). Banking as loan sharking, in brief, and financial crime in general, could be the object of analysis only if a single conceptual perspective was adopted embracing both white-collar and organized crime (Smith, 1980). That is what chapter 10 of this book will attempt.

In conclusion, by the end of the 1970s, incompetent muddlers, organization men, swindlers, and gangsters were all included among the market operators who facilitated or promoted financial delinquency.

The Keynesian era came to a close, leaving behind it the debris of financial illegality, the feeling that the economy could not be controlled, and the anxiety that failures and dysfunctions were soon to reach unprecedented levels when, with the end of interventionism and the rejection of Keynes, market 'freedom' was restored.

7

A Paper World

The 1980s and 1990s witnessed a proliferation of financial delinquency and parallel efforts to respond to and explain it. The customary double standard in the sanctioning of white-collar crime in general was attributed, like in previous criminological literature, to the status of the offenders, the difficulty of establishing their criminal intent, and the tendency to spare them the humiliation of formal punishment. A renewed and more intense emphasis on the victims, however, brought the debate to a higher level, with some authors suggesting that, when faced with the financial world, the doctrine of *caveat emptor* could no longer be taken seriously. This doctrine traditionally applies to buyers who may have incomplete information about a good or service they are purchasing or ignore the fraudulent intention of those selling them. The growing awareness of the prevalence of financial delinquency, instead, was associated with specific information (rather than lack of it) about the victimization it caused, as proven by the rise of consumer movements and campaigns exposing financial scandals in the public and the private spheres. Prophet Ezekiel's view that usury should be equated to rape (see chapter 2) was echoed by the proposal to include all forms of white-collar crime in the equation. While being two distinct victimization events, white-collar crime and rape, it was felt, shared some strikingly similar traits, including the impunity often enjoyed by offenders and the attempt to blame the victims (Geis and Stotland, 1980).

In this view, financial crime could become a 'social problem' as a result of individuals and groups expressing grievances or making claims with respect to some specific conducts in the financial sphere. In the process identified by Spector and Kitsuse (1982), social problems emerge as claims-making and entail, first, groups drawing attention to offensive or harmful practices, and second, the recognition of such offensiveness and harmfulness by official agencies or institutions. This chapter discusses the extent to which financial delinquency came to be regarded as a social problem in the 1980s and 1990s, returning in the concluding section to the issue of impunity and to the 'rape analogy' regarding financial crime.

Honest Players in Immoral Systems

The changes introduced in the early 1980s in the economic system reflected the conservative critiques of interventionist policies still in place as a legacy of the New Deal. What was to be described soon later as 'neoliberalism' posited a market model with units motivated by self-interest, capable of delivering coherent results and characterized by efficiency. This abstract model excluded instability, as it ignored the volatile nature of 'capital assets, financing arrangements, banks and money creation, constraints imposed by liabilities, and the problems associated with knowledge about uncertain futures' (Minsky, 1982: xii). In the previous decades, financial crises triggered responses by central banks acting as lenders of last resort, so that markets were stabilized through policies which increased liquidity and supported investments and consumptions. Up until 1980, therefore, financial debacles and bankruptcies were resolved through fiscal policies which prevented a deep depression, even though they failed to sustain employment, growth, and price stability. Throughout the 1980s, instead, the growing independence of the financial sector hampered rather than encouraged investment activity, as debts increased to the point of exceeding the borrowers' income. This form of 'Ponzi financing' was conducive to crises, as in the new climate governments supported capital formation rather than consumption: in a nutshell this was the 'Reagan road', leading to innovative financial practices and incessant experimentation. It was also the road leading to the belief that financial crises were systemic, rather than accidental, events. The financial world, ultimately, appeared as a 'paper world' committed to paying cash today and tomorrow, where cash in the future was exchanged for cash today.

The viability of this 'paper world' rests upon cash flows (or gross profits after out-of-pocket costs and taxes) that business organizations, households, and governmental bodies, such as states and municipalities, receive as a result of the income-generating process (Minsky, 1982: 63).

Financial crime throughout the 1980s and 1990s occurred within this 'paper world', where failure could only be prevented if profits exceeded debts, thus encouraging constant investment refinancing.

Drexel and Milken

The managing director of Drexel, a firm operating in Wall Street, was arrested in 1986 and accused of reaping $12.6 million in illegal profits from insider dealings. He eventually pleaded guilty to securities fraud, tax evasion, and perjury. The firm replaced him with a new director, who had also been arrested for similar offences committed during his time at another company. Investigators then turned their attention to Drexel's operations in its junk-bond department, which had been tolerated due to the company's generosity in funding the campaigns of political candidates. The company grew in wealth and power thanks to mergers and buy-outs that multiplied when the Reagan administration relaxed enforcement of antitrust laws, pioneering the use of junk-bonds, 'which carried high interest rates and high risk for buyers and large profits for Drexel' (Jackson, 1988: 96). In the 1986 elections, the company dispensed $253,500 to candidates and party committees, in this way accelerating the process that led to the prevalence of donors over voters and to lawmakers withholding legislative proposals that would damage the former. Drexel's donors and their beneficiaries saw themselves as law-abiding players in an immoral system.

Michael Milken was a star financier of Drexel, one of the wealthiest man in the US, who was asked by a House subcommittee to explain the origin of his riches. He invoked his right to remain silent, while the political candidate he had financially sponsored accepted a $2,000 speaking fee in an event in which he expressed admiration for his friend, who, he claimed, was constantly thinking about what could be done to make ours a better world (ibid: 96). Described as a wizard, Milken dominated the junk-bond market and used it to engineer a series of large takeovers, making over a million dollars within a five-year period (Punch, 1996). Known as competitive and arrogant, however, he played down his personality in court, where he appeared deferential and humble. He did not avoid a harsh sentence, although he served it 'in a minimum security prison where he was given light work and where he readily gained remission of sentence for good behaviour (being released after twenty-two months)' (ibid: 144).

The Savings and Loans crisis

In 1989 it was reported that groups of savings and loan operators across the US had defrauded customers and their organizations, stolen millions of dollars and billed the American taxpayers (Calavita and Pontell, 1992).

A savings and loan, or 'thrift', is a financial institution that offers deposit accounts, mortgages, and other personal loans to individuals. Established in the US in the 1930s with the purpose of helping with the construction of new homes after the big financial crisis, the Federal Home Loan Bank Board created a reserve credit system to ensure the availability of mortgage money and acted as the primary regulatory agency for federally chartered savings and loans. In 1985 the Board decentralized its power, allowing local banks to perform regulatory duties but also to promote the savings and loan industry. Among the causes leading to thrift fraud, some commentators indicated the general economic conditions, characterized by high interest rates and simultaneous slow growth. Difficulties in attracting new money were attributed to inflation overtaking the meager 5.5 per cent return on deposits. These difficulties combined with measures removing restraints on the industry, amid the liberalization and deregulation fervour prevailing in the early 1980s.

Throwing caution to the wind and armed with the brashness born of overconfidence, the deregulators undid most of the regulatory infrastructure that had kept the thrift industry together for four decades (ibid: 237).

Deregulation, however, was accompanied by an increase in the sums destined for rescue operations in case of bankruptcies. Savings and loan institutions, well protected by the law in case of insolvency, started to pay high interest rates to attract short-term deposits, although revenues from their own long-term deposits were lower. The law also authorized these institutions to increase their clients' loans up to a total of 30 per cent of their assets. In 1982, moreover, the requirement that thrifts should have at least 400 stockholders was dropped, along with the rule that no one could own more than 25 per cent of the stock. This opened the door to powerful entrepreneurs creating a virtual oligopoly in the business. In 1988 the collapse affected more than 500 insolvent savings and loans and in six months the industry lost about $7.5 billion.

Fraud in this sector of the financial world was divided into three categories: unlawful risk-taking, looting, and covering-up. The first type was associated with the willingness of operators to engage in unsafe and unlawful practices. Deregulation did, in fact, encourage high-risk activities, but savings and loans institutions transcended the limits officially established, cutting corners in monitoring both investment practices and loan disbursements. Looting, also described as collective embezzlement, consisted in funds being appropriated by employees for personal use at the expense of the institution, with the implicit or explicit sanction of managers. 'This robbing of one's own bank is estimated to be the single most costly category of crime in the thrift industry, having precipitated a significant number of the thrift insolvencies to date' (ibid: 242). Covering-up was also found to be widespread, and was often disguised as deals which were meant to provide a false picture of the institution's state of health. It should be added that the official regulations were already extremely permissive with respect to accounting strategies and bookkeeping procedures, thus fostering the search for further opportunities for deception.

Serious deficiencies were found in the way in which regulators and criminal justice agencies had dealt with the frauds. When abuse had been uncovered, the initial response would consist of a 'memorandum of understanding', a gentle suggestion to supervisors to act. If abuse was reiterated, a 'cease and desist' order would be issued, namely a timid and belated injunction often delivered after the institution had failed. The lack of formal enforcement action was coupled with extreme leniency towards prosecuted offenders. The problem was compounded by the institutional refusal to bolster stagnant regulatory resources: between 1966 and 1985, while known cases of irregularity and criminal activity in the thrift sector mushroomed, the staff tasked with the examination of cases declined. Explanations of this enforcement immobility revolved around political influence and networks of interest, with links between politicians and the thrift industry well documented. Monitoring and supervising the sector, ultimately, proved impossible, as officials were given conflicting responsibilities to promote the thrift industry and at the same time to regulate it.

Robert Maxwell

Maxwell built up a media empire formed of miscellaneous public and private units. His feverish acquisitions incurred substantial losses that he tried to cover by raiding his own firm operating in the area of pension funds. The Maxwell Communication Corporation, however, was in part owned by him and in part publicly owned, hence the peculiarity of his crimes straddling private markets and state agencies. Competition, indeed, was at the core of his operations, as he tried to overtake Rupert Murdoch, his Australian rival who owned News Corporation. The collapse of Maxwell's empire followed his death in controversial circumstances in November 1991, and was investigated by the Department of Trade and Industry, which took a decade to release an official report on the case. His operations were likened to classic theft on a grand scale, as he systematically plundered shareholders and his own company funds, appropriating the sum of £450 million. Among his directors was Labour Peer Lord Donaghue, who failed to notice what was happening, while his accountants, Coopers & Lybrand Deloitte, had nothing suspicious to report. Part of the sum stolen was transferred to Goldman, Sachs & Company, the American investment bank, which claimed to be unaware of the illegitimate origin of the money received. The City watchdog for the fund management industry had repeatedly warned that controls on pension funds should be tightened (Thompson and Delano, 1989; Greenslade, 1992).

The Bank of Credit and Commerce International

The BCCI was founded in 1972 by Agha Hasan Abedi, a Pakistani financier, and the Bank of America. It expanded quickly, growing into a large financial conglomerate, with offices in seventy-three countries and estimated assets of $20 million. When found to be insolvent in the mid-1970s, its managers were accused of having manipulated accounts, hidden losses, and concealed illegal investments. However, activities continued well into the 1980s, with services being offered to top politicians, ambassadors, intelligence agents, international organizations, influential businesspeople, and financiers. The decline of BCCI began in 1986, when a US Customs undercover operation was conducted. Investigators found evidence of money-laundering activities, theft from depositors, and unregistered payments to officials around the world in exchange for an unwritten licence to operate freely. Acting as financial guarantor, the bank was also involved in transferring arms to countries under embargo. A report commissioned by the Bank of England in 1991 concluded that the operations of BCCI were so complex that it was impossible to reconstruct its financial history. In the same year, regulators from five countries ordered the bank to shut down its offices, an action which affected the finances of a million depositors. Many of the protagonists in the scandal were never brought to court and Abedi, who was charged in the US and the UK, was never extradited from Pakistan. The real reasons why the US Justice Department refused for years to mount a full-scale investigation remain obscure (Truell and Gurwin, 1992; Adams and Frantz, 2000). Evil and blame 'were externalized', foreigners were demonized, Pakistanis and Arabs, corrupt Third-World politicians and bankers were regarded as the chief culprits. The Westerners involved in the network of business relationships claimed they had been deceived and were unaware of the illegal practices of the bank. Such practices were said to be incorporated in the traditional ways of transferring money through underground banking systems based on trust and close family ties (Kochan and Whittington, 1991). Yet, 'it is hardly believable that such a large number of intelligence-connected, astute, and well-informed individuals and agencies would not have known' (Passas, 1996: 68).

Individuals and Organizations

Criminological analysis of these events tended to focus less on individual acts damaging organizations than on new forms of financial delinquency associated with organizational structures. Of course, this period did not see the definitive decline of embezzlers acting behind a screen of respectability and reliability: in Canada, for instance, the author of the largest banking fraud carried out in the history of the country was a trusted individual who stole $10 million (Canadian) to feed his massive gambling habit (Ross, 1992; Punch, 1996). This notwithstanding, attention was mainly drawn to the emergence of new actors and alterations in the general climate in which pressures exerted by organizations over employees to 'perform' determined the blurring of the boundaries between orthodox and unorthodox practices. The new organizational dimension of financial crime was deemed to distort markets, penalize the financial world, and even to deliver a fatal blow to the economy as a whole (Reichman, 1993). Growing deregulation, it was felt, attracted young financial 'samurais' who could not distinguish between acceptable and unacceptable ways of making money and had not developed a minimum sense of civic duty. But was this simply a generational issue? The young generation of operators, in fact, acted alongside older colleagues, as proven by the involvement of highly experienced individuals employed by law and accountancy firms, 'so that collusion, illicit alliances, and illegal networks were developed' (Punch, 1996: 140).

The discussions that took place during the 1970s (see chapter 6) returned in criminology in the 1980s, when the analysis of organizations tout-court turned into the analysis of organizations as criminogenic sites. In the financial world, it was stressed, a climate conducive to crime is provided by the very nature of the business taking place, a business hinging on information, gossip, hidden truths, and misleading tips. In such an environment, organizations become populated by employees who are comfortable with deception and secrecy, and who are prepared to use both for their personal as well as their employers' benefit. The wave of acquisitions and mergers which occurred in the 1980s made information and gossip particularly precious, as advanced knowledge about them allowed insiders to anticipate the value of shares and buy or sell them accordingly. Detection of malpractice became problematic as the advocates of deregulation managed to impose a significant budget cut on the money destined for investigations (Shapiro, 1984). Ultimately, the widespread delinquency in the financial world provoked a very selective response, as authorities chose to tackle individual insider dealers rather than the complicit organizations encouraging them.

Routine, Cycles, and the Irrelevance of Persons

Explanatory theories of financial crime and corporate crime in general were inspired, among other things, by economic reasoning. For example, whether and how crime rates in the financial arena follow a precise pattern related to the economy became a matter of criminological debate. The analysis, however, focused on corporate crime and the crimes of the elite rather than, more specifically, on financial delinquency. We can only hypothesize that such analysis can be extended to cover the subject matter of this book.

Some authors regarded corporate offending as business routine, or as an inevitable corollary of capitalism, whereas others identified 'cycles of offending' somehow related to 'cycles of accumulation'. Advocates of the former interpretation seemed to put forward arguments which echoed the renowned Marxist notion of 'the decline of the rate of profit'. As accumulation was hindered by its own inherent mechanisms, recourse to crime became inevitable if these mechanisms were to be countered. Instead, advocates of the latter interpretation suggested that corporate crime is rife in difficult economic circumstances, which may be transitory or cyclical, when every effort is made to maintain profits (Box, 1983; Passas, 1990). We have seen in previous chapters that this assumption is questionable, as financial delinquency takes place even, or particularly, when profits escalate rather than decline. Strain elements due to capitalist competition were included in the analysis, and the attractiveness of illicit opportunities was said to increase when profitability declines. Similarly, it was remarked that 'firms in depressed industries as well as relatively poorly performing firms in all industries tend to violate the law to a greater degree' (Clinard and Yeager, 1980: 129). Other authors, however, cast doubt on this assertion: that firms in financial difficulty were more likely to offend than profitable ones had not yet found empirical corroboration (Braithwaite, 1985).

In his study of the role of middle management, Clinard (1983) found a variety of causes for the explanation of corporate unethical behaviour. The middle-management executives he interviewed felt that the source of this behaviour lay primarily within the corporation itself, not in external factors. External factors such as competition, or indeed unfair competitive practices, were deemed to be as unimportant in determining unethical behaviour as the poor corporate financial situation. Rather, 'the general theme expressed by most middle-management executives was that top management, and in particular the chief executive officer (CEO), sets the corporate ethical tone' (ibid: 132). Some 'financially oriented' top managers were more prone to chasing quick prestige and profits and therefore were more likely to engage in illicit practices. This occurred to a lower degree among 'technical and professional type' top managers. Finally, a distinction was drawn between the ethics of top managers who were occupationally unstable and moved from one corporation to another, and those who were more permanently established within one single corporation. The former were found to be more aggressive, 'interested in their own rapid corporate achievements and consequent publicity in financial journals; they have limited concern for the corporation's long-term reputation' (ibid: 137).

According to other interpretations, the study of corporate crime had to be coupled with the study of how 'trust' was distributed, maintained, and abused within both the social structure and specific organizations (Shapiro, 1990). The nature of the social structure, but also the specific layout of an organization, were deemed, under specific circumstances, conducive to abuse and malpractice. However, while the point was widely accepted that structural factors create conditions where abuse of trust occurs, the precise mechanisms that led to these conditions were not fully investigated. Nor were the mechanisms whereby, in the same conditions, some corporate actors did refrain from abuse. Were abuse and restraint related to the varying stringency of existing sanctions? (Pearce and Tombs, 1990; 1991). These issues brought us back to Sutherland's observation that the causes of corporate crime cannot be found in the institutional responses to it, just as the causes of tuberculosis are not found in the type of therapy chosen.

The difficulties encountered in explaining corporate and financial crime arose from the misgivings surrounding the precise identification of this kind of crime. On the other hand, they also mirrored the uncertainties surrounding the aetiology of all crimes. Nevertheless, attempts were made to identify causations which would be potentially applicable to all sorts of lawbreaking. This avenue was taken by Gottfredson and Hirschi (1990), who resumed where Sutherland had left off, by attempting to explain criminal behaviour with an all-inclusive theory. These two authors discarded the basic thesis of differential association, namely that crime is caused by culturally induced motives. Instead, they posited the 'propensity event theory', centred on differences between people in terms of self-control. Individuals endowed with the lowest self-control were said to commit the majority of crimes, irrespective of the type of offence. Financial delinquents, other white-collar offenders, street robbers, adolescent deviants, and prostitutes, therefore, were said to share a lack of self-control that manifested itself in a number of symptoms. Green (1993: 104) adopted this causation in his study of embezzlement and identified these symptoms as the following:

[R]isk-taking, or a quest for exciting and dangerous behaviour; simplicity, or an avoidance of difficult tasks; low frustration tolerance; physicality, or a desire for physical rather than mental activity; immediate gratification, or impulsivity; more concern with immediate than future pleasures; and self-centredness—looking out for oneself first or tending to blame oneself last.

Green also found further indirect support for this theory as an explanation for embezzlement. Propensity event theory, he explained, assumed that offenders have low self-control and that this condition is relatively stable over time. Offenders, in other words, do not display their criminal behaviour in one episode only, but manifest their low self-control in a career, on the one hand, and in a variety of offences, on the other. Thus embezzlers turned out to have been involved in other crimes prior to the embezzlement, a claim that Green substantiated through reference to other studies.

Coleman (1987) relied on a theory of white-collar and financial crime based on the hypothesis that criminal behaviour results from a coincidence of appropriate motivation and opportunity. Motivation was held to consist of 'a set of symbolic constructions defining certain kinds of goals and activities as appropriate and desirable and others as lacking those qualities' (ibid: 409). An opportunity was defined by the author as a course of action which is part of a person's repertoire of potential behaviours. Furthermore, he argued, a potential course of action becomes an opportunity only when there is awareness of it. Coleman discarded theories centred on the inadequacy of the biological make-up or the socialization of white-collar criminals, and considered the interactionist approach to be best suited for the explanation of their offences. The meaning that individuals attribute to a particular situation and to social reality, he pointed out, makes certain actions seem appropriate. Individual perceptions also include an anticipation of other people's responses to one's behaviour. Social behaviourists such as Mead (1934) had provided a crucial theoretical framework for this type of analysis. In performing a certain act, Mead suggested, one has to predict the reaction of others, and in a sense take over into one's self all the attitudes of others, or the generalized other. The adoption of this hypothesis led Coleman to identify rhetorical techniques of neutralization used by white-collar offenders, among which the 'denial of harm' was the most common. 'When convicted white-collar offenders are asked to explain their behaviour, they frequently claim that their actions did not harm anyone, and they have therefore done nothing wrong' (Coleman, 1987: 411).

Coleman was aware that interactionist analysis, while offering a convincing account of the ways in which white-collar offenders neutralize the symbolic constraints of their behaviour, failed to explain the origin of this behaviour. The author, therefore, suggested that a good start for this explanation would be to explore 'the relative strength of the culture of competition and the normative restraints on it among different groups and different organizational segments of society' (ibid: 434–5).

Availability of criminal opportunities and the knowledge of the techniques necessary to commit offences may account for both the motivation of this behaviour and its diffusion throughout an industry. For example, it was remarked that, unlike street crime, fraud is not an 'equal opportunity crime', 'and to the extent that there is disadvantage or discrimination by class, gender, ethnicity, or religion in occupying particular roles, the opportunities for particular types of fraud are correspondingly restricted' (Levi, 1987: 2–3).

Finally, explanations of white-collar and corporate crime were also located within the analysis of technological and bureaucratic development. The development of non-natural persons, such as corporations, was said to provide the backdrop against which powerful offenders operated (Coleman, 1982). The growth of corporate actors, it was argued, causes a structural change in society where 'natural persons' play an increasingly insignificant role. Corporations become pre-eminent actors: they substitute functionally for a natural person, can act in a unitary way, own resources, have rights and responsibilities. Natural persons could now gain mobility, as the fixed function in which they previously operated was taken over by functional units: corporate bodies. Continuity of functions was therefore no longer provided by individual persons and their skills, but by these growing corporate bodies. The changing distribution of roles among natural and corporate actors led to new relationships of power. According to Coleman (1982), these relationships produced four different kinds of actions whose nature and characteristics varied according to the actors involved. Actions performed by two natural persons constituted the first type, and were those to which we have all been socialized. The second type was characterized by actions in which two corporate bodies are involved. The third and fourth were those actions in which the two parties are a person and a corporation who perform respectively the role of subject and object. Unlike the other types of actions, these implied relationships which could be defined as asymmetric. In these relationships, one of the actors was endowed with very large resources compared with the other party. For example, a non-natural actor was in a position to control the conditions in which their relationships with natural actors took place. They also held more information regarding the nature of their relationship and the way in which this could be altered. Coleman's analysis suggested that this asymmetry provided the backdrop against which powerful offenders should be studied and their crimes analysed. According to the author, the 'irrelevance' of persons favours the increase of opportunities for corporate bodies to offend against them.

Trickle Down and Trickle Up

Outside the criminological community, a more general analysis focused on the economic system and its evolution, taking as a starting point a taxonomy that could provide some explanatory insight. Firms, households, and entire economies were divided into three types: hedged, speculative, and Ponzi. A unit with a hedged structure, it was pointed out, is able to honour all its debts through the income it generates; a speculative unit can pay back its principal debts only if it gathers new funds by selling assets or accessing new loans; a Ponzi unit, finally, cannot pay principal debts but only those incurred in new loans meant to pay off the former (Minsky, 1982). In the 1980s, it was felt that the economy had entered a Ponzi phase, in the sense that corporate takeovers were frequently carried out with the clear awareness that debts could never be comfortably serviced, 'and only with asset sales and divine intervention could bankruptcy be avoided' (Henwood,

1998: 222). But were operators as individuals thought to be the only perpetrators of financial delinquency, or was the financial sphere per se regarded as criminogenic? Let us examine examples of both.

The innovative nature of financial crime prevalent in the 1980s and 1990s can be detected in the original way in which embezzlement presented itself. With Sutherland, as we have seen, this specific offence was excluded from the category of corporate crime and isolated as crime committed by employees against employers or corporations. On the contrary, in the savings and loans crisis described earlier embezzlement assumed the features of a hybrid: a crime committed simultaneously by and against employers or corporations. Criminological analysis was charged with moral indignation in the face of illegal practices that led to buying sprees by perpetrators, who purchased luxury goods and villas. One such perpetrator threw a Christmas party costing $148,000, inviting 500 guests who were offered 'a ten-course sit-down dinner, roving minstrels, court jesters, and pantomimes' (Calavita and Pontell, 1992: 243). Beyond indignation, explanatory attempts hinged on deregulation and competition, interpreted as counter-values enticing individuals into risk-taking, unlawful adventure, gambling, swindling, and crime. As ideological imperatives, deregulation and competition were seen as incentives to invent new practices through which 'fiddling with money' would result in the creation of wealth and collective wellbeing. Even exorbitant profits made by crooks, according to the underlying philosophy (and echoing old discussions around luxury), would eventually 'trickle down', spreading wealth and happiness in the collectivity. However, reality showed that money accumulated in the financial sphere 'trickles up', 'as taxpayers foot the bill for the casino extravaganza' (ibid: 256).

Financial crime was, therefore, linked with the concept of criminogenic markets, created by changes in regulatory systems that caused instability while creating opportunities for abuse and fraud. In brief, systemic incentives were thought to be operating which led to collective looting (Akerlof and Romer, 1993). The analysis of this period would not be complete, however, without reference to Hayek's (1973) suggestions that the best government is a small government and that regulation only impedes innovation. Crime in the financial sphere, from this perspective, should be deemed an element of social order, a spontaneous action modelling new collective arrangements. Growth and evolution, in neoliberal thought, cannot be rationally established, they cannot abide by rules, but must be judged on the basis of what they produce. Rules of conduct, therefore, do not develop because they permit the achievement of a known purpose, but evolve because the groups practising them are successful in competing with others and defeating them. Those rules, in a given environment, allow a greater number of the groups or individuals practising them to survive. They indicate a propensity or disposition to act or not to act in a certain manner, which will manifest itself in what we call a practice or custom. Of course, such rules will always operate in combination, and often in competition, with other rules or dispositions, and only the rules of the victors will become part of the natural, spontaneous order connoting the 'Great Society'. In brief, social arrangements are the outcome of previous actions guiding individuals and groups in their struggle for survival and evolution, and as such are not subject to moral evaluation. Even when such arrangements are characterized by what seems to be iniquity, change will not result from forces acting outside society, but from endogenous factors spontaneously rectifying apparent injustice. According to Hayek, in sum, spontaneous order, that is markets, cannot be replaced by organizations, that is state intervention. And it should be clear that, in the liberalist tradition as a whole, the thaumaturgic force amending injustice and benefiting all is embedded in the pursuit of self-interest (Ruggiero, 2013). Financial crime in the neoliberal ideology, finally, can also be regarded as an 'externality', namely an activity that unintentionally damages unfortunate individuals who are not involved in the transaction being performed. Such 'collateral damage' must be accepted because, as we are told, 'some harm caused to others is even essential for the preservation of spontaneous order' (Hayek, 1973: 101). Law and legality, therefore, incorporate a range of conflicting expectations, some of which are bound to prevail, and we constantly have to decide which deserve priority. Decisions about committing crime in the financial sphere, in this view, will be part of an experimental process. Can we detect Bentham's voice behind Hayek's arguments?

It is within this justificatory framework that waves of financial criminal activity took place between the 1980s and 1990s.

A Financial Crime Compendium

New research was conducted on the victimization of the European Union, specifically on the illegal appropriation of finances by both legitimate enterprises and organized crime groups, who at times acted jointly (Passas and Nelken, 1993). The EU's agricultural expenditure in the form of subsidies represented (and still does represent) an attractive source of finance, and between 1971 and 1988, all countries of the Union reported numerous cases of fraud (Ruggiero, 1996). Meanwhile, in the period under consideration, the US and the UK produced a series of financial villains presented below in anthological form.

The brokerage house of *E. F. Hutton* engaged in a 'check-kiting' scheme, initially in an attempt to recapture some of the 'float', namely the interest made by banks on funds they held while waiting for a cheque to clear. Later the firm started issuing cheques before funds had been deposited. Hutton wrote very large overdrafts and pocketed the interest earned. In 1985, his operations were uncovered and he agreed to pay several million dollars in fines and restitution (Carpenter and Feloni, 1989; Stevens, 1989).

Charles Keating controlled Lincoln Savings and Loans, which collapsed in 1989 at a cost of \$2.6 billion. He funded political candidates in elections with the aim of ingratiating himself with regulators. His main exploits, however, consisted in securities fraud, selling directly from his branch uninsured bonds issued by Lincoln's holding company, American Continental Corporation. Keating's staff were complicit in selling unsafe products and continued to do so even when their company was teetering on the brink of collapse (Coleman, 2006).

Nick Leeson, a derivatives broker, caused the collapse of Barings Bank through fraudulent, unauthorized trading. The UK's oldest merchant bank was brought to its knees in 1991 and Leeson, after serving a six-year prison sentence, became a writer and an adviser in the area of corporate responsibility (Leeson, 1996; 1999). The liquidators of Barings sold his 'trading jacket' on eBay for \$21,000.

Salomon, Inc. admitted, in 1991, to an illegal scheme to manipulate the \$2.2 trillion securities market. The firm was the leading trader in government securities in the US. He violated the rule preventing a single company from cornering the market and buying more than 35 per cent of singular state bonds. Salomon illegally exceeded that limit and also traded bonds in the name of customers without informing them of the transactions. In 1992, he agreed to pay a $190 million fine and compensate his victims with another $100 million (Mayer, 1993).

Ken Lay was chairman of Houston Natural Gas: in 1986 he started acquiring other companies and eventually changed the name of the firm into Enron. Only in the new century did the Enron scandal emerge, but it is important to note how the preconditions developed. Thanks to the support of the Reagan administration, Lay managed to obtain the deregulation of the natural gas market and, after employing Jeff Skilling in 1990, turned the company into the nation's largest energy trader. The two men persuaded regulators that the revenues from long-term contracts could be regarded as immediate profits, even though the money might not materialize for years (Coleman, 2006). The development of this case and its criminal elements will be discussed in more detail in next chapter.

The list could continue for several pages and include a variety of other crimes, but little would be added to the qualitative aspect of the phenomenon. It is more important, perhaps, to outline some specific developments in the areas of regulation and auditing which underlie the brief compendium presented.

In the US, the major auditing firms were known as the Big Eight, which became the Big Six in 1989. Soon after this, more than 50 per cent of their income came from consulting, rather than auditing or accounting activity (Soll, 2014). In other words, they became de facto partners of their corporate clients, who were less interested in audits than in guidelines leading to increased profits. The partnership gave shape to a business environment impervious to official monitoring, where countermeasures would destabilize not only financial operators but entire professional sectors connected to them through the provision of auxiliary services. Laws, regulations, informed journalists, and the concerned public could not counter a coalition of forces so densely opposed to financial transparency. Acquisitions and mergers, moreover, had created large conglomerates which became increasingly 'unauditable', requiring armies of accountants and skilled investigators capable of orienting themselves in the maze of increasingly complex operations. Nobody seemed to 'keep up with the ever-mutating, bacteria-like financial tools and tricks of banking' (ibid: 204).

During the 1980s there was a multiplication of derivatives, their features, and use. In previous years a derivative was a contract that 'derived' its value from the performance of an underlying entity, normally a material good or product. Derivatives were used to neutralize price movements and traditionally entailed that one of the parties involved in the contract actually sold and the other bought a certain quantity of 'underlying'. Innovation meant that no material, physical underlying had to be transferred from one party to the other, and that its monetary value could be exchanged, thus making transactions volatile. Without the obligation to sell and buy a material god, derivatives grew in diversity and their value was attached to all sorts of things: 'changes in the price of a car insurance, the likelihood of a power cut or the outcome of a sport event' (Gallino, 2015). The Wall Street crash of October 1987 occurred against this backdrop.

The crash marked the end of a five-year 'bull' market that had seen the Dow Jones Index rise from 776 points in August 1982 to a high of 2,722 in August 1987. Although 15,000 jobs were lost in the financial industry, the intervention of the national reserve avoided a subsequent recession and it took two years for the index to recover completely. A number of explanations were offered as to the causes of the crash (Itskevich, 2002). Among these, first, illiquidity: operators were unable to find buyers to purchase stocks that sellers wanted to get rid of at certain prices. Second, the taxation of corporate takeovers, with corporate investors rushing to sell shares whose value they predicted would plummet. Third, the lack of synchronization between the derivatives market and the stock market. The owners of the former did not really own stocks, but only the right to buy and sell them at certain established prices. Certainly, investors had been carried away by the euphoria that shares would keep rising, but it was also explained that many were unable to get to their trading desks that day because of the disruption caused by the storms over the previous night. Sell orders turned into a flood, as investors tried to cash in on the profits made over the previous years. 'Irrational exuberance' was the definition given by regulators who also reminded investors that shares constitute long-term investments and that they should stay away if they could not cope with short-term volatility (Hughes, 2012).

Financial trading inhabited a special cultural space that identified profit with masculine virtue, shares with adventure, and the
world with a global site where time was the new frontier. Dealing
on the prices whizzing into the future, traders operated at a temporal edge. This risky business lent a charisma to speculators,
who were celebrated as independent and determined individuals.
'The marriage of individual cunning and risky profit cuts a figure of daring in a routinized world. Adventure capitalism has
long linked heroism to the regeneration of wealth' (Zaloom,
2012: 180).

Restaurateurs and Customers

Further contributions from the sociology of organizations
focused mainly on micro-sociological aspects. As organizations become more complex, it was noted, responsibilities are
decentralized, while their human components find themselves
inhabiting an increasingly opaque environment in which the
goals to pursue and the modalities through which one is expected
to pursue them become vague and negotiable. Organizations may
be 'mechanistic' or 'organic', the former operating in conditions
of relative stability, the latter adapting themselves to changing
conditions. Illegal practices may be the outcome of such changing conditions, as organizations are required to incessantly devise
new ways of reaching their ends and, consequently, to innovate
by reinventing or violating rules. On the other hand, they are
composed of individuals and groups pursuing their own interests,
although internal conflicts are rarely officially displayed and are
hidden behind public images of harmony. Alliances taking shape
and dissolving, contingent interests, and a permanent antagonistic climate characterize the daily existence of organizations,
whose goals are as indefinite as is the outcome of the power strug-
gles taking place within them.

By 'decoupling themselves' from their constituent parts, financial organizations attempt to meet their goals while operating
in a highly unpredictable environment. In this way they assume
a structure consisting of loosely coupled entities. The different
entities keep a relative independence, and a loosely coupled structure allows organizations to deal with the vagaries of business.
Decoupling, particularly encouraged by geographical expansion,
mergers, and acquisitions, also entails that the parent companies

dissociate themselves from the practices adopted by their subsidi-aries or partners. Where such practices are illegal, organizations may therefore claim their innocence and invoke ignorance of the type of operations being conducted by subsidiaries or partners.

One of the crucial characteristics of white-collar and corporate crime in general is also found in financial crime: ambiguity. The fact, for example, that the perpetrator has justification for being present at the scene where the crime takes place distinguishes this type of offending from conventional predatory crime (Nelken, 1994; Clarke, 1990). In sum, difficulties in classifying financial offenders are compounded by difficulties in discovering that an offence has been committed in the first place.

Invisibility, in turn, contributes to making the field of study indistinct, classification formless, and typologies fuzzy. It has long been noted that invisibility describes the condition of both finan-cial criminals and their victims. The perpetrator is made invisible by the circumstance whereby the setting of the offence does not coincide with the setting where its effects will be felt. This is also the case because the time when the crime is performed and the time when the damage caused becomes apparent do not corre-spond. On the other hand, victims themselves can be described as invisible in that they are both absent from the scene of the crime and are frequently unaware of their own victimization.

In the analysis of the moral and managerial component of human behaviour within organizations, Punch (1996: 2) high-lighted the culture of competition providing opportunities, motivations, and rationalizations for rule-breakers. He also emphasized the ambiguous and manipulative nature of man-agement, matched by the incoherent character of organizations themselves, which may present a clear image of their objectives and practices to the outside world, but in fact operate in a con-tingent manner whereby the legitimacy of ends and conducts are constantly redefined. Summing up his argument: 'the corpora-tion, and the business environment, are potentially criminogenic'.

Firms cannot be seen as machines controlled by individuals who know exactly what they want, calculate how to maxi-mize profits, and enforce decisions consistent with this aim. They are not immediately and effectively responsive to mana-gerial instructions and market incentives, nor are they unitary entities. On the contrary, they are constituted by 'a number of small societies comprising many people with different interests, opportunities, information, motivations and group interests' (Schelling, 1984: 29). For this reason, firms have to be disaggregated, entered, and the process governing them monitored. With this premise, some authors argued that individual responsibilities had to be dealt with and incentives and sanctions imposed directly on those involved in specific transactions. However, there were difficulties in locating responsibility, as financial firms were constituted by a labyrinth of agents and roles and linked together and/or delinked from a central coordinating operator. It was felt that managers may be impotent, or pretend to be so, or even take refuge behind their presumed impotence. When the conduct of a company victimized someone, who was to blame? It was like watching a bad film and wanting to complain, but to whom? There were cases in which the warnings given to employees by managers not to act as delinquents were not taken seriously because they sounded inconsistent with the routine actions of the firm: those giving orders did not appear to really want their orders to be heeded. In sum, delinquent behaviour in organizations was said to occur not because managers were unable to monitor performance, but because they lacked the moral authority to establish the desired behaviour. On the other hand, unorthodox behaviour in organizations could also be hidden by managers who sought to avoid alarming customers. Finally, blaming the victims of financial crime, it was contended, amounted to blaming customers for failing to distinguish healthy from unhealthy eating, rather than blaming a restaurateur serving them poisoned food (ibid). Let us see how these observations were translated into criminological reasoning.

The Ubiquity of Financial Crime

Studies focused on the status of offenders and institutional responses to their conduct produced mixed findings. The examination of criminal cases was deemed essential to establish the characteristics of white-collar criminals and the degree of harshness with which they were punished. Of course, the outcomes of such studies depended on the specific sample used, so that, for instance, concentrating on women offenders, the conclusion could be drawn that theirs were typically offences resulting from occupational marginality (Daly, 1989). On the other hand, studying a variety of illegal conducts adopted by white-collar workers of varying status and occupational positions could even lead to the conclusion that such offenders were sentenced more severely than their conventional counterparts (Wheeler, Weisburd, and Bode, 1982). In these cases, researchers could polemically remark that Sutherland's idea around the leniency incurred by white-collar offenders was mere rhetoric, 'reality' demonstrating otherwise. Indiscriminate samples in terms of status and position were bound to prove that white-collar crime was committed by people in the middle class rather than the upper class of society (Weisburd et al, 1991). But by focusing on high-rank offenders, for example antitrust and securities violators, these conclusions could be easily overturned, thus providing support to Sutherland's view (Hagan and Parker, 1987).

Critics of Sutherland's analysis attempted to reformulate the very concept of white-collar crime, calling for specific attention to violations of trust. Common definitions, it was argued, 'confuse acts with actors, norms with norm-breakers, the modus operandi with the operator' (Shapiro, 1990: 347). Crimes cannot be defined by the characteristics of their perpetrators, even if among these the variable respectability is included. Respectability itself may, in fact, possess diverse meanings according to the social groups and actors sharing those meanings, while the focus on offenders was seen as an obstacle for the understanding of the deviant acts and the techniques utilized to perform them.

Offenders clothed in very different wardrobes lie, steal, falsify, fabricate, exaggerate, omit, deceive, dissemble, shirk, embezzle, misappropriate, self-deal and engage in corruption or incompetence (ibid: 358).

But again, extending definitions of white-collar criminality to individuals of all social conditions was seen as an offer to powerful actors and organizations to conceal their offences and shape benevolent public perceptions of them (Friedrichs, 1996).

Business is business, was the prevailing slogan, entailing an appreciation of lawlessness in markets which, presumably, contain their own regulatory mechanism allowing for the harmless co-existence of self-interested actors. To say that markets, in this way, are depicted as jungles is offensive to jungles, where there are commandments and where wolves restrain themselves from killing their own cubs. The maximization of profits, on the other hand, can hardly be presented as a justificatory argument, in that it contradicts a general principle that determines how we judge ordinary people. We are entitled to demand from financial organizations the same decency we expect from a teacher or a cleaner, and we would not condone doctors who promote and spread disease in order to maximize their income.

An integration of criminological approaches attempted by Braithwaite (1989) addressed corporate crime from the insights of strain, labelling, subcultural, and control theories. Following this attempt, financial crime could be interpreted as the result of failure to achieve increasing profits and pressure or strain to do so illegally. Financial criminals, from this perspective, commit offences as an alternate means of achieving success (Benson and Simpson, 2015). Such means have to be made available by the specific subculture in which offenders are immersed and require the knowledge of the techniques and the justifications needed for offending. 'Thus, strain, the availability of subculturally endorsed illegitimate means and enforced conformity to deviant subcultural values are criminogenic forces that foster corporate crime' (ibid: 89).

At the centre of this and other explanatory attempts there is a view that what causes white-collar, corporate, and financial crime is a form of 'philosophy of injustice' embraced by offenders. This philosophy tends to regard laws and regulations as unnecessary and unfair, or as moralistic impediments that interfere with freedom of enterprise. Financial crime, in this view, becomes like an 'exercise of justice', a practice that allows economic actors to survive and society as a whole to prosper. Intertwined with a powerful culture of competition, this philosophy assumes that all actors operating in markets are enjoined to violate norms and that individuals or groups failing to do the same would give competitors unfair advantages.

Cultures of competition, however, may be fruitless if concrete opportunities to commit crime are unavailable. Such opportunities vary in attractiveness, a variable influenced by a number of factors: the size of the potential gain, the likelihood of detection and punishment, the compatibility of the criminal act with one's beliefs and values, and the availability of alternatives, including legal, opportunities (Coleman, 1987). Competition and opportunities, in their turn, are not only fostered by greed, a quality commonly and perhaps rightly attributed to white-collar criminals.

In the financial sector offenders may be mainly motivated by fear, resulting from the uncertainty surrounding them. This is a crucial aspect characterizing the existence of financial actors, whose mood and acts are affected by the contingent economic and political conditions, by the assessment of the immediate financial circumstances, and by the forecast of future economic development. Financial crime, therefore, could be partly deemed to be the outcome of fear for the future, in the sense that offenders confront and control the inexorable sense of contingency and insecurity generated by their awareness of the future. Humans are the only animals who are aware today of the hunger they will feel tomorrow; by the same token, financial delinquents have an obsessive relationship with their future, therefore they try to accumulate and augment the high income they already possess for fear that future events may lead to them losing it (Ruggiero, 2015).

The relationship between gender and white-collar crime, only briefly alluded to earlier, became the object of analysis particularly in respect of the victimization process (Gerber and Weeks, 1992). Women's victimization in the financial arena goes back to the nineteenth century, when institutional sexism made them particularly vulnerable to fraud. When involved in the financial sector, women would be excluded from top positions and from the learning processes that yield experience and build defences. Keeping them inexperienced was the best way to expose them to deceit and crime. Dubious financial products were circulated among female small investors, particularly widows and unmarried women, who after being duped, had no resources or status to defend themselves in court (Robb, 2006). In the 1990s research focused on how differences in gender roles affected legal protection, access to redress, and victimization (Szockyi and Fox, 1996), not only in the financial arena but in all those productive spheres aimed at women's consumption: pharmaceuticals, products and services related to birth control, health, cosmetics, diet products (Croall, 1992). 'In summary, the gendered nature of white-collar victimization patterns mirror the gendered nature of white-collar offending (Benson and Simpson, 2015: 221).

Leniency for financial offenders, as already noted, was explained with the fervour and success of the deregulation movement, whose goal was to get the state 'off the back' of business, 'which meant, among other things, cutting back on government supervision and regulation of the economy' (Coleman, 2006: 93).

A responsible firm wishing to comply with some social standards and abide by the remaining regulations was said to refuse to
do so unilaterally for fear of offering advantages to competitors.

In brief, a large part of the literature produced in the 1980s
and 1990s responded to the growing neoliberal movement by
pointing out its criminogenic philosophy and by noting that
the emphasis on quick profits at all costs eroded the boundaries
between licit and illicit practices. Related to this critique was the
concern that the growth of the financial sector marked an irre-
versible process damaging the 'material' economy, namely the
productive apparatus which guaranteed employment and relatively harmonious social relationships. The expanding 'paper
world', in sum, was deemed to be dysfunctional, a harbinger
announcing waves of criminality involving powerful and powerless individuals alike. Financial expansion was seen as an
attempt to delay the crisis of capitalism, therefore a symptom
of maturity or obsolescence of the dominant productive system (Harvey, 1989). Little attention was devoted to suggestions
that financial growth was a recurrent feature in the evolution
of market economies, which traversed productive phases, then
slowed down, experienced stagnation, developed financial accumulation and, eventually, returned to a novel productive phase
(Braudel, 1984; Wallerstein, 1988; Arrighi, 1994). From this
perspective, financial crime possesses the flexibility and eclec-
ticism displayed throughout the history of market economies
and is far from being a characteristic product of neoliberal ideologies. A permanent feature of economic systems in general,
rather than a symptom of its critical phase, financial crime, in
this view, is not only a deviant solution to economic crises or a
response to the decline of profits, but also the likely outcome of
periods of growth. More the result of optimism and abundance
than of gloom and deficit, financial crime may expand because
economic expectations rise, creating what comes to be perceived
as an 'entitlement'. This persuades offenders to believe that, in
prosperous times, everyone has a right to pursue wealth and that
no external forces should interfere with that pursuit. Finally,
if Keynesian-style systems characterized by intervention in the
economy are regarded as the opposite of neoliberal systems, little evidence exists of the absence of financial crime from the
former (see chapter 6).

In conclusion, if financial crime and rape possess similar characteristics, for the similarity to apply we have to think of the form known as gang rape, where the individual perpetrator hides behind a herd, responsibilities are hard to allocate, and where the very fact that rape has been committed is hard to prove.

8

Psychopaths and Thrills

The wave of financial crimes inaugurating the new century can be attributed to a series of causes, including the changing social composition of investors, operators, and managers. Two decades of market worshipping, praise of greed, and laudatory sermons for privatization were bound to have an effect. The degradation of the private and public spheres is normally imputed to the immorality of emerging upper classes, which find the cost of their reputation very low due to their previous low status and the relative lack of disapproval within their group of origin. In other words, for the newcomers the cost of corruption and unethical conduct is not deemed as high as that characterizing persons of established high status. In the financial sphere, a similar phenomenon is said to have occurred during the early days of currency and derivatives trading, when 'barrow boys' landed on the dealing floor of the City of London.

With roots in the working-class East End these traders drew on the hard-bargaining tactics of the street trades and the raucous manners of the London docks that once provided material sustenance for the district's young men ... moving from physical commodities to more abstract ones, the task, they argued, was the same: to best your opponent for the best price (Zaloom, 2012: 182).

The generation populating stock markets at the turn of the century, instead, was incubated in neoliberal philosophies and had absorbed, in its educational experience, the unscrupulous trading strategies developed in the previous decades. The debate around financial delinquency in the twenty-first century does contain aspects of this 'generational hypothesis', but as we shall see in this chapter is also inspired by a number of interpretations, old and new, centred on organizational, economic, and cultural issues.

Fraudulent Bookkeeping

The use of creative accounting tricks continued into the new millennium, producing, in the new context, plain, old fraudulent bookkeeping. However, the case of WorldCom, followed by the collapse of other corporate giants such as Enron and Parmalat, which can be seen as pure deception and fraud violating accounting rules, can also bring other aspects to the fore.

WorldCom

One of the largest long-distance communication and data providers, WorldCom was found to have improperly recorded around £7 billion profits in its books. This was only part of the accounting horror that was to unfold, as evidence emerged that the company had manipulated its own reserves, creating what amounted to a slush fund. Reserves had been inflated and transferred under the heading of profits, so that its market credibility could receive a boost. John Sidgmore, the Chief Executive, blamed the former financial officer, Scott Sullivan, and the former director, David Myers. Both had already been fired for filing the routine expenses of the company as investment capital. They had been shamed, handcuffed, and paraded in front of TV cameras. The false financial statements they had engineered showed a healthy condition depicting optimistic prospects for future profits. Arthur Andersen, the same accounting firm that managed the books of Enron, failed to detect the irregularities and claimed that relevant information had been withheld from them. Losses had been hidden and only a long, comprehensive audit made it possible to give an accurate picture of the fraud. WorldCom announced that it had to write off $50 billion from its accounts, a sum that amounted to the 2001 gross domestic products of Hungary and the Czech Republic put together.

The founder of WorldCom was Bernie Ebbers, a former milkman, bouncer, and gym trainer, who expanded his small company through acquisitions of several firms in the telecommunication industry. He was indicted in 2004 and sentenced to twenty-five years' imprisonment in 2005. Despite the magnitude of the fraud, the way in which it was accomplished was relatively mundane: the impressive growth through acquisitions was carried out by using the stock of WorldCom, which had to continually increase in value to make operations possible. The longer the deception lasted the more complicated it became to continue it, also due to the high expectations of investors in terms of the company's performance. Ebbers' personal interests played a role in the fraud, as the falsification of accounts brought him enormous gains (Di Stefano, 2005).

Enron

In April 2001 Enron's CEO was ranked by *Worth* magazine as number 2 among his peers in the world. A global leader in the production and distribution of energy and the seventh world conglomerate in the stock exchange, it appeared three times on the front cover of *Time* in a few years as one of the most dynamic firms in the world (Blackburn, 2002). The company's stock had tripled between 1998 and 2000, after engaging in 'structured finance', namely complex deals involving the creation of a number of partnerships. These allowed Enron to operate tax deductions and transfer debts onto shell companies. The personal profits of top executives amounted to half a billion dollars thanks to a variety of their high-risk investments and financial exchanges involving so-called raptors. These acted as protections in case the stock of the partner entities declined, but were almost entirely funded by Enron, therefore they were directly dependent on the parent company's stock value. When the protective network of partnerships began to show its weaknesses, the losses were finally revealed, and in December 2002 Enron went bankrupt, exposing at the same time the failure of accountants, watchdogs, and auditors.

Its board defaulted on its oversight duties. Outside accountants ceded their independence and violated their profession's rules. Outside lawyers approved misleading deals and failed to vigorously pursue crucial allegations of accounting misdeeds ... the media were blinded by its image of success. (Coleman, 2006: 95).

Arthur Andersen, a limited partnership formed in 1913, had been the auditor for Enron since 1985 and had seen the company grow into the seventh largest in the US. The relationship between the two organizations had become more than friendly, with personnel moving from one to the other, thus creating a network of complicity and a conspiratorial climate. Andersen became an accomplice in fraudulent accounting and in manipulating annual reports. The chain of partnerships created by Enron was declared by Andersen to be formed by independent entities, while actually it only served to hide the company's true financial condition and enrich its executives (Fox, 2003; Schwartz and Watkins, 2003; Squires et al, 2003).

Arthur Andersen was one of the Big Five of America's accounting firms, with 350 offices in eighty-four countries and 85,000 employees. It was receiving $52 million a year in auditing and consulting fees from Enron, its major client. It displayed a façade of honorability by recruiting Harvard professors of organizational behaviour and business ethics (Toffler and Reingold, 2003). The accounting firm was mentioned in an official dinner by President George W. Bush, who said that there were good news and bad news from Iraq: 'The good news is that Saddam Hussein is willing to let us inspect his biological and chemical warfare installations. The bad news is that he insists Arthur Andersen do the inspections' (Soll, 2014: 201). Although highly disturbing, the Arthur Andersen case was not deemed any worse than cases involving the handful of other accounting firms responsible for external audits of almost every large corporation in the US (Geis, 2013). Large banks, however, with their own high-paid teams of internal creative bookkeepers and lobbyists, could always remain one step ahead of the auditors.

Parmalat

Milk-processing giant Parmalat, dubbed Europe's Enron, was found in 2003 to have accumulated losses amounting to $14 billion, victimizing some 130,000 small investors. Calisto Tanzi and his family, who controlled the company and also owned Parma football team, during the 1980s and 1990s had converted what was initially a small business into a global dairy and food firm. However, in the early 2000s the first sign of irregular bookkeeping emerged, as a financial statement listing €4 billion allegedly deposited in a US bank proved mendacious. Other forged documents came to light, until Tanzi and some of his family members were arrested. Several executives were also brought to court, including chief financial officer Fausto Tonna, who addressed journalists present at the trial with the following words: 'I wish you and your families a slow and pain-ful death'. A series of court cases followed, despite attempts by Tanzi and his accomplices to destroy documents and bribe witnesses. Parmalat's auditors and bankers were the object of a class action brought by US creditors, who found that the company had established a complex web of offshore subsidiar-ies to disguise its financial position. Among the accomplices of Parmalat, investigators identified Bank of America, Citigroup, Morgan Stanley, Deutsche Bank, and UBS, but eventually they were all acquitted (Hooper, 2008).

Metaphors for Our Times

The generation of businesspeople emerging from two decades of neoliberalism, perhaps, was led to associate success with criminal conduct. This 'generational hypothesis' is based on the belief that justification of 'greed' and pressures towards financial growth acted, for the new ascending class, as a propulsive force, blur-ring the boundaries between speculation and crime. Whether public attention to the cases examined above managed to rees-tablish such boundaries is hard to determine. Financial offences, in the current century, seem to occur as a result of the enthusiasm and optimism accompanying the long cycle of deregulation and the growing emphasis on large, fast profits. This enthusiasm is linked with favourable calculations by offenders, whereby unor-thodox choices appear to rationally respond to market demands. The cycle of financial delinquency we witness today, therefore, could be interpreted through rational choice theory, which rejects deterministic explanations and focuses on decision-making pro-cesses (Shover and Hochstetler, 2006). Financial delinquents assess their potential gains and judge them consistent with the prevailing climate and philosophy, considering the possible averse consequences as negligible. Crime becomes an act of faith, an expression of ideological loyalty towards the ruling political phi-losophy. The goals of that philosophy and those of delinquency align to create a whole, a systematic behavioural guide adhering to the dynamics of the marketplace and to the prescriptions of the economy. Financial criminals, as goal-oriented individuals, decide to act after assessing the circumstances that may favour their violations, while the nature of what they try to achieve will enable them to get away with the means they utilize. Situational explanations are, however, counterbalanced by other interpretations (Geis, 2016).

Following the suggestions of control theory, we could argue that there is no distinction between a pharmacist stealing drugs from a carpenter stealing lumber. The causes of the two conducts, it is assumed, are the same: a contextual opportunity and a lack of self-control on the part of the perpetrator. However, it could be retorted that financial delinquents, during the course of their career, display a significant dose of self-control before embarking on delinquent acts. Their shared culture, in effect, revolves around ideas of deferred gratification, calculation, and restraint, and their propensity to commit financial crime does not make them likely to offend in other arenas, for example in cigarette smuggling or the trading of stolen goods (ibid). However, to say that the financial acts of delinquency prevailing in this century are the product of individual lack of self-control is limiting, as is the assumption that such acts are confined to creative accounting tricks, that is, plain, old, fraudulent bookkeeping.

Bernie Madoff

A stockbroker who engineered a gigantic Ponzi scheme, Madoff is currently serving a 150-year prison sentence. In 1960 he founded his investment company, attracting investors among ordinary people as well as celebrities. The company gained a reputation for its 10 per cent reliable returns and by the late 1980s was handling more than 5 per cent of the trading volume on the New York Stock Exchange. Quick to adapt to technological innovation, Madoff Securities was among the first to introduce computers in the financial trading business, contributing to the establishment of the National Association of Securities Dealers Automated Quotations (NASDAQ), of which he became a chairman. As the business expanded he employed an increasing number of family members, including his niece, appointed as a rules compliance lawyer for the trading division.

In December 2008, Madoff informed his sons that he intended to increase the bonuses destined for his senior managers and, when asked where the money would come from, he revealed that a branch of the company was running an elaborate Ponzi scheme. He was reported to the federal authorities by his own sons and was arrested and charged with securities fraud. He had lost $50 billion of his investors' money, and in 2009 he pleaded guilty to, among other things, investment adviser fraud, money laundering, perjury, and theft from employees benefit plans.

Surely, Madoff went well beyond fraudulent bookkeeping and poses the old dilemma with which even eighteenth-century observers engaged: is financial crime caused by the individual characteristics of offenders or is it embedded in organizational cultures and arrangements? Madoff was well integrated into the financial world and his conduct could be seen as neither strange nor particularly deviant. 'It must be understood within the context of the values and practices of present-day finance capital. Rather than being an outlier, Madoff's career is something of a metaphor of our times' (Young, 2012: 68).

Psychopaths

That Madoff committed his crimes after WorldCom, Enron, and Parmalat had been punished may show that financial delinquents have a short memory, or/and that punishing corporations operating in the financial arena only has a short-term effect on individual perpetrators as well as the industry as a whole. Surely, faced with high recidivist rates, the judicial system has to admit to its inadequacy to fight financial delinquency. Therefore, one may well invoke leniency of punishments and the limited number of persons being charged to provide an explanation.

Alternative interpretations of the phenomenon revolve around the belief that large organizations operate in an inherently criminogenic environment, or that they tend to be led by individuals with particular personality traits conducive to crime. Continuing an analytical trend established decades earlier, some commentators would associate narcissism with elite white-collar offending (Perry, 2013). Other authors working on the topic at the turn of the century put forward a more reckless, all-embracing hypothesis.

Images of disgraced and handcuffed Scott Sullivan, David Myers, Tanzi, and Madoff may lead to the inference that voracious, individual businesspeople are responsible for financial debacles, thus absolving the system in which they operate. By contrast, suggestions were made that the corporation itself is a pathological and dangerous organization. As a legally designated person, the corporation pursues the monomaniacal goal of promoting self-interest and invalidating moral concerns. We would find such traits abhorrent, even psychopathic, in a human being, 'yet curiously we accept [them] in society's most powerful institution' (Bakan, 2004: 28). The corporation compels its human appendices to dissociate themselves from their own values, abandon feelings of empathy, and enter a form of schizophrenia. Its psychopathology manifests itself in a number of characteristics:

- it is irresponsible: in an attempt to satisfy corporate goals, everybody else is put at risk;
- it is manipulative;
- it is grandiose: always insisting that 'we are number one, we are the best';
- it lacks empathy: it shows no concern for its victims;
- it does not recognize the effect of its action as its own;
- it is unable to feel remorse.

It is difficult, of course, to know exactly how prevalent psychopathy is among business leaders, although there is evidence that the rate is higher in corporations than in other social groupings (Babiak and Hare, 2006). On the other hand, if organizations with the characteristics identified by Bakan (2004) find themselves in situations that offer opportunities for offending, then we should not be particularly surprised when they take advantage of those opportunities. Corporate psychopaths find ideal contexts in which individuals can lie, cheat, manipulate, thrive on thrill-seeking, and need constant stimulation. Such individuals are driven by what they perceive as the vulnerability of others and experience a perverted pleasure from hurting and abusing their victims (Babiak and O'Toole, 2012). Their grandiose vision may be misconstrued as self-confidence, enthusiasm, and energy, all characteristics denoting a bald entrepreneurial spirit: this is why they are highly prized in business environments and sought after by companies. As managers, corporate psychopaths are said to exert abusive supervision, causing disaffection among those being supervised (Boddy, Ladyshewsky, and Galvin, 2010). However, selective processes may be in place whereby it is the disaffected rather than their psychopathic managers who are disposed of in corporations. The latter, in a sense, possess what are presumed to be the characteristics necessary to succeed in the business world. In this respect, think of the work of Sombart (1915), who depicted entrepreneurs as not simply pious and thrifty (as Weber would), but as exceptional individuals who manifest a particular type of psychological disposition. Theirs are 'instinctive passions' such as acquisitiveness, hectic activity, the desire to plunder their neighbour. To Sombart, the 'desire to plunder neighbours' was exemplified by the speculator, a character which is both devious and proper, peripheral and central to the entrepreneurial spirit. Speculators possess a new power, the 'power of suggestion', and this alone enables them to realize their plans. Instead of exerting overt might or fear, they set hope.

[The speculator] sees visions of giant undertakings; his pulse beats quickly like a person's in a fever ... His soul may be said to be in a condition of lyrical enthusiasm. And the result of all this? He carries others along with him, who help him to realize his plan (ibid: 92).

Speculators perform the simultaneous roles of employer, inventor, and demand stimulator. One feels the echo of modem advertising, but also that of seductive financial advisers. These characters resonate with Melville's confidence man, who is the quintessence of financial adventure and characterizes the epic deeds of the new American frontier: he promises enormous revenues to those who risk their money in the adventures he engineers (Melville, 1984). Turning this fictional character into a contemporary observation:

This is not to say that all corporate leaders are crooks, but on the other hand being a crook may not necessarily disqualify one from getting ahead in the corporate world (Benson and Simpson, 2015: 61).

Thrill, Suitable Targets, and Rationalizations

While 'thrill seeking' is listed by some authors among the traits of corporate psychopaths, it is included by others among the ingredients of everyday life, of consumerism and, ultimately, of the 'carnival of crime'. Financial crime, in this perspective, produces seductive excitement, becoming a form of transgression and subversion: 'Bank fraud and theft, joyriding, manipulating the stock market, all contain the thrills and spills of edge-work' (Presdee, 2000: 62). Excitement and desire, according to this 'cultural' criminological perspective, keep the momentum of the economy, and financial criminals, like their conventional counterparts, respond to their uninteresting life by committing senseless acts.

What they pursue is a Disney-like world where fun and pleasure are immediately attained.

Financial delinquents, however, need specific opportunities in order to act, including a suitable target and a lack of capable guardianship (Felson, 2002). Money is an ideal target, as it is portable, valuable, and fungible, namely it can be exchanged for something else. Financial crime, in brief, is inspired by 'lure' and a 'lack of credible oversight' (Shover and Hochstetler, 2006). This formulation is closer to traditional characterizations than it appears to be, as it describes financial crime as the result of significant opportunity structures: offenders have legitimate access to the location in which the crime occurs, they are spatially and temporally separated from their victims, their actions have an appearance of legitimacy, and their context is devoid of capable guardianship. Deception, abuse of trust, concealment, and secrecy constitute the techniques utilized by financial criminals, which, in their turn, echo the specific techniques 'learned' by white-collar offenders examined during the course of the previous century.

In the cases examined earlier, offenders did not devise their own rationalizations but simply applied existing sensibilities and judgments to their own behaviour. Even without verbalizing them in the form of defence, they had absorbed justificatory notions which were taken as a given in their specific context and were perfectly suitable to rationalize their own experience. Theirs were examples of how, in order to strive for the triumph of the prevalent economic thought, egoism had to be the core inspiring principle of action. WorldCom, Enron, and Parmalat, however, were only highly publicized scandals among less known delinquent episodes which received inadequate attention despite the immesurable damage caused (Markham, 2006; Simpson, 2002).

In criminological analysis, corporate cultures and structures encouraging organizational crime, on the other hand, are seen as permanent features of the financial world, where known and unknown forms of delinquency are described as 'control fraud' (Sullivan, 2015). This type of fraud entails not only the victimization of customers and competitors, but also the manipulation of internal and external control with the aim of preventing detection (Black, 2005). Such manipulation becomes possible when companies manage to persuade auditors and accountants that frauds are in fact safe and profitable investments and that, therefore, they can hardly be distinguished from acceptable financial practices.

The complicity between financiers and accountants, as shown for instance in the Enron case, was of a criminal but also of an ideological nature, and led to a shared perception of the legitimacy of the operations being conducted, ultimately offering a potent rationalization for the crimes being committed.

Interrelated Contexts

The financial offences committed in the current century are also made possible thanks to the use of two techniques. The first permits firms to include in their balance sheets future earnings which may or may not actually materialize. The second allows them to pay managers in stock instead of cash, thus turning the earnings of the organization into personal profits. The latter technique is intended to attract talented personnel and to create a situation where the interests of shareholders and managers coincide. But it also gives managers the opportunity to manipulate the value of stock, thus benefiting themselves, shareholders, and the organization at the same time. Hence the embarrassment of financial firms, which cannot allocate guilt to individual agents whose practices, after all, benefit all the actors involved. Illegal practices, in this case, can be seen as survival strategies or as collective responses to general problems constantly affecting markets.

The interrelated contexts that can help understand financial crime include what Sullivan (2015) identifies as the societal context, the control context, and the organizational context. The first refers to the overall political–economic environment, the second to lack of control mechanisms to prevent crime, while the third refers to the processes and internal arrangements leading to fraud. The societal context sees the prevalence of non-intervention philosophies, which blindly rely on market self-regulation, thus encouraging experimentation, opacity, risk-taking and, ultimately, autocracy. The control context, as we have seen, is characterized by regulators organically linked to financial firms with which they share an appreciation of innovative strategies and justifications for unorthodox operations. This conflict of interest (Van Niel, 2009) contributes to the creation of a criminogenic environment. Finally, the organizational context is formed of norms of conduct, established ways of interacting, and networks of complicity that make individual responsibility unimportant. Collective crime, therefore, seems an appropriate definition that can be applied to the cases discussed earlier.

These interrelated contexts provide the basis for financial crime and simultaneous cover up of wrongdoing.

More money could be made through illegitimate means than legitimate business operations, as fraudulent behaviour became normalized ... stock values were artificially inflated through overly complex and fraudulent accounting practices ... shell corporations to hide debt and make the company appear profitable when it was actually losing money (Sullivan, 2015: 180).

Let us now focus on other cases.

A Concise Florilegium

Adelphia Communications was charged in 2002 by the US Securities and Exchange Commission (SEC) with what was described as one of the most extensive financial frauds to take place at a public company. Adelphia had fraudulently hidden billions of dollars in liabilities from its financial statements, inflated earnings to meet Wall Street's expectations, and concealed stock purchases and the acquisition of luxury estates in New York and elsewhere. Adelphia was the sixth largest cable television provider in the US and provided telephone services to thirty-two states. Self-dealing by the Rigas family, the major proprietors, included the use of the company's funds for personal loans, and sham transactions backed by fictitious documents stating that debts had been paid, while instead they had been shifted to other family-owned entities. 'This case presents a deeply troubling picture of greed and deception at a large, publicly-held company', said SEC director of enforcement (US Government, 24 July 2002).

The chief financial officers of *Tyco International Ltd* were indicted for reaping $600 million through a racketeering scheme involving stock fraud, unauthorized bonuses, and forged expense accounts. In 2002, managers were also accused of concealing $14 million spent in improper loans to themselves (Ross-Sorkin, 2002).

This type of financial delinquency was not an exclusive characteristic of US business, as the following cases will prove. However, the suggestion was made that US events acted as experiments and were replicated by a number of other corporations throughout the world, all giving the impression of prosperous business through fraud or false accounting, all showing a constant increase in the market value of shares, irrespective of production performance (Gallino, 2005; 2011).

Kirch Media was the primary subsidiary of Bavarian-based Kirch Gruppe. It was created in the 1970s, and became prominent in 1984, when the German state relinquished its broadcasting monopoly. It rapidly became the second largest broadcaster in the country, entering the digital pay-television market in the mid-1990s. Protected by friends in the Bavarian local government, it received funds even when the number of subscribers dangerously declined. It purchased broadcast rights for movies and sport events from various foreign media companies, committing itself to unrealistic financial deals. In April 2002, the company was declared insolvent (Taneja, 2014).

The collapse of Kirch Media affected other companies in the sector: *EM.TV & Merchandizing*, based in Munich, was charged with concealing the true state of its finances. In 2000, the company had acquired a competing firm but subsequently, in 2003, lost $600 million (*Animation Magazine*, 1 April 2003).

Dutch *Ahold* was the world's third largest food retailer, with a market value, in late 2001, exceeding €30 billion. In 2002, its value plunged by 63 per cent, and the company came under investigation by various authorities, including the US SEC. Its bosses were described as vain and secretive, and were accused of aggressive management and accounting irregularities. Ahold's chief executive and finance director resigned after it was discovered that the company's profits had been overstated by more than $500 million. *The Economist* (27 February 2003) welcomed the case because, at least, Europeans could no longer smugly believe that corporate malfeasance was an exclusive American vice.

French media giant *Vivendi International* collapsed in 2002, when its shares plummeted and its chairman resigned. Originally a water company, it was transformed by Jean-Marie Messier into the world's largest media group, but the ambitious expansion brought €19 billion of debt. Lack of clarity in the company's strategic development prompted Moody's, the credit rating agency, to cut Vivendi International's debt to junk status. Stock markets across Europe fell while it emerged that, among the other irregularities, the company had pretended to dispose of shares, but instead of selling them, it had used them as collateral for a loan. In a message to Vivendi staff, Jean-Marie Messier said: 'I am leaving the scene, with a broken heart, in the hope that this will soothe the divisions in the boardroom and the permanent suspicion of the market' (Tiefgarne, 2002).

Lernout & Hauspie, a Belgium high-tech conglomerate, came under scrutiny when $9 billion of its stock market value was wiped out, leading to the suspension of the company's trading on the stock exchange. The firm produced speech and language software used in telecommunications, cars, and the internet. Facts had been concealed from the auditors and 'errors' had been made in the financial statements for the previous three years. The co-founder of the company Pol Hauspie resigned along with two other board members, while further irregular dealings carried out in Southeast Asia came to light. False sales in Korea had been recorded, with the profits forming around 25 per cent of the company's revenues. The new interim director stated: 'Our team is anxious to resolve these recent controversies affecting the company's financial statements, so we can continue to maintain and extend our leadership position' (*Associated Press*, 24 November 2000).

These cases, which follow an imitative pattern, took place in a grey area where criminalization was not certain and illegal practices became accepted routine (Ruggiero, 2015b). They occurred in a process leading to their normalization. The authorities, in this process, ignored the illegality of certain practices and implicitly invoked legal pragmatism, thus departing from precedents. In practical terms, they protected certain sectors of the economy which were deemed too important for the general wellbeing. Financial delinquents too seemed to invoke legal pragmatism, committing what can be termed 'foundational crimes', namely conduct inspired by an 'experimental' logic and driven by a consequentialist philosophy. They adopted illicit practices with the awareness that they were indeed illicit, but with an eye to the social and institutional reactions that might have ensued. The intensity of such responses would determine whether violations were to become part of a 'viable' routine or be carefully avoided. Some violations, in sum, possess a 'founding force', namely they are capable of transforming the previous jurisprudence and establishing new laws and new types of legitimacy (Derrida, 1992). In this sense, foundational financial crime restructures the legal and the political spheres while playing a legislative role.

The Irresponsible Firm

Throughout the 2000s, deregulation and privatization led to the unprecedented international expansion of business, while freedom of enterprise came to be identified, among other things, with freedom from the bonds of location. The process was enhanced through the establishment of a number of international agencies and the ratification of agreements aiming to ban all measures that might restrict international trade. It is in this climate that in economic sociology the phrase 'irresponsible firm' kept resounding.

An 'irresponsible firm' is a firm which assumes that it cannot be called to account by any public or private authority, or by public opinion, for the social, economic, and environmental consequences of its activity (Gallino, 2005). Irresponsible firms prosper thanks to the emphasis on maximization of profits at any cost, and in the short term, of their market value in the stock exchange, irrespective of their budget or revenues and of their productivity. Although 'maximization at any cost' appears to benefit all shareholders, including small ones, in practice throughout the 1990s and 2000s it resulted in the disproportionate creation of wealth for large shareholders and managers and in losses for small investors. Further, irresponsible firms experience changes in their functioning and governing apparatus, including the return to the direct power of the proprietors, along with family-type property and capital. New investors, however, also comprise institutional actors: private and public pension funds, investment funds, and insurance companies (Prins, 2004). The managerial phase of the firm, according to Gallino (2005), was superseded when proprietors felt that unsatisfactory revenues (between the 1960s and 1980s) required more aggressive practices. Hence, proprietors started to exert increasing pressure on managers, who devised strategies prioritizing the creation of stock value above any other objective, even if this was to the detriment of small investors. The social costs of irresponsible conduct by firms are difficult to measure due to the intricate web of concessions, affiliations, and the 'placelessness' of finance. In brief, while transactions are globalized, financial regulations and institutions are not. The result is a global society formed by a number of financial protectorates, where the absence of a credible central power and a set of universally accepted norms leaves nation states in the role of spectators. In this way, while in the past states controlled their own territories in order to monitor the wealth produced, today it is no longer the state which decides how to tax wealth, but it is wealth itself which decides how and where to be taxed (Cavallaro, 2004). The events of 2007–8 and after unfolded against this background.

2008

Many commentators agree that the major factors determining the 2008 financial crisis were financial engineering and rosy assumptions concerning housing prices (Scheinkman, 2014), with banks lending money to borrowers and then selling the right to receive repayment to third parties in the form of credit default swaps (CDSs). Banks lent recklessly to borrowers who lacked the ability to repay (referred to as 'subprime'). Meanwhile, investors were lured into buying collateralized debt obligations (CDOs), which are akin to insurance policies, guaranteeing a return in the event of a default on the part of the original mortgage borrower (Reinhart and Rogoff, 2009). 'Speculators (including banks) with no interest in the underlying loans began to buy CDSs as a means of betting on whether those loans would be repaid' (Platt, 2015: 4).

The crisis proceeded in parallel with the creation of new projects, viable or otherwise, that could show profits on balance sheets, so that numbers would appear favourable and investors could be attracted. However, if institutional efforts were made to prosecute some of the cases presented earlier, the 2008 crisis triggered no such efforts, officially due to lack of resources, as public money, we were told, was now being directed towards anti-terrorist activity. Regulating business became a negligible task (see chapter 9). Criminal prosecution was avoided and negotiating with financial delinquents prevailed, as banks were deemed too essential to the economy to be brought to account for their conduct (Barak, 2012).

The idea is that banks are essential to the economy, and with the economy being stubbornly fragile, prosecuting frauds would destabilize a weak recovery. These prevailing political-economic attitudes of government officials and politicians allowed fraud to flourish in the name of stability (Sullivan, 2015: 182).

Prior to the 2008 crisis, lenders of last resort, such as central banks and the Federal Reserve in the US, would only support traditional commercial banks. With the crisis, however, non-commercial banks, also known as shadow banks, were supported too. Being unregulated, the shadow banking network had been a major protagonist in initiating the crisis, offering low-quality products and promising high returns. Investment banks, structured investment vehicles, hedge funds, non-bank financial institutions, money market funds, and exchange-traded funds are all components of the shadow banking system and their risky operations escaped the control of regulators (Zaidi, 2016). Shadow banking is not a single, identifiable system, but a constantly changing and largely unrelated set of intermediation activities pursued by very different types of financial market actors.

One aspect of the crisis was associated with the repeal, in the US, of the Glass-Steagall Act which provided a clear distinction between commercial and investment banking. Introduced in the Depression era, the Act was in place for sixty years, until it was no longer deemed appropriate under the new economic conditions and repealed in 1999 during the Bill Clinton presidency. This provoked the blurring of the boundaries between regulated banking operations and shadow banking activities.

The Financial Meltdown and White-collar Crime

We should resist the temptation to single out the most proximate suspects and pin the blame only on them. This was the message experts launched to the public when the crisis exploded: to punish greedy bankers, lax government officials, and other villains would be 'too facile a response' (Rajan, 2010: 4). The basic principles guiding the free-enterprise system were sound, and the crisis was precipitated by systemic factors. Responsibility for the crisis, it was asserted, 'includes domestic politicians, foreign governments, economists like me, and people like you' (ibid). What enveloped everyone, official sources announced, was a form of collective mania, but everyone did what was sensible to do given the circumstances. The problem, in the last analysis, was caused by *fault lines* in the economy, similar to those breaks in the earth's surface where tectonic plates come into contact and collide. The first fault line was the rising income inequality and the political pressure this created for easy credit. But easy money and public policies came into contact with a competitive, sophisticated, and amoral financial system, thus causing a deep fault line. Second, consumption was supported by countries structurally inclined to export, like Germany and Japan, and the goods they offered tempted people who simply could not afford them. Fault lines in the economy, from this perspective, could only be avoided by striking a balance between the role of governments and that of markets.

A modern, sophisticated financial sector understands this and therefore seeks ways to exploit government deficiency, whether it is the government's concern about inequality, unemployment, or the stability of the country's banks. The problem stems from the fundamental incompatibility between the goals of capitalism and those of democracy. And yet the two go together, because each of these systems softens the deficiencies of the other (ibid: 18).

The incompatibility between capitalism and democracy formed the basis for some criminological analysis. Hence, the financial crisis was conceptualized as an inherent phenomenon to market economy, while white-collar crime and its consequences were compared with the impact of conventional criminality. Friedrichs (2015), for example, reiterated his 'inverse hypothesis', arguing that the proportion of criminological attention to a form of crime varies inversely with the objectively identifiable level of harm caused by such crime. Of course, it was contended, humans may well be driven by an animal spirit to make irrational choices, irrespective of economic gain. However, adding to that spirit, the very structure of the financial system was deemed responsible for encouraging practices with varying degrees of intent, liability, and wrongfulness. The exemplar case of Goldman Sachs, in this respect, showed how an iconic American investment bank sold debt obligations that were designed to fail and then betted on their failure. This was only one form of wrongdoing, in a context where some financial operators appeared to constitute a variant of organized crime, as their fraudulent activities were conducted for years exactly like conventional organized criminals conduct theirs, namely on a continuing basis.

Anomalies and Inherent Instability

For those who find the idea that capitalism and democracy are incompatible too coarse, other arguments may refine the analysis.

As we have seen, financial regulators develop their thinking in close and constant relationships with the entities they are required to regulate. They examine the same data and adopt the same models and conceptual frameworks; as a consequence, they perceive new financial products and the risk associated with them as part of market innovation. Before the 2008 crisis, moreover, they tended to monitor the activities of smaller and new firms, leaving the established and larger ones to conduct their own internal risk assessment. The latter, experiencing a period of relative stability, assumed that a stable condition was a permanent feature of financial markets. This assumption led to increasingly risky actions, which spread across the system through imitation and competition, thus giving the impression that risk itself had been finally uprooted from the financial realm. Debts risks, in fact, were passed on through the sale of insurance against the possibility of default. Mortgages were originated, securitized, and distributed. With the first operation lenders offered mortgages and supposedly ensured that the borrower was creditworthy. With the second, the mortgage was sold to another institution, a so-called 'packager' who combined it with other products to create a marketable security. Finally, these were sold to investors, in this way, presumably, spreading the risk (Dorn, 2010). The safety of such products was endorsed by rating agencies which eventually recognized their 'unfortunate errors'. The crisis was compounded by the tolerated practice adopted by banks to transfer debt and risk to an off-balance-sheet subsidiary. Light-touch regulation, invoked by financiers and politicians in unison (Tomasic, 2009), completed the picture, determining what is termed 'regulatory capture', whereby agencies became the captives of those they were supposed to regulate.

In criminological circles, the abysmal knowledge about financial crime (and white-collar criminality as a whole) in popular, institutional, and academic contexts was underlined. It was noted, for example, that criminology 'spends only 5 per cent of its time researching, teaching, and writing about white-collar crime while devoting 95 per cent of its time to blue-collar crime' (Barak, 2015: 1). Financial crime was directly linked to the deregulation of transactions that were previously criminalized. The invisibility of the victims was reiterated, as was that of corporations, whose 'invisibility' as offenders is determined by their limited liability. The expansion of state safety nets, supposedly meant to avert future crises, turned into an encouragement to take yet more risks:

We have become trapped in a repeating game in which participants continue to seek ever higher and more risky returns while 'banking' on the state to fund any losses in a crisis (Barak, 2012: 134).

According to another general argument, neoliberalism and globalization provide a criminogenic combination due to the anomic climate they spread. Global anomy theory is referred to as an explanatory tool for all sorts of international, cross-border criminality (Twyman-Ghoshal and Passas, 2015). Similarly, financial crimes are included among the 'crimes of globalization', and related to the international policies and philosophies endorsed by institutions such as the World Bank and the International Monetary Fund (Friedrichs, 2015). In this sense, financial crimes and crises are seen as inherent and cyclical features of advanced economies rather than anomalies or rare occurrences. Inherent instability, however, is intertwined with financial crime, although economists are often unwilling to acknowledge the relationships between the two. Changes in market philosophies and regulatory norms open up opportunities for fraud and abuse, but the question remains whether such opportunities present themselves in a cyclical pattern or constitute a permanent option in financial markets. True, at times criminal practices may become the object of public attention, and the stigma attached to them may act as a temporary deterrence. But such practices re-emerge at times in different forms or in different places.

The fact that criminogenic markets don't just disappear despite often vigorous campaigns to eliminate them suggests that they are connected to larger social institutions and ideologies. The broader question, then, concerns the underlying conditions and processes that create and re-create criminogenic markets over time and make them resistant to reform (Tillman, 2015: 265–6).

We have seen in a previous chapter Minsky's instability hypothesis: success leads to excess, which leads to failure. Prosperity encourages risk, while the memory of past financial crises fades, making operators succumb to euphoria and rule out the possibility of failure. Adventurous and speculative sprees follow, with riskier strategies expanding and regulatory bodies bowing to the hectic activities of those they are supposed to regulate. Increased risk-taking, in brief, develops simultaneously with increased regulatory relaxation, which is composed of three dimensions (Palley, 2010). The first sees regulators sharing with financial institutions concerns that rules hamper economic development. The second makes financial products and practices escape regulation by virtue of their innovative and unfathomable nature. The third is characterized by regulatory capture (as mentioned earlier), and consists of banks and institutions co-opting public and private agencies designed to oversee them. Note that 'capture' is mainly used in the analysis of corruption, and describes situations in which criminals spread their practices across institutional bodies until they, as it were, 'capture' the entire state (Gounev and Ruggiero, 2012).

These processes are triggered by the financialization of a growing number of economic sectors, all subjected to the financial logic, in an expansionist dynamic that invades areas after areas of the economy. 'Once it has subjected much of the economy to its logic, it reaches some type of limit, and the downward curve is likely to set in' (Sassen, 2013: 33).

Networks of Greed

Crises are also determined by the increased willingness of all participants to take financial risk. As more products are offered, customers are encouraged to incur larger debts, while euphoria turns into the belief that previous crashes have honed the skills to control events. Blaming the victims is still part of this process, whereby ordinary investors are depicted as avaricious individuals who ignore the principles of caveat emptor. If at times such investors may feel anger for having been duped or betrayed, often they see themselves as victims who have contributed to their own victimization (Dodge and Steele, 2015).

From another perspective, financial crimes and crises can be included among those injurious actions carried out by private agents with the support or direct complicity of public actors (Michalowski and Kramer, 2006). Termed 'state-corporate crimes', these actions, in the financial sphere, can be interpreted as the outcome of consortia involving institutions of governance (auditors and regulators) in cooperation with economic actors, in sum: public–private criminal partnerships.

The financial sector is the locus where the elite forges connections and networks and where the constant movement from one occupational group to the other is promoted. This sector displays the sedimentation of partnerships, alliances, solidarity, and complicity among representatives of formally different spheres. It is constituted by a social space hosting lawyers, legislators, politicians, entrepreneurs, and other elitist professionals who amalgamate their values and forge their ethical allegiances (Ruggiero, 2015a). Two illustrious examples of these networked partnerships include former Labour Prime Minister Tony Blair, who is now an adviser to JP Morgan, and former US Secretary of State Condoleezza Rice, who has been recruited by HSBC (Luyendijk, 2015). Corruption of financial markets, it would appear, is incorporated into political systems of governing: it stems from access to powerful institutions, rather than from illegal actions attempting to circumvent them (Johnston, 2005). As routinized crime, therefore, financial crime shapes powerful alliances whose political and economic influence grows in combination with the revenues it produces.

Drawing on critical criminological analysis, we can term these alliances 'networks of trusted criminals' (Friedrichs, 2007), as they are based on long-term interactions between representatives of the elite who have had numerous chances of proving their mutual reliability. The individuals interacting in such networks show that they are desirable partners in cooperative endeavours, thus establishing behavioural regularities and guaranteeing the predictability of the outcomes of interactions. They build their reputation by publicizing their skills and potential to benefit others in joint ventures. The dynamic giving shape to these networks makes the distinction between white-collar and corporate criminals difficult to draw (DeKeseredy, 2011), as in both cases offenders benefit themselves as well as the company employing them. This became manifest during the 2008 crisis, which has spawned an array of other analyses and studies.

The 'networks of greed' emerging during the crisis were already holding sway during the previous decades, when criminogenic conditions in financial markets rapidly developed. Such conditions, as we have seen, were associated with deregulation, senseless credit expansion, and lack of control. An added factor analysed in criminology is the level of corruption predating and accompanying the crisis. In a quantitative study addressing EU countries, the impact of bribery on the financial crisis was examined (Alibux, 2016), while in more general contributions linking social theory and criminology, the financial crisis was seen as simultaneously avoidable and inevitable. 'A better social liberal government and a more informed public', it was argued, 'could have prevented the capitalist system tipping over into a crisis' (Hall, 2012: 86–7). Or perhaps, it might have just delayed the process, because crises are unpredictable, unless drastic systemic change is invoked through massive public support (ibid). This view was inspired by classical arguments that financial domination is necessary to break social bonds and subjugate the entire society. In a 'financialized' society,

solidarity and security are no longer seen in terms of the public or the collective but in terms of the individual protecting property rights and achieving a sense of security through the accumulation of money as a storehouse of value (ibid: 44).

The crisis was also inscribed in the generalized 'Ponzi culture' that continues to create massive harm to the economy, a culture that 'still finds willing believers in the illusion that huge returns on meager investments are available without a risk' (Will, 2013: 45).

In journalists' work as well as in movies, we find descriptions of financial operators as individuals who are socially dysfunctional but honest in their contorted way, as people who profitably cultivate their own ignorance (Wood, 2016). In Adam McKay's film *The Big Short*, we are shown the following epigraph supposedly from Mark Twain: 'It ain't what you don't know that gets you into trouble. It's what you know for sure that just ain't so'. Michael Lewis (2011), in the book on which the film is based, praised the traders' ignorance who trusted the effectiveness of the financial packages they designed or just used ignorance as a strategy, a way of knowing just enough. Knowing just enough meant to sell those packages and continue to offer loans without recording them on the books. Ignorance, with respect to financial institutions, took on the form of confidence and patience: rescue would inevitably come. It should be noted that the idea of taxpayers bailing out bank bondholders was perhaps not particularly controversial in past eras, when the two groups were socially similar or overlapped. Today there is no correspondence between those who benefit from the banking system and 'those who stand to bail it out when things go wrong' (Martin, 2013: 238).

In *Swimming with Sharks*, journalist Joris Luyendijk (2015: 3) took a journey into the world of bankers, where 'billions and billions had been spent to bail out the industry yet nobody had gone to prison'. He found that employees of banks and other financial firms risked losing their jobs, being sued, or suffering severe damage to their reputation if they were caught speaking to the press. Most did not make enormous amounts of money, but nursed the hope to become like those who did, and their acts were therefore the result of imitation. He also found a deep divide between those employed by investment banks and those working in retail or commercial banking, with the latter being regarded as dull and unadventurous. Their understanding of the crisis came from the media, as many had assumed that, thanks to the new generation of complex financial products, 'risk has spread over so many points that the system as a whole was stable' (ibid: 71). Investment banks were divided into three layers. There was a top, relatively small group known as the 'front office', supported by an apparatus of lawyers, accountants, and analysts. All support services were provided by the 'back office', while the 'middle office' was formed by 'risk and compliance' employees responsible for internal controls.

Compliance is there to make sure everything is done by the book. Risk managers monitor the risks that investment bankers take or are proposing to take, saying 'no' to overtly reckless plans and pressing 'stop' when activities get out of hand' (ibid: 69).

Compliance department staff were seen as linesmen are seen in football, losers running back and forth along a line, stopping players from scoring but, at the same time, as individuals useful for reassuring the shareholders and taxpayers, namely those who shoulder the real risks. One analyst added that capitalism without the possibility of failure is like Catholicism without a hell.

Among the findings of this journalistic journey, some echo observations made by academic researchers, as for example the high mobility of personnel in banks and financial firms. Many interviewees had moved to three or four institutions by the age of thirty-five, learning how to be disloyal in order to make their way up. Similarly, we have seen in previous pages that academic work links white-collar crime with occupational instability. The lack of job security in the financial sphere, we are shown, turns into the destruction of human capital and ruthlessness. Echoing the metaphor of financial crime as rape (see chapter 7), an interviewee described a lucrative deal as 'rape and pillage', or 'slash and burn'. Militaristic terms abounded: bankers worked in the trenches, they took no prisoners. Echoing analyses equating business with war or evoking the image of Von Clausewitz in the boardroom (Ruggiero, 2013; 2016), we are told the story of employees of a large financial firm being flown to Las Vegas for a weekend of military-style self-celebration. The firm's best performers were invited to the podium to be honoured. But first they were shown a clip of a war movie, and then a guy stepped forward and began shouting:

We are gonna rip the skin off competitor X. And we'd be expected to go, fists pumping in the air, 'Yeah!' Next he shouted: 'we are gonna fuck over competitor Y!' and we'd go 'Yeah' (Luyendijk, 2015: 114).

Finally, resonating with an argument that cultural criminologists would immediately endorse, some of the interviewees remarked that they were persons who wanted to swim with sharks and see if they could survive. They needed to see themselves coping and developing when challenged by harsh, achievement-driven standards. 'Happy bankers are those who don't do it for the money but for the thrill' (ibid: 213).

In the next chapter we shall see whether the responses to the 2008 crisis managed to reduce opportunities to experience such a thrill.

9

Various Shades of Grey

A frenzy of regulatory proposals followed the crisis, while the basic question loomed persistently: can financial markets be controlled? A related question was: will markets always be one step ahead of regulators, shifting their operations from one sector of the system to another and from one country to the next? (Will, Handelman, and Brotherton, 2012; Friedrichs, 2013; Davies, 2015). Before attempting to answer these questions, a preliminary look at the system to which regulatory efforts are addressed is necessary.

The contemporary financial system extends globally and penetrates all social and natural spheres. It has been described as a mega-machine developed over the last decades that accumulates and maximizes, in the form of capital and therefore of power, 'the values that can be extracted from the highest possible number of human beings and echo-systems' (Gallino, 2011: 5). It enjoys the power to decide what has to be produced, in what quantity, how, where, and when. The mega-machine constituting industrial capitalism had as its engine the manufacture of goods, while the financial system relies on the production of money. As noted in a previous chapter, it is controversial whether the predominance of the financial over the productive sector follows a linear or a cyclical process, namely whether it characterizes the evolution of market economies in general or successive phases thereof (Arrighi, 1994). It seems that the constant companions to such predominance are periodical crises and bubbles (Bilginsoy, 2015; Scheinkman, 2014).

The first component of the financial system consists of bank holding companies, which simultaneously control banks and insurance firms, offer loans, and sell a variety of stocks, derivatives, and other products. The second component consists of institutional investors, who mainly manage pension funds and hedge funds. Both components can trade securities, which include equities, bonds, certificates of deposit, investment trusts, and credit default swaps. The third component is constituted by private banks, that assist 'high net worth individuals' (HNWIs) and provide an array of services and products, including investment management, insurance, and consultancy in cross-border operations. 'Having made a pile of money, most HNWIs spend most of their time worrying about how not to lose it. Private banks are geared towards helping them to hang on to it and grow it' (Platt, 2015: 47). This component, already alluded to in the previous chapter, is also known as grey or shadow banking, is impervious to regulation and public scrutiny, its size is unknown, and its balance sheets are far from transparent. The grey sector offers:

a mountain of derivatives which, for some reason, are not budgeted, is formed of thousands of companies devoid of a proper organisational structure, are often set up by banks solely for the purpose of moving revenues out of the official accounts (for this reason they are also known as vehicles) (Gallino, 2011: 10).

It is against this background that responses to the 2008 crisis will be examined (Ruggiero, 2015b).

Preventing Future Crises?

Not all financial activities can be labelled as criminal, although they may be socially harmful. Responses to the crisis, one would assume, should be capable of tackling both criminal and non-criminal harmful activities carried out in the financial sphere. Let us see, in the broad summary below, how the authorities formulated their responses.

The Basel Committee

The primary international forum for the coordination of financial regulation is the Basel Committee on Banking Supervision, based at the Bank for International Settlements—the so-called central bankers' bank (Martin, 2013). In Basel, regulatory weapons to mitigate financial hazard have been designed in the past, such as rules requiring banks to keep a specified quantity of cash or highly liquid securities in their portfolios.

This requirement has the function of a tax, in the sense that it imposes a cost on banks that decide to act in an adventurous manner. It is like the tax some would like to impose on polluting industries. However, in the financial sphere all rules are extremely difficult to enforce, because they are normally non-binding rules. Moreover, some commentators would endorse the argument that all regulatory measures, particularly those making banking operations more costly, have a perverse effect. If banks are required to raise capital as a form of guarantee to avoid crashes, the argument goes, the cost they incur will make future crushes even worse. This will mean scarcity of liquidity, therefore a restriction in the ability of banks to give loans. And of course, loans and other forms of credit given to entrepreneurs are essential for the economic recovery. According to this view, therefore, regulatory measures in response to a crisis actually exacerbate future crises.

In December 2009, the Basel Committee reiterated that banks retained insufficient capital reserves and showed poor efficiency. Harmonizing reserves, monitoring standards of bank liquidity, and establishing a 'leverage ratio'[1] were among the suggestions made. The issue of assessing and predicting risk in financial operations was also raised.

The document released by the Basel Committee caused some commentators to observe that it is not enough to 'tighten a screw here and put in a new nail there': the entire ship of banking regulation needs a thorough overhaul (Hellwig, 2010). Moreover, the regulatory community was accused of sticking to a tradition of discussing issues only with the bureaucratic cognoscenti, without even trying to explain to the public at large the effects that the new measures were expected to produce.

As for the proposed measures oriented towards prediction of risk, these were deemed ineffective, because risk cannot be reliably measured.

---

[1] In finance, leverage is a general term for any technique to multiply gains. Most often this involves buying more of an asset by using borrowed funds. The belief is that the income from the asset will exceed the cost of borrowing. As the 2008 crisis demonstrates, this involves the risk that borrowing will be larger than the income from the asset, causing loss or even collapse.

Managers Directive

In July 2011, the European Parliament and the Council of Europe issued an 'Alternative Investment Fund Managers Directive'. The Directive regulates EU managers who deal with hedge funds and private equity funds; it establishes general operating conditions and limits to leverage, while calling for transparency and stricter supervision. It also fixes a ceiling for remuneration and bonuses for bankers and brokers, while requiring the appointment of independent risk managers and evaluators. Although EU countries were expected to turn the provisions of the Directive into national legislation, most member states failed to do so. Asset managers employed in the UK regard the Directive as an obstacle to competition and, in their opinion, it will reduce the number of overseas agents operating in the EU.

Regulatory bodies

Discussions following the immediate aftermath of the crisis indicated that reform had to focus on the relationship between governments and independent regulatory bodies. The faults in the administrative and regulatory machinery already mentioned (see chapter 8) were detected. As a remedy, suggestions were put forward to set up committees formed of politicians and professional economists, with a view to exercising overall control over business conduct, on the one hand, and over systemic issues, on the other (Goodhart, 2008). One such committee set up in 2012 in the UK was the Financial Services Authority (Wilson, 2014), which does not tackle shadow banking, with the latter therefore attracting an increasing number of traders who feel that the restraints introduced prevent them from operating otherwise.

Cross-border consequences

Short-sightedness meant that the crisis was initially regarded as affecting individual countries, while its cross-border consequences were almost totally neglected. Bailing out banks was perceived as a domestic issue and it remained unknown how the loss burden arising from transnational transactions might be handled. Only later were international changes invoked, through a 'Memorandum of Understanding' on cooperation for cross-border financial stability, prompting the joint action of supervisory authorities, central banks, and EU countries' finance ministries (Praet and Nguyen, 2008). The Financial Stability Forum took the lead in this process, recommending stricter monitoring of liquidity and risk, and enhanced transparency. However, such recommendations were accompanied by an underlying belief in the disciplinary role of markets, thus displaying an implicit scepticism towards the very measures suggested. Authorities were asked to investigate whether adding new requirements to adaptive market practices would be advisable or might end up being redundant. Market practices, in brief, were and are still deemed 'adaptive' and self-disciplined, irrespective of the damage caused. The type of transparency advocated was linked to the capacity of public authorities to gather information, assess liquidity, and appraise performance. Transparency, therefore, did not entail stricter institutional control but rather the possibility of quantifying potential losses and covering them with public funds. This appeared to be the only acceptable state intervention tolerated by financial institutions. The network established by the Financial Stability Forum was therefore required to gather data around financial practices, to 'encourage mutual exchange of information that are necessary for the proper execution of the mandate of each institution' (ibid: 371). The rescue operations made it clear what the mandate of governments had to be. Due to the global dimension of the crisis, authorities in all the countries involved were asked to cooperate to resolve the crisis situation.

Internationalization of finance meant that all national bond markets were affected, and in countries such as Ireland and Spain domestic taxpayers found themselves footing the bill for bank recapitalization that benefitted foreign bondholders. In sum, responses to the crisis, at least in Europe, took the form of austerity packages producing further increases in unemployment and growing public unrest (Calhoun and Derluguian, 2011; Turner, 2013).

When, on 31 January 2011, Anglo-Irish Bank—which had been recapitalised to the tune of 25.3 billion euros by Irish taxpayers—repaid in full and on schedule a 750 million euro bond to its investors, the distribution of risk under the new regime of sovereign credit support for banks was on stark display. The total cuts to welfare spending in that year's Irish budget amounted to a little over the same amount (Martin, 2013: 238).

In the past, it was acceptable that ordinary citizens helped bond-holders, because almost everybody, through pension and mutual funds, was a bondholder. But with the growing polarization of wealth, an elite has taken shape which retains large quantities of assets and then, when in trouble, expects to be bailed out by those who retain little.

In brief, the need for, and the form of, public intervention were and still are taken as an undisputable given. The principles enunciated by the Forum reaffirmed 'the primacy of private sector solutions', but 'when a strictly private-sector solution cannot be found, public funds have to be mobilised' (Praet and Nguyen, 2008: 372). Authorities, by intervening, do not have to rescue those harmed by the financial crisis, but simply attempt to strengthen market players' confidence. Finally, it was felt that public intervention could not be restrained through ex ante rules, but had to remain 'open' to contingent necessities emerging by future crises. With this, state intervention in support of financial markets was not only definitively ratified, but all qualitative and quantitative limits to that intervention were lifted.

Regulating Europe

'A crisis is a terrible thing to waste', goes the motto, meaning of course that errors committed in the past can bring to more efficient arrangements. Not so in the UK, where light-touch regulation is still preferred and where reform finds an impervious terrain, showing how the conflicting interests of EU member states are significant (Begg, 2009). Regulating financial operations is problematic for the EU because of the clashes between national sensitivities. Disagreements are hard to avoid when discussing how best to reach a coherent approach to cross-border risks and burden-sharing. 'The UK has sought to avoid a dominant role for EU bodies in supervision which could pose a competitive threat to the City of London' (ibid: 1121). The new European System of Financial Supervisors outflanks the problem by granting an enhanced role to national supervisors. No changes in this specific area can therefore be recorded.

Changing the rules amounts to interfering with both domestic and European legislation. A further problem arises from the fact that the Euro area and the EU have different forms and intensity of membership, so that the interplay between monetary policy and financial regulation is complicated and 'raises questions about which institution should take the lead at EU level' (ibid: 1114).

A further issue affecting European integration is that, as we have seen, ultimately taxpayers bear the risk of financial market failures. Because taxpayers are national, not European subjects, it is at the national level that austerity measures are designed as a result. Yet, financial operations involve a number of countries simultaneously, hence the unfair situation in which those nations burdened with cuts and penalties find themselves. For instance, the collapse of a bank in an EU country may lead to calls on taxpayers from other member states to foot the bill, but the negative reaction in the latter can be easily predicted. For this reason, authorities designing new regulations hesitate and fail to take action, thus exacerbating risk for future failings.

The Volcker rule

In early 2009, President Obama appointed an Economic Recovery Advisory Board, chaired by Paul Volcker, a former Chairman of the Federal Reserve. The Board was tasked with making proposals for the reform of the financial sector.

In the UK, the newly formed coalition government, in June 2010, created an Independent Commission on Banking under the leadership of the eminent Oxford economist Sir John Vickers. The Volcker and the Vickers groups had slightly differing views but ended up recommending similar policies, specifically the separation of banking activities into distinct sectors. It should be noted, as we have seen in a previous chapter, that in the US such separation was ratified by the Glass-Steagall Act 1933, passed in response to a crisis affecting many commercial banks. The Act was partially repealed in 1999 by the Financial Services Modernization Act, with the result that the distinction between commercial and investment banks was eliminated, 'turning the financial markets into a free-for-all and establishing a criminogenic environment' (Barak, 2012: 12).

The Volcker and the Vickers groups drew a line between client-oriented and proprietary banking, retail and wholesale markets. The Volcker rule is understood as a ban on proprietary trading by commercial banks. Volcker argued that banks engaged in high-risk speculation were damaging the entire system and that the growing use of derivatives had to be halted. The rule has never been implemented and, in the US as well as in the UK, a reduction rather than a prohibition of hedge fund ownership by banks was introduced (Goldstein, 2014). European Union countries have also discussed the rule, reaching the conclusion that limitations rather than a total ban on hedge funds dealing by banks are acceptable. In both Europe and the US, however, the very discussion of the Volcker rule has caused an exodus of traders from large banks to small hedge fund dealers, thus reproducing the grey financial area that contributed to the crisis in the first place.

In the UK, the distinction between investment banks and retail banks has not marked the decline of 'packages', which are still available while regulators are impotent. They are underfunded and have little experience: at times they ignore what exactly they have to check or regulate. It is bankers themselves who advise clumsy regulators as to what they should look into (Dermine, 2013; Prins, 2014).

The Haldane doctrine

The Executive Director for Financial Stability at the Bank of England, Andrew Haldane, admitted that the financial crash made 'the riches be privatised and the rags socialised'. But it was nobody's fault: 'For the most part the financial crisis was not the result of individual wickedness or folly. It was not a story of pantomime villains and village idiots. Instead, the crisis reflected a failure of the entire system of financial sector governance' (Haldane, 2013: 21). Putting events in historical perspective, he also explained that in the first half of the nineteenth century the business of banking was simple: the owners-managers backed the bank's losses with their own personal finances. Shareholder funds (so-called equity capital) protected clients from loss and bank directors excluded investors who were financially weak in facing risk. Things changed with the emergence of giants embracing the 'too big to fail' doctrine.

At the start of the 20th century, the assets of the UK's three largest banks accounted for less than 10 per cent of GDP. By 2007, that figure had risen above 200 per cent of GDP. When these institutions hit problems, a bad situation can become catastrophic. In this crisis, as in past ones, catastrophe insurance was supplied not by private creditors but by taxpayers. Only they had pockets deep enough to refloat banks with such huge assets. This story has been repeated for the better part of a century and a half; in evolutionary terms, we have had survival not of the fittest but the fattest. I call this phenomenon *doom loop* [emphasis in original] (ibid: 22).

In Haldane's view, ownership and control of banks have been left in the hands of a myriad of agents and brokers taking high risk and receiving large incentives. In this situation, while the losers are easy to identify, the beneficiaries should be found among small-term investors lured into quick-profit operations. His proposals for reform hinged on reshaping risk-taking incentives on a durable basis and increasing the equity capital of banks. Such measures would increase the banks' capacity to absorb loss and reduce the risk they can take. The proposals of the Basel Committee mentioned earlier constituted, in his opinion, a significant piece of reform in this respect.

Bank governance and control, in Haldane's argument, should be improved through increasing expertise and granting more power to risk committees. Voting rights within banks should be extended to wider groups of stakeholders, thus establishing genuine principles of democratic governance. Of course, pluralism in boards of governors comes at a cost: consensual decisions are slow to reach and action can become ineffective. But this is balanced by the benefits pluralism produces in avoiding catastrophic errors.

In his evolutionary analysis, Haldane highlighted the increasing role played by 'economic formality', with mathematics underpinning models, and predictions and concepts being formalized to the point of shaping a theological doctrine. Businesses, in the past, would have on their boards experts in the area in which they operated. Now, he noted, all businesses, irrespective of the area, employ experts in economics and financial matters. On the contrary, it should be acknowledged that even experts have imperfect information and are surrounded by uncertainty, and economists in general should have a narrower view of themselves (Davies, 2012). Ultimately, a good leap forward was achieved in splitting up banks and diversifying their activities, with the distinction between retail and propriety institutions. As for the 2008 crisis, Haldane concluded, mistakes were made, although they were 'honest', not fraudulent mistakes, and anyone would have made them given how uncertain the world is.

Critics of the Haldane doctrine noted that the amount of public funds spent to rescue financial firms outweighed the annual expenditure for social security and education and was almost equal the expenditure for health (MacKenzie, 2013). The Basel Committee, moreover, has never been effective in enforcing rules and has been too generous to banks in establishing the amount of liquidity these were prompted to possess (Pinto, 2014). Challenging Haldane's view that individuals and boards of governors were not to be deemed responsible for the crisis:

The bonus culture requires radical change, much more than the response Haldane suggest. Senior bank executives and board members should be liable to charges of negligence and reckless lending in the event of bank failure and subject to suspension. Unless we get rid of the chancers and rogues, the most determined regulation will have no effect whatsoever (ibid: 231).

The Financial Services Act 2013

Why financial misconduct should attract criminal liability is contentious. The perception that financial crime is 'less criminal' than other conventional criminal activity makes even the Financial Services Act introduced in the UK in 2013 of dubious validity. Optimistic commentators may argue that the Act continues the British long-standing tradition in tackling large-scale illegality in the world of finance (Wilson, 2014). However, critics suggest that most available legislation is unable to deal with the variety and scale of financial malpractice, whose nature and multifaceted characteristics are not sufficiently understood (Mirowski, 2014). Moreover, prosecuting managers who opt for high-risk practices proves ineffective because financial operations, by definition, involve risk-taking. Finally, the Financial Services Act 2013, as might be expected, totally ignores the grey financial area which, in the UK, still constitutes a large sector of the financial sphere as a whole.

The EU regulatory framework and the UK

EU institutions, notably the Commission, the European Parliament, the Council of the European Union, and the European Council, responded to the crisis with a set of some forty legislative proposals inscribed in a general regulatory framework (some of them are mentioned above). One of the key measures was the establishment of new European Supervisory Agencies (ESAs) which, since their inception in 2011, showed several fundamental weaknesses. These include lack of authority, insufficient independence, marginal influence over the shape of primary legislation, poor flexibility in the correction of legislative errors, and inadequate funding and resources. Critics argued that such weaknesses were due to political pressures to take prompt action and to make the financial sector pay for the crisis (House of Lords, 2015). The amount of new legislation, its broad range, and the speed of its introduction produced a number of inconsistencies, and some of its provisions were regarded as disproportionate or misguided. Governments were concerned about the cumulative effect that such a huge programme of reform would have on the financial world, and in the UK, with its largest financial sector in the EU, fear grew that the implications would be immense. Reluctance to adopt the framework was based on the negative repercussions the new rules would have on growth and prosperity. The energetic reactions of the UK authorities can be summed up as follows.

The prosperity of the City of London and the financial services industry it hosts was said to serve the interests not only of the UK but of the global financial market as a whole. The Commission, therefore, was urged to focus more on the overall impact rather than the quantity of its legislative output. A key component of 'better regulation' should be to ensure that a full assessment is undertaken of the impact of substantive amendments to legislation. Impact assessment of major legislative revisions was therefore loudly invoked. The European Parliament was described as being 'prone to occasional popular (and populist) reforms that have not stood up to scrutiny' (ibid: 6). National self-interest had to be safeguarded, it was intimated, and if the regulatory framework continued to leave taxpayers at risk of the failure of a large and complex financial institution, a flexible approach was needed. This would have to ensure that 'the right balance be struck between reaping the benefits of increased transparency and ensuring that the market is able to operate in an effective and efficient manner' (ibid: 9). Transparency, in brief, risked tarnishing economic efficiency.

Flaws were highlighted in the design of the new consumer protection tools, rendering them ineffective. For example, excessively detailed disclosure requirements were criticized, and while enhanced protection for consumer deposits in the event of a bank failure was lauded, it was also remarked that risks can never be eliminated. On the other hand, complete consistency across the EU in the form of the single rulebook was seen as unrealistic, because the specific characteristics of the markets of individual member states would require otherwise. 'Good regulatory design requires that rules appropriately reflect the specific features of particular market segments' (ibid). For example, some financial services providers (including certain asset managers) would be disproportionately affected by restrictions, due to the significant increase these would imply for their operational costs. Real estate funds, private equity funds, and venture capital funds would be particularly hit.

The UK authorities called for impact assessment before reforms were introduced and, while acknowledging the public outcry the crisis had generated, they stressed the leading role of the financial market in bringing economic prosperity and creating jobs. The costs imposed on growth, therefore, had to be assessed. Increased burdens on the financial sector would reduce the flow of credit towards productive sectors and generate a chilling effect on competition: regulatory reform, in sum, was too expensive. Moreover, reform was also deemed excessively 'politicized', part of an ideological, hostile campaign launched against market freedom. This hostility was manifested in the 'mirage' of a fixed regulatory framework, which in reality could never control a constantly evolving sector: regulation had to keep up with this evolution, not the latter with regulation. It was then asserted that the shadow banking sector, in its various shades of grey, played a pivotal role in the economy, offering a much-needed alternative financial driver to the regulated banking sector. Regulating shadow banking, therefore, would prejudice its benefits to the wider economy.

This was the cocooned environment in which a new wave of financial delinquency occurred in the UK, as we shall now see.

Business as Usual

Authors remarking on the lack of major prosecutions of companies or individuals after the crisis pointed out the influence of large financial institutions on law-making and regulation, as well as the high status of potential defendants (Pontell, Black, and Geis, 2014; Rakoff 2014). Examinations of recent transnational responses highlighted how the complexity of cross-border financial linkages made rules difficult to implement. This was due, among other things, to the persistent tensions between transnational measures and national policies. The ongoing power of private actors (grey banking), moreover, was said to have made regulatory responses fall short of what was needed (Porter, 2014). However, among the concerns of agencies and individual senior operators supporting new bank regulations were: 'cyber risks' which may have systemic implications, the survival of the 'too big to fail' credo, the future low levels of interest rates caused by excessive regulation, and the growth of non-bank, or shadow institutions taking on the role of financing the economy. As we have seen, the growth of shadow institutions is testified by the fast move of intermediaries and operators towards alternative financial firms in response to the 'threats' of the Volcker rule. On the prospect of declining rates of interests for investors, commentators failed to predict how this would encourage new forms of financial criminality as a way of making up for the interests lost. The following section lists some of these new forms, proving the apparent inefficacy (or the efficacy?) of regulations in the UK.

Zombie funds

The City regulator called in lawyers to scrutinize the announcement of an investigation into 30 million pension and investment policies. The news sent shares in leading British insurers tumbling (Collinson and Osborne, 2014). The policies scrutinized were sold in the 1980s and 1990s and savers were trapped by penalty charges of 10–12 per cent and in some cases more than 20 per cent if they wanted to move their money. The first two years of contributions by savers covered commissions earned by salespersons and annual charges were around 4 per cent per year. These policies are still in use and the regulator assured financial firms that no compensation for customers would be imposed. Loss by savers is called 'market value adjuster'. Customers, in brief, are trapped in funds where the annual bonuses have often fallen to zero and where they do not have access to their savings until retirement age. Regulators, on the other hand, cannot review the millions of policies individually; they cannot remove exit penalties without an ad hoc piece of legislation; they are impotent when it comes to introducing change in sales practices, and cannot apply current standard retrospectively, let alone calling for compensation of savers.

This case prompts two observations. First, investigations such as this determine a plunge in share values; therefore they are feared by firms as well as customers, with the former pointing out the damaging effects that any attempt at regulation may produce. The status quo, in this view, is deemed less harmful than any sort of external intervention. Second, disappointment and fear by savers may lead competing firms to offer their own services, persuading people to move money out of their pensions to their own schemes. Such unsolicited offers of help may hide yet more speculative or even fraudulent purposes.

Libor interest rates

The 'London interbank offered rate' (Libor) was involved in criminal activity (illegally establishing currency exchange rates) affecting more than a dozen institutions on three continents. Investors were outraged when the scale of the offence was revealed, with Barclays Bank being asked to pay a hefty penalty for moving the exchange benchmarks and thus gaining illicit profits (Ruggiero, 2013). An enquiry led to three employees being charged by the Serious Fraud Office (SFO) for conspiracy to fix Libor interest rates. According to the SFO the offences took place between August 2006 and September 2010, therefore before, but also well after, the effects of the 2008 crisis came to light (Bowers, 2014). City trader Tom Hayes was sentenced in 2015 to fourteen years' imprisonment, becoming the first person to be convicted by a jury for rigging the Libor interest rate (Hickey and Grierson, 2015).

Co-op Bank

The Co-op Bank had a £1.5 billion deficit in 2013 and was bailed out by hedge fund investors and the wider Co-operative Group. In 2014, the Bank admitted that it needed a further £400 million to balance its accounts (Armitage and Goodway, 2014). Mis-selling of pension schemes and interest-rate-hedging products were cited, as well as breaches of the Consumer Credit Act 2006. Shareholders, largely consisting of hedge funds and institutions, will be required to foot the bill.

The Co-op Group was itself in turmoil after the resignation of its chief executive. The situation further alienated the ethical investors traditionally attracted to the Co-op Bank's previous collective ownership structure. Some charities began looking for alternative places to bank after the hedge funds became the majority of shareholders. The Co-op Bank announced that it had to cut 1,000 jobs from its 10,000-strong workforce and close thirty of its branches.

Cases such as this may become more frequent in the future due to the changing features and compositions of the National Audit Office (NAO). The NAO warned that a brain drain from Britain's City watchdogs led to their employing thousands of inexperienced staff. A report published by the NAO expressed grave concerns that a third of staff at the Financial Conduct Authority had less than two years' experience while a quarter of leavers from the Bank of England's Prudential Regulation Authority were rated top performers. It went on to note that it would be vital for both watchdogs to attract and retain the right staff to cope with the challenges arising from the financial crisis. The report stressed the importance of effective oversight of an industry that is valued at more than £234 billion. Regulated firms paid £664 million in the 2013–14 financial year to keep their regulators running, 24 per cent more than in the previous year. The increase was said to result from expensive and time-consuming investigations. Therefore, firms can claim that regulation is wasteful. Problems are compounded by the realization by some regional directors of the astronomical levels of remuneration enjoyed by top managers before and even after the crisis. But, as some commentators sarcastically remarked: 'The rich deserve to be rich' (Krugman, 2014).

Lloyds Banking Group

One of Britain's biggest banks cost victims of the payment protection insurance (PPI) scandal tens of millions of pounds by wrongly cutting their compensation awards. Lloyds Banking Group, which is 33 per cent owned by the taxpayers, cut pay-outs to victims who were mis-sold the notorious insurance policies intended to cover loan payments if borrowers found themselves unable to work (mentioned earlier as CDOs). Loans were mainly linked to property mortgages. In many cases, the fine print meant that customers could never make a claim. This was a case of a taxpayer-sponsored bank depriving taxpayers of their rightful compensation by using a loophole (Harper, 2014).

This case shows that the banking system itself is the root cause of severe instability. More than three quarters of bank loans are linked to property and this creates a self-fuelling boom-and-bust cycle. The availability of credit pushes up property prices and, as prices rise, further speculative borrowing and buying are encouraged, thus pushing prices up even more and well beyond what is sustainable in the long term. When the bust comes, the spiral goes into reverse and the deleveraging causes huge pain throughout the economy. The role of banks in economic textbooks is to provide capital to entrepreneurs to build businesses. That happens very rarely. We can even suggest that today, the role of banks is to finance speculation in second-hand property.

Channel Islands

The Channel Islands, particularly Jersey, Guernsey, Sark, and the Isle of Man, continue to play their role. Described as 'the worst tax dodgers', they are inaccessible to foreign authorities engaged in investigations into tax evasion and financial fraud. In the Isle of Man there are thousands of completely unsupervised companies whose owners are hidden. In Guernsey and Sark it is common for local residents to act as bogus 'nominee' directors for tax-dodging companies. 'The Channel Islands make so much money that islanders enjoy a standard of living twice higher than that on mainland Britain. A vast service industry has sprung up, involving lawyers, solicitors, accountants and banks' (Christensen, 2011: 177). Money to the Channel Islands also arrives in the form of payments to supposed suppliers servicing entrepreneurs based on mainland UK or in other countries. In general, tax havens are regarded as prominent features of the globalized capital market and their very existence continues to create a 'criminogenic environment in which illicit financial flows are easily disguised and hidden amongst legitimate commercial transactions' (ibid).

In the British territories there are still 3 million companies whose owners are unknown. It is also unknown who actually lies behind trusts and foundations, due to ownership secrecy remaining inviolable.

Office of Tony Blair

Evidence of how the borders between legitimate and illegitimate practices are uncertain was provided by controversial news relating to the companies owned by former UK Prime Minister Tony Blair. In 2010, while holding the role of Middle East peace envoy, he acted as a business mediator between Chinese leaders and a Saudi-owned company for which he worked, PetroSaudi. Arranging and advising on deals for investors is a regulated corporate function, and Blair was not authorized to cover that function. He was paid £41,000 a month and a 2 per cent commission on any contracts he helped to secure (Ramesh, 2016). Income channelled through a complex network of firms and partnerships controlled by Blair rose more than 40 per cent in 2011 to more than £12 million. Of this, almost £10 million was paid for 'management services'. The money was transferred via a network of firms and financial vehicles. Accountancy experts questioned the arcane nature of the network's finances, which makes it difficult to trace where its money is coming from or where it is being spent. Windrush Ventures is the name of the pool of companies linked to the 'Office of Tony Blair', but exactly what sort of 'management services' are provided, and how the companies generate their income, is impossible to determine. On the other hand, Blair has provided advice and consultancy to charitable foundations for poverty relief projects in Sierra Leone and Rwanda, creating his own Africa Governance Initiative. He has also advised heads of states and global corporations, which has led to criticism for the way his private and philanthropic activities tend to merge. He has lucrative consultancy contracts with luxury goods firms and insurance companies in Switzerland, has undertaken work for the royal family of Kuwait, an investment firm in Abu Dhabi, and an oil company in South Korea. Blair is taking advantage of laws allowing him, as a promoter of charitable activity, to limit what his companies and partnerships are required to disclose, with the result that his accounts are far from transparent (Doward, 2012).

Glencore International

International aid is supposed to benefit small businesses and vulnerable peoples, for example the aid provided through the World Food Programme (WFP), which is aimed at feeding the starving and committed to buying food from very poor farmers and whose finances consist of donations. However, during the 2011–12 period, more than £500 million ended up in the hands of a London-listed commodities trader, Glencore International. This conglomerate, which buys up supplies from farmers and sells them on at a profit, was in that period the biggest single supplier of wheat to the WFP. 'In the latest half-year financial results, Glencore, which previously attracted controversy for environmental breaches and accusations of dealing with rogue states, reported that revenue from agricultural products doubled to $8.8m' (Neate, 2012). Betting on rising wheat prices, lobbying for bans on exportations from some countries, taking advantage from droughts, and investing in agricultural 'products futures' allow giant food wholesalers to capitalize on 'inert' donation finances and turn them into profit. As a technique of rationalization, wholesalers might well mobilize the argument that they are less corrupt and more ethical than arms producers, because they at least provide food, not weapons.

Flash brokers

'Flash brokers' manage to beat regulators through high frequency trading, which is not just regarded as risky; '[i]t is a form of legalised theft, designed to allow traders to skim profits from other investors' (Surowiecki, 2014: 37). Put simply, an investor intending to buy shares, fractions of second before hitting the "enter" button, may find the price of those shares higher. Orders to buy, in other words, are captured by other traders who buy the wanted shares and resell them at higher prices (Lewis, 2014).

Tesco

Giant supermarket chain Tesco was involved in an accounting scandal, having released false data on profits in order to reassure shareholders and attract new investors. Huge losses were suffered by pension funds, traders, small investors, and staff holding shares. At the basis of the irregular accounts was the practice of demanding financial contributions from suppliers and recording these payments 'creatively', thus faking a healthy financial situation while sales declined. Companies such as Tesco are not required to disclose supplier contributions in their trading statements. About £700 million were wiped off the stock market value of the company, and while shareholders were defrauded, annual salaries amounting to around £1 million were still given to senior managers after the investigation was launched (Wood, 2014).

In 2016, it was more precisely revealed that Tesco had deliberately delayed payments to its suppliers to boost profits. The company breached the legally binding code governing the grocery market with the result that some suppliers had to wait two years for millions of pounds. By holding money owed to suppliers, Tesco was able to overstate profits, thus presenting its business as healthy. Shareholders lost tens of millions of pounds after the company admitted it had mis-stated its profits. Pressure to meet financial targets drove the company's conduct, which agreed a $12-million deal in the US to settle a shareholder class action suit over its accounting fraud (Butler, 2016a; 2016b).

Barclays Bank

This large banking institution was accused by a campaign group of encouraging international fraudsters through its loose security procedures. The Bank allowed individuals holding unchecked international passports to open accounts and set up fraudulent businesses. One example was a multi-million pound fraud against holidaymakers who booked villas and homes in exotic resorts and transferred money through the bank, only to find that those villas or homes did not exist or were not for rent. Campaigners posing as potential investors found that Barclays staff were extremely lax when examining applications, at times only requiring a foreign driving licence as ID. Fraudsters from around the world are attracted to the bank and, after opening their accounts, they can comfortably operate from anywhere they choose (Brignall, 2014).

Sir Philip Green

The collapse of BHS, a high street chain, revealed the operations of owner Sir Philip Green and his associates, who took enormous sums out of the business, including pension funds, and then sold the company for £1 to Dominic Chappell. The purchaser was a former bankrupt businessman who had no experience in the retail sector. When BHS had called in administrators, in March

2016, 11,000 jobs had been put at risk, and a $541-million pension deficit had been found. Under the Pension Act, the regulator has the power to ensure that pension liabilities are not avoided or unsupported, but the case could lead to years of courtroom battles. The news that Green was buying a £100-million yacht to replace his old one did not reflect favourably on his reputation, or the way he is perceived by the public (Davies, 2016).

Harley Street

The property on 29 Harley Street in London is home to a company named Formations House, which manages the businesses of over 2,000 other firms and provides them with an official postbox and answerphone. Formation House literally 'creates' companies, which are both easy and cheap to establish in Britain, and the process is almost entirely unmonitored (*The Guardian*, 19 April 2016). As the law requires that companies must have at least one real person as a director, company formation agents sign up people who, for a fee, declare themselves directors of newly created companies. Formation House creates companies not only in the UK, but also in Gambia, Hong Kong, the Seychelles, the British Virgin Islands, Ireland, the US state of Delaware, Panama, Gibraltar, Jersey, the Isle on Man, Belize, and Mauritius. The companies created are impossible to penetrate for anyone trying to discover who really owns them, and act as vehicles for money launderers and tax evaders. Moreover, they may also be set up by large-scale swindlers whose business consists merely of taking money from gullible investors. At 29 Harley Street (ironically not far from Sherlock Holmes's residence) developers from the US and shipping companies from the Netherlands are among those who have been robbed of their money. This extreme example of grey banking shows how, even within generalized illegality, opportunities for yet further illegality are provided.

The Balloon Effect

Proposals for regulation, as we have seen, moved risk into increasingly unregulated areas, but this paradoxical outcome of the 2008 crisis was never acknowledged by the authorities. For example, the European Securities and Markets Authority (ESMA, 2014) expressed optimism, documenting improving market conditions, bolstered by a combination of macroeconomic prospects and liquidity support measures from central banks. Risks, supposedly, are now below those observed in the more acute phases of the crisis. In this chapter, by contrast, it has been argued that many of the measures proposed to prevent future crises were contested, amended, or scrapped. When applied, their potential effect was neutralized through the creation or expansion of areas impervious to regulation. The phenomenon possesses some similarities with illegal drugs markets, where enforcement targeting one substance or distributing route merely directs business towards other substances and routes, like a balloon 'bulging' here or there according to where it is squeezed.

The suggestion that banks should hold significant quantities of cash or highly liquid securities in their portfolios was countered with the argument that higher resources would expose banks to higher loss in case of further financial crises. Despite reforms introduced in the banking sector aimed at safeguarding customers and small businesses and the separation of retail and property banks (gov.uk, 2014), debts were and remain saleable commodities, and the 'maturity gap' which contributed to the collapse is stationary or widening. The proposed limits for remuneration and bonuses for bankers and brokers was met with the objection that such limits hamper competition and reduce the number of capable managers prepared to work in the financial sector.

Orthodoxy spawned a series of shared assumptions regarding feasible and desirable forms of regulation (Tombs, 2015a), while the appointment of growing numbers of regulators was criticized for the lack of skills and professionalism the new appointees display. Even the Financial Services Act 2013, as we have seen, may prove relatively effective when faced with some extreme forms of misconduct occurring in the official banking system, but may be totally inadequate in getting to grips with the grey sector of the financial world as a whole.

The notion that international financial markets need international regulatory tools was rejected because rules can only be established nationally and can never be totally harmonized. Where new rules were implemented, financial markets witnessed an exodus of traders from large banks to small hedge fund dealers, namely to the grey areas that contributed to the 2008 financial crisis. Finally, disappointment and fear on the part of savers is leading to emerging private firms (yet more grey banking) to offer unsolicited help, often hiding yet more speculative or fraudulent purposes.

The lack or ineffectiveness of new regulations may also be the result of the lack of substantial organized and ideological opposition to market philosophies, whereby policies continue to be tailored around the needs of bankers rather than citizens. The global economy, in brief, is no longer subject to political control: on the contrary, it is politics that has placed itself at its service. Echoing a religious creed, the prevailing motto is: there is no salvation outside the market (Todorov, 2014). Against this ideological backdrop, licit or illicit financial operations, both causing social harm, may be destined to continue undeterred as long as those conducting them can claim that such operations benefit not themselves but markets, namely society at large. In this way, as Touraine (2014: 74) has remarked, financiers can step outside the framework of legality and enter the world inhabited by 'drug cartels, arms dealers or cigarette smugglers', while their acts become 'part of the powerful surge in an expanding illegal economy'.

Whistleblowers such as Hervè Falciani, the employee of a Swiss bank who passed clients' details to tax investigators and personally to Christine Lagarde, head of the International Monetary Fund, are still in danger of prosecution (*Associated Press*, 2013). In the UK, large corporations continue to pay derisory amounts of tax despite their gigantic profits, tax incentives are still being offered to foreign companies with a view to attracting foreign investment, and this tax competition is triggering a race to the bottom which contributes to making the boundaries between white-collar and organized crime increasingly blurred. This is the result of increased corporate tax competition among states (Farnsworth and Fooks, 2015), whereby large companies continue to be the biggest 'welfare queens', and tax breaks, grants, loans, and subsidies constitute what can be termed 'corporate welfare'. Corporate theft and fraud continue undeterred with the complicity of accountancy firms and the full cooperation of regulators: even when tax avoidance schemes have been declared unlawful not one accountancy firm that designed and marketed them has been disciplined (Sikka, 2013). Despite official condemnation of 'banksters', nation states failed 'to examine—let alone act upon—their harmful and criminal risk-taking' (Tombs, 2013: 168). With risk operations still prevailing, and with the self-assurance of operators denying such risks, it is not just 'waste' being produced but a dynamic leading to the infection of the whole financial system (Skidelsky and Skidelsky, 2012).

There is no contemporary Solon in view: that is to say, there is no novel democratic arrangement supervising the financial world and making sure its operation are fair. Regulation in one area of the financial system encourages deregulation in another, while the growth of hidden networks of business may well be the result of recent legislative efforts in the UK. Elsewhere too the number of shadow banks has grown exponentially, with more than 80 per cent of their activities taking place in the advanced economies of North America, Asia, and Northern Europe. Estimates for the year 2015 suggested that the shadow banking sector handled $36 trillion across twenty-six jurisdictions in high risk conditions (Zaidi, 2016).

This growth may in fact offer organized criminals novel opportunities. The claim that markets are adaptive and self-regulating accompanies this perverse process. The following example is indicative of the bleak future ahead: HSBC, Britain's biggest bank, agreed to pay a record £1.2 billion to settle allegations that it allowed terrorist organizations and drugs traffickers to move billions of dollars around the financial system (Rushe and Treanor, 2012).

The next chapter will focus on similar cases occurring in the vertiginously expanding area of money laundering.

10

The Hidden Wealth of Nations

Crises, crashes, and bubbles may be endemic or cyclical, they may follow regular or unpredictable patterns, or may also be determined by intermittent periods of financial optimism or gloom. Attempts at reform, as we have seen, have resulted in the expansion of grey areas of banking which are yet more impervious to reform and regulation. With the bail-out philosophy still protecting adventurers in the financial domain, a push to even greater adventurism is certainly provided by the Bank Recovery and Resolution Directive introduced in January 2016 in the EU countries. The Directive establishes the bail-in principle, namely the obligation on customers to directly rescue their failing banks (Amato and Greco, 2015). Whether this new measure will also lure investors towards more unregulated institutions remains to be seen. Untouched by this and other directives, however, one significant area remains where finances can move at ease: it is the area hosting money laundering, tax evasion, and bribes which do not follow intelligible cycles or patterns. This furtive area, undeterred by public outrage and regulation, is the focus of the current chapter.

Money Laundering

Criminological contributions around the issue of money laundering tend to focus on the use of the finance industry by criminal groups who try to turn their illegal profits into legitimate assets. This specific form of financial crime, therefore, is deemed an appendix of organized crime itself, namely an auxiliary, if integral, component of illicit markets. Banks have traditionally provided money-laundering services, at least until the introduction of piece-meal legislation, throughout the 1990s, enjoined them to report suspicious transactions to the authorities, particularly when large sums are involved. Splitting up the sums into less suspicious tranches remains a practice utilized by organized crime groups, who make large numbers of small transactions at various financial institutions, a practice also known as 'smurfing'. Organized groups can also use the services of numerous individuals to convert cash of small denominations into larger bills, a process also described as 'refining' (Gilmore, 2004). However, investments into the official economy are viable alternatives. Money can also be laundered through casinos, whether already operating or purposely established by criminal groups and, for the more aesthetically sensitive, through art. The latter is an attractive sector for money laundering because of the large monetary transactions it presides over, its confidentiality, and the illegal activities endemic in it, including theft and forgery (De Sanctis, 2013).

If legislation has forced conventional organized criminals to resort to more sophisticated techniques, the alternatives available are not exclusively utilized by them, but have opened up opportunities for a myriad of other financial delinquents. The resort to non-bank institutions, for example, as will be discussed in the following pages, involves a variety of actors whose profile is not so neatly identifiable.

Money laundering can be regarded as a service provided by the official economy to organized crime, in an exchange producing mutual entrepreneurial promotion. Organized crime, however, may be able to 'capture' financial institutions, set up close partnerships with bankers or open up its own banks (Ruggiero, 1996). In the sensational, if not totally anomalous, 'Sindona case' that occurred in Italy in the late 1980s, it was not organized crime which took advantage of the financial system but, vice-versa, bankers holding mafia money who defrauded the organization by making the illicit funds evaporate (Cipriani, 1989; Lodato, 1992).

Illicit funds invested in the official economy are said to determine market distortions, with unprofitable enterprises surviving thanks to the injections of the criminal funds and legitimate businesses penalized by unfair competition (von Lampe, 2016). On the other hand, market distortion is also the consequence of a variety of white-collar crimes taking place in the financial industry. These crimes may escape attention due to the assumption that the bulk of money being laundered is drug-connected. Looking at the exemplary case summarized below, a number of other criminal connections come to light.

Los Cammellos

A group of cocaine wholesalers bought quantities of illegal drugs from Peruvian producers and sold consignments to a number of distributors based in Europe. Los Cammellos, the name given by investigators to this group, had business contacts with partners residing in Germany, Spain, France, Switzerland, and Italy. Payments for consignments took place courtesy of the mediatory role of Swiss banks. In the Italian component of this business, Los Cammellos relied on importers who 'mixed' the drugs with industrial machinery and frozen fish, the items they dealt with in their official trade. The money was physically brought to Switzerland by couriers, and from there transferred on to accounts in Miami and New York. Later, parts of the proceeds returned to Italy, specifically to Sardinia, where connected investors were active in the up-market layer of the construction sector through 'Smeralda 94', a company building luxury homes on the beautiful Emerald Coast. Among the individuals charged with criminal offences were entrepreneurs, developers, financiers, members of traditional organized crime groups, and local politicians (Pinna, 1999).

The exemplary nature of this case lies in its combination of conventional criminality, political corruption, and tax evasion, the three charges faced by some of the protagonists. As far back as the 1990s, therefore, it was becoming clear that, amongst the various operations determining the international pool of dirty money, proceeds from drugs could not be considered the most prominent (Arlacchi, 1994). Of greater relevance were the portions of 'hot' money derived from tax evasion, corruption, bribes, flight capital, and the proceeds of hidden economies, as distinguished from overtly criminal economies. Perhaps, since the 1990s, awareness of the illegal circulation of a large variety of funds, their amounts, and origin, has grown, as shown by more recent accounts. The list of actors engaged in money laundering, in such accounts, includes public officials hiding bribes or stealing public funds, corporations hiding profits, and top managers concealing earnings, while attention is drawn to a variety of transactions: those conducted with the intent to promote unlawful activity, those conducted with the intent to engage in tax evasion violations, and those designed to conceal the nature, location, source, and ownership of funds (DiMartino and Roberson, 2013).

This notwithstanding, the fight against illicit finance is shaped by its very origin, namely by its polarized concern towards funds deriving from conventional criminal activity. In the popular imaginary, but also in official rhetoric, is it not easy to dissociate money laundering from the war on drugs, with the result that the fight against dirty finance continues to convey an image of clean but vulnerable financial institutions being soiled by contaminating criminal attacks. The ambiguity of this image is compounded by frenetic activity aimed at curbing the monetary operations conducted by terrorist groups, which are increasingly described as violent entrepreneurs rather than religious or political combatants.

In contrast to popular or official rhetoric, a growing number of cases being prosecuted fall within the realm of corruption and tax evasion rather than organized crime and terrorism, suggesting a proliferation of money-laundering strategies that can respond to differentiated demand. For example, there are professional money launderers, whose number and the range of customers they serve is unknown. There are members of organized criminal groups who stay away from financial institutions and opt to invest their proceeds in further illegal activity or in mere consumption, not necessarily conspicuous. Moreover, the findings of specific research on money from drugs disprove the transnational nature of the laundering process, which appears mainly to remain a local endeavour (van Duyne and Levi, 2005). When criminal profits are inserted into the official economy, for example in the construction sector or through the acquisition of real estate, fronts unrelated to the illegal underground are used, including businesses experiencing difficulties. Such businesses may ultimately be acquired by criminal groups as their original owners become insolvent and, at the same time, subject to blackmail threats. A portion of criminal proceeds, on the other hand, finds its way into the bank accounts of accomplices in the economic sphere as well as in political circles, so that the task of laundering is entrusted to official actors who are normally more successful in such operations. In this way, it becomes nearly impossible to ascertain whether the funds being laundered originate from organized criminal activities or from corrupt economic and political initiative.

Intermediary figures in the financial world offer services to a range of customers, from the underworld as well as the upperworld. Their ability consists in accelerating the mobility of money rather than assessing their origin, also because they, in turn, may interact with other intermediaries linked in a relatively long and tangled chain. Lawyers and accountants are components of this chain and often act as 'enablers', whether in an active or passive fashion (Middleton and Levi, 2015). The source of the funds being laundered tends therefore to fade in a vortex of moves that protects deals and transactions: mobility means that the culpable are never found on the crime scene. This characteristic, which is commonly attributed to white-collar criminals, may well denote the operations of conventional criminals in the financial world.

Officially triggered by the urge to fight drug traffickers and seize their profits, anti-money-laundering measures, while criticized for obstructing business (Gill and Taylor, 2004), proved unable to separate the revenues of organized crime from those of white-collar offenders. Such measures, perhaps unwittingly, in fact encouraged the connubial unification of the two. As a result, the traditional caution, uncertainty, timidity, and fear in dealing with white-collar offenders may well extend to the treatment of conventional criminals, as money laundering, perpetrated by indistinct actors, is one of the few activities 'that connect Al Qaeda, Colombian drug dealers, Credit Suisse, and Enron officers' (Levi, 2014: 439). In brief, the effects of this specific kind of financial crime are not confined to the business sphere, but spread to the criminal business world, exerting a tantalizing attraction on illicit entrepreneurs. It is a type of financial delinquency that provides motivations for, enables, or even indirectly 'creates' other types of delinquency. Let us examine some elements of this process.

Furtive Money

Tax evasion and money laundering share a set of techniques and are carried out through the mediatory role of similar, if not identical, financial operators. Of course, they may entail distinct processes: for instance, the former aims at hiding the existence of legally earned profits, therefore at making it illegal. The latter, on the contrary, involves the transformation of illegally earned profits into legally acquired earnings (UNODCCP, 1998). Tax evasion, in sum, has to minimize the financial success of those performing it, while money laundering has to maximize the sums officially presented as legitimate earnings. It is commonly assumed that the major actors involved are, respectively, legitimate entrepreneurs (tax evasion) and organized crime groups (money laundering), although the former too find it often necessary to hide not just their legitimate, but also their illegitimate earnings. This is the case when they have to disguise or hide money given or received as bribes or kickbacks, or in general when the money spent or earned is associated with illegal market practices. States may also perform money-laundering operations, when they hide financial transactions associated with illegal political practices at the international level (the clandestine financing of friendly parties or allied ruling elites abroad).

Conventionally divided into three stages, the laundering of money entails, first, the removal of the illicitly earned profits from the place these have been acquired; second, their layering, namely a series of transactions which conceal their origin; third, their integration in the legitimate financial channels. Virtual banking makes such operations easier than before, offering the opportunity to open anonymous accounts and establish shell business entities. Offshore trusts and companies (which will be revisited later in the chapter) may act as vehicles through which the funds are moved before reaching the major financial centres.

Regarded as a tabloid-like description of money laundering, the three-staged model has been critically re-examined in its distinct components. The removal of illicitly earned profits and their 'placement' into the financial system, it is noted, ignores the fact that often the money involved is already in it when the crime is committed. Insider dealing, illegal payments for contracts, bribes, and kickbacks involving politicians and business are examples of how those benefiting from crime find their profits already safely 'placed' in the financial system. As for the stage of 'layering', the assumption that a long series of complex transactions guarantees the proper 'cleaning' of dirty money neglects how simplicity may also offer an effective service. Finally, 'integration', which is supposed to allow criminals to enjoy the proceeds of their acts, overlooks the reality that this stage is frequently indistinguishable from the activity preceding it. In brief, it should be reiterated that the three-staged model may apply to conventional criminal activities such as drugs trafficking, which typically is a cash-generating crime, but it is inadequate when faced with non-cash generative crimes, 'such as bribery, tax evasion, market manipulation, and cyber-crime—crimes which have become much more prevalent since anti-money laundering guidance was first issued over twenty years ago' (Platt, 2015: 27).

We have seen how money-laundering legislation across the world, originally designed to fight organized crime, can end up encouraging it. Such legislation revolves around the notion of 'suspicion', whereby financial institutions are required to adopt a risk-based approach in judging the honesty of their customers and report to the authorities suspect money launderers. How this requirement fails to cover several forms of financial delinquency is illustrated by the following example. Corrupt politicians can hide bribes by setting up front companies that disguise their identity as final beneficiaries of the companies' activity. The bribes received remain in the same bank accounts and are used as collaterals for loans, that the corrupt politicians can then invest in the purchase of luxury property. No suspicious movement can be detected here, as the money was already legitimately circulating before being wired to the front company.

In a model of money laundering suggested by Platt (2015), the finance industry offers criminals a chance to achieve all aims they deem desirable: success in the perpetration of a crime, avoidance of detection, benefit from the crime, and retention of that benefit. The process is informed by a number of different 'disconnects'. First, the beneficiaries of the crime are disconnected from the act committed if they create a company administered and controlled by a firm. Second, they can transform the cash acquired into costly goods. Third, they can disconnect from the property purchased if they set up a trust company, so that the trustees become the official owners of those properties. Some specific financial services empower criminals to achieve yet further disconnects. These include:

- foundations, officially devoted to charitable purposes, which can manage money from 'donors';
- correspondent accounts, which are kept by one bank for use by another and can be used by customers to transfer money in foreign currency;
- shell banks, which hold licences in poorly regulated financial centres;
- loans, which can be repaid using illegal proceeds;

- investment funds, whose ownership may not be registered and can be redeemed to a third party;
- letters of credit, which are used to 'grease the wheels' of international trade and facilitate money laundering, for example, through over invoicing (overstating the price of the goods bought and sold as a means of transferring funds);
- private banks, which offer total discretion.

Zero-tax Countries

It is in the area of private banking that some illuminating examples are found. *Tax & Finance*, based in Lugano (Switzerland), continued to advertise its services as fiscal consultancy, despite being investigated, in 2015, for promoting tax evasion and money laundering. Among its customers were known sports personalities, show business celebrities, entrepreneurs, and politicians (Randacio, 2015). Branches of the bank are found in London, Milan, Buenos Aires, and Dubai, where customers escape vetting and suspicious operations are not regarded as such. In 2013, the French budget minister resigned after it was revealed that he hid his money through a similar fiscal consultancy firm, as did the treasurer of the party in power in Spain for illegally siphoning funds through the private banking circuit. In the US, giant corporation Apple was found by Congress to have evaded tens of billions in taxes by manipulating the location of its profits (Zucman, 2015a; 2015b). These cases proved that there is a growing flux of elite and corporate profits towards zero-tax countries.

Corporate tax rules were established by the League of Nations in the 1920s and stipulated that taxes had to be paid in the countries were profits were made. Corporations that manage to report profits in Bermuda, therefore, pay no tax at all, although they make no sales or run no office there. Zucman (2015a) gathered data on international investments, balances of payments, bank reports, and accounts of multinational companies with a single objective: to expose the true activities of tax havens and their social costs. He found that 55 per cent of the foreign profits of US firms were 'made' in a handful of almost zero-tax countries. As a result of tax avoidance US firms are able to save $130 billion annually, 'contributing to a decline in the effective corporate tax rate from 30 per cent in the late 1990s to about 20 per cent today' (Sunstein, 2016: 38).

In Europe, investigations targeted the tax deals offered by Ireland and Luxembourg, although the fundamental mechanism that allows tax evasion remains untouched: corporations are not taxed on their global profits, but it is their subsidiaries (officially operating in havens) which are taxed as if they were independent entities. In Europe, tax evasion is unaffected by what was presented as a 'courageous' measure adopted in 2005 whereby citizens earning interests outside their country of residence had to be reported to the tax authority of their own country. Known as the Savings Tax Directive, this measure excludes dividends and is systematically outflanked through the use of shell companies and trusts which make it impossible to trace precisely the owners of funds.

The social costs of such tax deals and irregularities manifest themselves, first, in market rigging: large firms distort competition by paying low tax rates while smaller businesses have to face statutory rates. Second, low taxation for corporate actors translates into austerity measures for entire populations. This upward redistribution of wealth, in turn, exacerbates inequality.

Londongrad

The UK is certainly not a zero-tax country, at least not for all. This notwithstanding, it is regarded as one of the major final destinations for laundered funds from across the world. This is due to its reputation of respectability and professionalism, and to the discretion with which it offers its services. The variety of expert and skilled agents populating the City of London, including lawyers, accountants, advisers, mediators, and fiduciaries, can cater for a diverse clientele, from members of organized criminal groups to corrupt politicians and entrepreneurs. Funds derive from drug trafficking, illegal trade in arms, people smuggling, stolen art work, protection rackets, and all other activities in which organized crime is engaged. This was also the opinion, expressed in 2015, by the head of the National Crime Agency (NCA) Keith Bristow, who warned that Britain's economy, the security of its financial sector, and its reputation for probity were in jeopardy because of the emergence of London as a world centre for criminal financial activity. Profits from crime linked to international terrorism were also said to find hospitality in London (O'Neill, 2015). The revelations were accompanied by the decision to investigate law firms for their role in money laundering and other forms of economic crime by large-scale criminal organizations (NCA, 2015).

Echoes of these warnings came from the business world itself, which described London as the money-laundering capital of the world: the City, it was stated, helps corrupt officials and criminals from across the globe hide trillions of dollars of their ill-gotten gains. Among those who shared this view was one of Russia's most prominent businessmen, Alexander Lebedev, the Russian-born owner of *The Independent* and the *Evening Standard*. Lebedev claimed that London-based banks have helped hide more than $6 trillion in corruption payments and criminal proceeds since the turn of the millennium, and argued that the City was now the epicentre of a global financial services oligarchy (Wilson, 2014). The City of London, however, is not alone in providing such services, as it competes with financial centres such as New York and Tokyo. All three centres engage in 'off-shore activities', a term that does not refer to the geographical locations in which certain financial activities are carried out, but to the judicial status of the financial centres themselves (Talani, 2011). The crown dependencies and the British overseas territories are components of the money-laundering network, as they enjoy autonomy in the sphere of taxation and discretion in financial issues (Palan, 2003).

The City of London, therefore, is part of a large network spread around the world, the remaining shards of the British Empire. It is organized in concentric rings. The inner ring consists of the three crown dependencies of Jersey, Guernsey, and the Isle of Man, where transactions are carried out with the assistance of legal staff and accountants based in London. Much of the activity consists of tax evasion and money laundering for a large variety of unidentifiable customers. The next ring is constituted by satellite centres situated in Britain's fourteen Overseas Territories, of which half (Anguilla, Bermuda, British Virgin Islands, Cayman Islands, Gibraltar, Monserrat, Turks & Caicos) are recognized tax havens.

The havens themselves are usually fairly regionally focused: so the Crown Dependencies heavily target Europe, Middles East and Africa, while the Caribbean havens will more commonly target the Americas (Shaxson and Christensen, 2015: 74).

This large network encapsulates a significant part of irregularly circulating money and the hidden wealth of nations, while keeping the City of London dissociated from the dirty business committed elsewhere on its behalf. Various other havens such as Hong Kong, Luxembourg, and Switzerland, while not British, still feed large volumes of business to the City (ibid).

According to the director of Tax Justice Network, wealthy elites from former Soviet Union countries have shifted ownership and control of their assets, however obtained, into offshore companies registered in either the UK or in British secrecy jurisdictions, allowing the UK's capital city to earn the nickname, 'Londongrad'. Collectively, these secrecy jurisdictions act as hidden conduits for dirty money originating from countries across the world, and when reaching London the origins of this money can be untraceable, being hidden behind a complex of secretive offshore bank accounts, companies, and trusts (Christensen, 2015). London achieved this position after overseas territories and crown dependencies, for decades, were ignored or supported in the process of becoming secrecy jurisdictions. The decline of the formal Empire, poor trade, and lack of investment in productive sectors pushed the country into the swamp of finance. As a result, the UK, together with Switzerland and Singapore, all regarded as 'clean performers' in respect of the corruption index established by Transnational Transparency, display the highest secrecy index measured by the Tax Justice Network.

James Ibori

An example of the international dimension of financial secrecy is offered by a graphic novel based on a real case that occurred in Nigeria (Manes and Dojmi, 2015). In the novel there is negative character, a well dressed big man who acts as a boss. We see him first in a London inner city area, where he is a small con man, and then we encounter him in Nigeria, where he has become governor of a southern state of the country. There is also a positive character, a small honest businessman, Dotun Oloko, who is working on a documentary on corruption, and we see briefcases full of banknotes, oil wells, Western financiers, and bursts of bullets. The honest man investigates the career of James Ibori, former governor of the Niger Delta, elected in 1999 and arrested in 2010 on corruption charges. Ibori engaged in a colossal laundering operation by transferring the funds stolen into the international financial circuit with the complicity of private and public institutions of the Western world. The money was found in a US private security firm called Emerging Capital Partners, which also managed funds entrusted to them by Western institutions including the UK Department for International Development and the European Investment Bank. When Oloko handed the material he collected to the British authorities, nothing happened, or rather, he was stalked, threatened, and put under surveillance. The UK authorities, which eventually apologized, revealed his identity to those Oloko was exposing.

Inefficiency

Complicity or inefficiency? It would appear that failure to investigate wrongdoing is connected to the vested interests of financial institutions and their unwillingness and/or inability to select customers. But can the causation of this type of financial crime be associated with a mixture of official complicity with offenders and inefficiency in combating them?

Mundus Bank

A scenario proposed by the Royal United Services Institute (RUSI) outlined a fictional money-laundering network which exemplifies real-life experience. Fictional Mundus Bank operates in fifty countries where, with around 3,000 branches, it serves a total of over 30 million customers. The Bank processes around 2 million international transactions per day and files about 100,000 suspicious transaction reports each year. These reports are sent to the relevant national authorities in charge of investigating suspicious financial activities. The case begins with Mundus Bank detecting a pattern of round-figure payments (highly unusual in everyday trade) into two bank accounts in its Singapore branch. Mundus then discovers that the money has arrived to Singapore from a UK money service business (MSB) and has been sent by a textile entrepreneur based in Paraguay who is also engaged in business deals with China. In six months, 102 payments are recorded amounting to $5.7 million. The account in Singapore also receives funds from Mexico, apparently after selling electronic items in that country. In total, there are sixty-seven payments in about eight months, amounting to $3.3 million. Other funds are deposited into the Singapore account for goods purportedly exported to Hong Kong from a firm based in the United Arab Emirates. Fifteen payments are recorded in this case and the amount of money involved is around $2 million. Despite this unusually intense financial activity, the network appears to be formed of only four Mundus account holders, who operate in diverse lines of business and have customers in various jurisdictions with a reputation for poor transparency. 'For example, the true source of funds paid out of the UK MSB was a Paraguay-based firm, with a nominee director domiciled in Panama' (Ellis and de Oliveira, 2015: 4). This nominee director is also connected to other companies registered in the British Virgin Islands whose nature of business is unknown.

This hypothetical but realistic case shows the enormous difficulties encountered by investigators, particularly in terms of information sharing, leading RUSI to identify as the main challenges: 'Data-protection restrictions, insufficient resources, low levels of co-operation and inefficiency across the system' (ibid: 5). RUSI's recommendations advocate a new model for information sharing guided by the principle of effectiveness and based on three pillars: a clear legal framework; improved resourcing; and facilitated co-operation between public and private sectors and internationally' (ibid: v).

One does not expect some etiological considerations from a study mainly addressed to the investigative aspects of money laundering, hence the necessity to look elsewhere for an understanding of the contexts in which it occurs, its features, and causes.

The Resource and Finance Curse

It is not always the case that countries possessing natural resources manage to turn these into earnings useful for their national development. Oil-rich countries like Nigeria, for instance, 'suffer more conflict, lower economic growth, greater corruption, higher inequality, less political freedom and often more absolute poverty than their resource-poor peers' (Shaxson, 2007; Shaxson and Christensen, 2015: 1).

This paradox of 'poverty from plenty' also affects some countries with large financial sectors. Oversized finance, despite propelling massive and rapid circulation of funds, has no effect on human development indicators. The UN Human Development Index shows that the poorest performers tend to be resource-dependent economies and finance-dependent ones (UN, 2011).

Inequality, absolute poverty, life expectancy, education, and health are not affected by the growth of the financial sector. In fact, the reverse may be the case, in the sense that oversized finance displaces resources from productive and service activities to abstract accumulation. The 'finance curse', in this way, manifests itself in 'country capture', whereby entire sectors of the economy are crowded out, hollowed out, and made ancillary to fictitious, impalpable, ill-distributed wealth. Financial centres, therefore, develop sectarian interests which clash with national collective interests, leading countries to what Keynes saw as a casino-like economic growth.

Like a 'cuckoo in the nest', large financial sectors damage manufacturing, agriculture, and tradable non-financial services, raising local price levels and hampering entrepreneurial innovation and initiative. The predominance of finance also causes a visible brain drain, as the high salaries offered divert the better skilled and educated from more socially useful occupations. Objects of 'capture', therefore, are countries, economies, and human capital, in a quiet coup which 'involves a sophisticated political and societal consensus shaped by a usually rather deferential media' (Shaxson and Christensen, 2015: 19). Resources are poured into the dominant sector, where the pursuit of sheer monetary rent turns into government priority.

It is in this climate that the boundaries between acceptable and unacceptable practices tend to fade, as every new financial strategy, whether socially damaging or not, comes to be equated to pure ingenuous innovation. Against this backdrop, large companies access financial markets less with the intention of stepping up productive activities than as an attempt to enact forms of capital engineering and speculation. Financial markets, therefore, no longer feed the economic growth by putting funds into companies, but take away potentially productive funds from them (Kay, 2013). They do so while pursuing 'safety', an unambiguously good thing except in the financial world, where safety is intended from 'taxes and criminal laws'.

More specific features denoting the pursuit of safety relate to criminalization–decriminalization dynamics, which have been discussed earlier. In brief, we are faced with a type of delinquency utilizing experimental techniques which, by stretching the range of acceptable practices, aims at simultaneously stretching the contours of legislation. In this way, such delinquency is capable of 'founding' a new form of legitimacy.

A variety of foundational crimes fall into the economic domain and pertain specifically to the financial sphere. Others occur in corporate practice, whereby violating the rules often results in new rules being devised, in a race which sees the law chasing the economy, rather than vice-versa. In the financial sphere, new rules are made to be broken, as an effect of competing actors similarly making and breaking rules. Decriminalization ensues, as the new practices prove profitable and restrictions are consequently deemed too onerous. The examples that follows shows some significant outcomes of the simultaneous process of rule-making and rule-breaking.

Google

Controversial tax laws in Ireland, the Netherlands, and Bermuda boosted Google's offshore deposits to some $43 billion. Meanwhile, the company agreed a deal with British tax authorities to pay £130 million in tax arrears, namely payments amounting to a tax rate of a mere 3 per cent. Italy and France issued Google with larger tax bills, but Wall Street analysts were confident that the company would continue to hide profits in Bermuda, thus officially showing lower taxable income. 'Google's tax structure means income from many overseas markets, including £4,6 billion from the UK, is booked through Ireland. Much of it is bounced through the Netherlands and back to Ireland and Bermuda' (Bowers, 2016a: 2).

Panama

The leaking of millions of documents revealed details of operations conducted over forty years in offshore tax havens. The Panamanian law firm Mossack Fonseca was at the centre of the revelations, which provided information about some seventy current or former heads of state and their tax evasion. Iceland's Prime Minister resigned, while Vladimir Putin's circle was proven to engineer unorthodox wealth acquisition mechanisms. Representatives of FIFA (the International Football Federation) were also listed in the documents. Mossack Fonseca, initially, claimed to be shocked by the way the services it offered had been abused by customers, but was also surprised that offshoring arrangements were so vulnerable to investigative journalism and, perhaps, to prosecution (Leith, 2016). British and London-based banks emerged among the most active customers of the Panama firm: HSBC, Coutts, Rothschild, and UBS being among the top ten banks who set up around 15,600 shell companies to help clients conceal their finances. HSBC had been fined £28 million in 2015 for allowing customers to launder money in its Swiss private branch, while in Panama it set up more than 2,300 offshore companies. Its chief executive was among the customers of Mossack Fonseca, which concealed his pay and dealt with his tax affairs. Coutts, the private arm of publicly owned Royal Bank of Scotland, set up 500 paper companies through its Jersey agency. UBS, the Swiss group with most of its investment banking operations in the City of London, set up more than 1,300 offshore companies. The Luxembourg International Bank was involved through Experta, which offers corporate and trust services, while other British-based institutions included Credit Swiss Channel Island and Rothschild Trust Guernsey (Goodway, 2016). The Panamanian firm also laundered money derived from notorious bank robberies and other organized criminal activities (Bowers, 2016b; 2016c). Fonseca's customers avoided paying tax by hiring Bahamas residents as fronts. UK ex-Prime Minister David Cameron and his father Ian appeared in the leaked papers, along with six members of the House of Lords, three former Conservative Members of Parliament, and dozens of donors to UK parties. Ian Cameron was a director of an investment fund named (how ironic!) *Blair*more Holding Inc, which had among its customers an adviser of Robert Maxwell and the Rolling Stones. In thirty years, Blairmore never paid a penny of tax in the UK on its profits (Garside, 2016).

The British Virgin Islands continued to license Mossack Fonseca despite knowing the firm was unable to establish who owned the companies on its books, while a British banker set up a secret offshore finance company allegedly used by North Korean leaders to assist in arms sales and the expansion of its nuclear weapon programme. The revelations also touched Ukraine's President Poroshenko, who was elected in 2014, in the aftermath of the political upheaval in the country that led to the annexation of Crimea and open conflict with Russia. While the war was taking place, Poroshenko moved his assets into an offshore company in the British Virgin Islands. The leaks also contained information about how some leaders from a number of countries used foundations and other firms registered in Panama to anonymously own mining companies and real estate (Schmidt and Lee Myers, 2016).

Commentators argued that, despite the trail of evidence detailing specific financial crimes, leading economies will keep refusing to address the problem at its source. The UK overseas territories and crown dependencies, it is still felt, cannot be shut at a stroke, because the official banking system thrives on the benefits of offshore centres. But as reformers stressed:

To tackle the cancer of corruption at the heart of the global financial system, tax havens need not just to reform but end. Companies, trusts and other structures constituted in this shadow world must be refused access to the real one, so they can no longer steal money and wash it back in. No bank accounts, no property ownership, no access to legal systems (Brooks, 2016: 28).

Mobility and Crime

This suggestion echoes similar proposals and practices adopted in the realm of conventional organized crime, thus ironically locating financial delinquents in the same category of offending. In the fight against criminal organizations, the key variable 'mobility' is associated to the ability of offenders to shift from illicit to licit business and efforts are concentrated on the channels making this shift a smooth one. Severing the links between criminal and official entrepreneurs is of paramount importance for this fight, which as we have seen includes the severance of the links granting criminal proceeds access to the financial world. In the case of white-collar offenders operating in finance, however, severing the links between legitimate and illegitimate practices may be harder, for the reasons tentatively explicated below.

The old 'fraud triangle' posited by Cressey (1950), which identified opportunities, motivations, and rationalizations as the enabling factors of white-collar criminality, may well be inadequate for the explanation of contemporary financial delinquency. Granted, tax evasion, corruption, and money laundering are performed in local or global contexts in which opportunities for hiding one's resources abound, and where the skills of facilitators may make investigation hard. In general, fraudsters may be motivated in their action by the decreasing availability of legal opportunities, or by a system of rewards based on what is achieved rather than how. The acts performed by fraudsters, moreover, may intensify and expand when social and institutional responses are hesitant or non-existent. High pressure in organizations is often cited as a crucial catalyst for fraudulent conduct, although it has also been hypothesized that the enactment of such conduct is hampered by 'a fraud-inhibiting inner voice'. Furthermore, research on offenders convicted for financial statement fraud, corruption, bribery, embezzlement, and accounting fraud appears to reveal a lack of rationalization, but rather a 'guilty conscience after the crime' (Schuchter and Levi, 2015: 184). Contrition after the crime, however, may be the supreme form of manipulation by offenders aimed at tempering the indignation meted out to them, and often does not guarantee desistence from reoffending. Again, a parallel can be drawn with conventional organized crime, when members of mafia-like structures become turncoats only to eliminate competitors and continue or even escalate their criminal career (Dino, 2006).

Rationalizations of tax evasion, bribes, and money laundering, however, often revolve around the 'iniquitous' nature of the state and its invasive fiscal policies. They are fed by the belief that wealth must freely circulate in order to reproduce itself, and that taxation aimed at funding collective welfare exacerbates the unwillingness of the beneficiaries to fend for themselves through enterprising efforts. Pressure, in its turn, does not only derive from particular organizations or professional enclaves, but also from the general political culture, whereby large-scale offences are tolerated if small-scale ones are treated benignly, in a process leading to mutual acceptance between different social groups. The degree of harm respectively caused, which is incommensurable, becomes symbolically equal: those committing small illegalities condone those committing large ones. 'Condemning the condemners' turns into 'condoning the condoners' (Ruggiero, 2000: 122).

Mobility is a crucial variable for the understanding of the types of financial criminality examined here. Mobility describes the privileges enjoyed by offenders as well as the object of their offending. Such offenders are the real 'sans-papiers', as they can freely circulate, undocumented, and cross any border, with the purpose of hiding and valorizing their money. Disadvantage, by contrast, amounts to immobility, namely lack of possibilities to establish geographical and social links. It is this polarization, this substantial asymmetry that creates a climate conducive to tax evasion and money laundering. Wealth includes the ability to multiply one's affiliations and access a variety of social worlds, and is fostered by the resulting expansion of choices offered to mobile individuals and groups. A polarized distribution of mobility means drastic limitations for some, whose efforts to form links and multiply affiliations are impeded. And this impediment is one of the most significant aspects of what we call social exclusion. Mobile individuals and groups, on the contrary, develop opportunities by expanding the circle in which they operate, by entering other circles which intersect with yet other ones, in a geometrical progression leading to increasing and ever new possibilities.

Inequality, in brief, lies on differences in mobility, hence the power of financial markets and operators: funds are moved at a pace that is unimaginable to other economic spheres, let alone other social groups. Finance and its crimes are embedded in an insatiable process which is portrayed as natural, implying that people themselves are naturally and categorically insatiable (Boltanski and Chiapello, 2005). Insatiability, in turn, borders on crime.

Mathematical Morality

Money laundering is going viral, an epidemiological metaphor suggesting that a number of financial corrupt practices are amalgamated and meshed in hidden operational circuits where actors from diverse backgrounds meet and cooperate. Looking at the universe of *money laundering as network*, there are many aspects that need to be unveiled.

Financial institutions and money launderers are two entities involved in a game and, let us assume, represent two sets of interests. They are both intelligent and try to outmanoeuvre each other through choices determined by expected rewards. Money launderers will acquire confidence and even temerity if the payoffs and losses produced by their action are not only acceptable, but desirable. Their behaviour, in sum, is not dictated by law or ethics, but is inspired by a form of mathematical morality associated with the maximum outcomes the game can yield. Applied to military affairs, this 'theory of games of strategy' analyses choice under a system of rewards, with participants who are aware of potential winnings and losses (Williams, 1954). Financial institutions and money launderers, for example, are aware of this zero-sum game, and while bearing in mind the game matrix, namely the rewards and penalties, would normally act with a certain degree of prudence. Supposing the two players pursue antithetical goals, they will be satisfied when both obtain the maximum outcome from their choices. According to this theory, when this is achieved, the game is said to have reached a *saddle-point*, and when the players depart from this point they may suffer unnecessary loss, the situation becomes fluid and someone, anyway, will ultimately suffer.

We can argue that the incorporation of diverse forms of financial delinquency within *money laundering as network* has achieved a saddle-point, allowing all actors involved to derive the maximum benefit they can achieve within that specific organizational setting. Corrupt officials, organized criminals, and financial institutions, in brief, all achieve satisfying results in the network. Some detection will be successful, some charges will be pressed, some bankers or drug traffickers will be punished, but the network as a whole will have achieved what could reasonably and rationally be achieved under the given circumstances. The apotheosis of accumulation is the final goal, of course, and this requires the participation of many operators, irrespective of ethnicity, social origin, occupation, and culture: all have to turn their action into capital, or even 'become' capital.

Like in all networks, in money laundering people work together to accomplish some desired aim, and they can do so through carefully designed strategies or improvisation, although theirs must always be a coordinated effort (Czarniawska, 2008; Hatch, 2011). In this sense, money laundering appears to be composed of parts and elements (criminals, lawyers, bankers, politicians, and entrepreneurs) whose interactions produce outcomes that transcend their specific role and characteristics. 'In other words, a system has properties that cannot be fully known by examining its parts in isolation' (Hatch, 2011: 14). The interactions between the different parties change their singular culture, creating a group identity of varying strength, connecting them through practices, experiences, and symbols. It is the opening of cultures to each other that produces change in the network, giving rise to the phenomenon of 'emergence', namely a set of values which cannot be traced back to the original values held by the components of that organization.

Financial crime, here, becomes a kind of administrative behaviour, where decision-making is based on intelligence, design, and choice. Alternatives and consequences may be partly unknown, means and ends poorly differentiated, but some choices are more likely than others to approximate the desired result. Working procedures, however, will sooner or later take shape as the most effective way to achieve goals, and these procedures will be based on decisions that participants in the network would not make in their personal life. In a 'Weberian' fashion, decisions will become impersonal, as they possess validity only in relation to the survival and perpetuation of the network itself, rather than merely of its constituents. Ultimately, money laundering, as administrative behaviour, requires a form of loyalty, whereby the perpetrators replace their own aims with the general objectives of the network to which they belong.

Networks and Hybridity

The above description postulates a configuration that has attracted intense analytical effort. Criminological investigation into networks reveals contacts, interactions, cultural proximity, and operational partnerships among constituents. Participation in networks does not exclude membership in more structured organizations, but may provide added value in terms of information, mutual aid, and criminal opportunities. Research has unearthed networks of drugs dealers, identifying core participants and peripheral agents, but also discovering a degree of fluidity leading participants to avoid fixed roles and tasks. It has also helped to clarify how networks affect criminal careers, produce leaderships, and adapt to changing markets and law enforcement (Natarajan, 2006; Morselli, 2009). When addressed to conventional criminality, network analysis, although at times describing ephemeral or fluid connections, nevertheless depicts relationships among relatively homogenous individuals who are bound together by specific subcultural ties. In financial crime, however, networks are better understood as informal assemblages made up of ties and nodes through which information is transmitted, knowledge is transferred, ideas are exchanged, and constant innovation is produced. What prevails in them is a philosophy motivating a praxis, rather than a culture shaping a lifestyle. Such networks are characterized by a degree of openness and by loose ties, which may lower trust but increase innovation, thanks to the diversity of those involved. While most criminological analysis of networks depicts crystallized configurations or compartmentalized entities, when this analysis is addressed to the financial world it faces open, chaotic, and unformed interactions. Those operating in financial delinquent networks enjoy a plurality of memberships and connections and a form of multi-positionality.

They concentrate power, in the sense that the power each person can draw from membership in a specific entity is multiplied, both through multiple memberships and through the personal relationships that ensue (Boltanski, 2014: 251).

The concepts of 'criminal social capital' and 'criminally exploitable ties', in this respect, can provide additional elements to the analysis (McCarthy and Hagan, 2001; von Lampe, 2016), as they hint at potential resources that can be mobilized in order to enhance the possibility of success and the prediction of outcomes. Some qualifications are necessary, however, particularly in respect of the different identities of those providing such capital and ties.

Money from organized criminal activity, bribes, and tax evasion flows in the same pool, in networks that gather individuals from a variety of social and occupational backgrounds. Financial networks imply the existence of consortia of highly heterogeneous groups and individuals, each with a distinctive goal and culture, who may establish common goals on an occasional or long-term basis. Actors operating in them are socially 'fuzzy', in the sense that their exploits and careers overlap with those of others who are apparently radically different from them. Financial networks are the reflection of grey areas hosting diverse cultures, identities, and motivations, areas in which diverse activities develop points of contact, common interests, and strategies between licit, semi-licit, and overtly illicit economies. These are 'dirty economies' consisting of encounters which add to the respective cultural, social, and symbolic capital possessed by criminals, politicians, and entrepreneurs, who interlock their practices.

Typically heterogeneous in nature, financial networks provide 'the strength of weak ties' by following the model of a matrix, where each actor is connected to two key partners: one who will help to enact the specific operation at hand, the other who will provide the general skills irrespective of the specific operation to be carried out. This model, which is common in engineering, design, and consulting firms, adapts well to changing environments and allows operations to be started and completed with the involvement of a limited number of persons (Hatch and Cunliffe, 2006). Fast and flexible, the matrix model does not require any substantial change in the overall structure of (in our case) the financial institution, and projects can be carried out in isolation from one another, although through an identical philosophical praxis.

Money laundering as network brings to mind the idea of hybridity, namely the mixing, morphing, and mimicking that stretch identities and breach boundaries.

[H]ybridity is a kind of constant of human interaction and group formation, a meta-datum of what happens through countless crossover processes occurring at many different levels and across the ages (McLennan, 2016: 151).

Hybrids hosting criminals of all social backgrounds, financial institutions involved in money laundering are particularly resilient, as they absorb anomalies and disturbances, and while undergoing change, they retain the same function (Hazan, 2015). Adaptable, they shift notions of risk and responsibility while incorporating new actors and their subculture (DeVerteuil and Golubchikov, 2016). In the speculative philosophy of Whitehead (1978) we find a constant effort to grasp these ideas of hybridity, resilience, persistence, and change. For him, stability and innovation, permanence and flux, are mutually implicated, in a process of reciprocal contamination. A symbiosis is reached when different social groups and institutions connect, shift their allegiances, and establish new coalitions through negotiation (Schwanen, 2016).

Fuzziness

Developments in the financial world, finally, may be consistent with the evolution of modern bureaucracies, which make the employees' definitions of their role uncertain and fuzzy. The separation between units, tasks, and specializations tends to fragment responsibility, with employees ignoring (or choosing to ignore) how their duties relate to the general goals of their employers.

Employees who question the ethical or legal implications of their work are told to carry out their duties and not to worry about things that are the responsibility of top management (Coleman, 2006: 213).

In the face of *money laundering as network*, it remains an open question whether criminal conduct is more likely to occur in competitive markets or whether it is more prevalent in oligopolistic ones. In the former, with many different companies struggling to achieve success, crime rates may be high, but they may be so also in the latter, where large companies have more opportunities to dictate the moral (or immoral) tone of business conduct. In the financial sphere, however, it is the mere growth of organizations and the expansion of their members and customers which may play a crucial role. This growth causes an increase in practices and experiences within organizations, along with the possible subjective interpretations of rules and procedures guiding them. As a result, and in order to avoid a decline in performance, financial institutions are forced to step up coordination and reduce ambiguity (Davidson Reynolds, 2016: 7). This can be done through the introduction of new and more detailed rules, which will create yet more ambiguity and offer increased opportunity for violations. So, the germination of new rules and procedures, which supposedly brings new and more robust formalization, in fact causes an expansion of grey areas where diverse actors can conduct deviant experiments.

The type of financial crime examined in this chapter shows how two main conceptions of 'status structure' can simultaneously be in place. The elitist conception seems to apply to the upper layers of the financial world, where all factors that define an individual's status are positively correlated and all highly valued characteristics co-exist. In this case, the components of the financial world are arranged in a hierarchy. The pluralistic conception, on the other hand, seems to describe a situation in which there are several power centres, and those wielding power are prepared to negotiate among themselves: financiers, politicians, entrepreneurs, and criminals are all invited to the negotiation table.

11

Conclusion

I am aware that the chapters composing this book may be useful as a diagnosis, rather than a cure. There are, of course, discussions on what the future is likely to bring and which responses to financial delinquency should be put in place. As stated at the outset, the choice in this volume to apply the definitions 'delinquent' and 'delinquency' to the financial world might be seen as a first step towards denouncing the harm produced by those operating in that world. Proposals to force banks to hold the total of the reserves they engage in the varied investment portfolios have also been put forward. This, in a sense, would constitute a radical exacerbation of the regulatory measures suggested by the Basel Committee (see chapter 9). The Volcker rule has also been mentioned by reformers, who believe that a drastic division between banking activities would remove resources from speculative ventures and direct them towards productive ones. Finally, the idea of abolishing off-shore and grey banking has also been timidly aired (see chapter 10). As we have seen, however, it took centuries for financial activities to find hospitality in the Western consciousness, and if we adopt Gramsci's slogan around the optimism of the will and the pessimism of reason, we may be tempted to state that, equally, the centuries of financial crime are counted. This conclusion intends to sketch some of the reasons that form the basis of such pessimism.

Thieves avoid keeping the property they steal in their home, but if the object of theft is money, as noted by Montesquieu (1989), precautions become unnecessary: once they have it, money no longer belongs to the victim, but to its new holder. Money enjoys a special charm among criminals, but also among phlegmatic, calculating financial operators. When social activist, anti-war campaigner, and counterculture icon Jerry Rubin (1971), together with his 'co-conspirators', tossed dollar bills from the balcony of the New York Stock Exchange, brokers suspended all trading, lost their emotionless calm, and scrambled for unearned money. Rubin himself, however, eventually became a successful business-man: an early investor in Apple, by the early 1980s he was a multimillionaire (Sen, 2015).

This book has described similar scrambles, involving dishev-elled operators, rational investors, far-sighted financiers, and ruthless impostors. Crises, crashes, and crimes punctuate the history of money, from its slow incorporation into the Christian spirit through to its exclusive predominance in economic activity. Becoming a religious phenomenon by itself, financial accumulation managed to rid itself of guilt and, when events showed its harm-ful effects, explanations and justifications crowded the minds and writings of authoritative commentators.

In the seventeenth century, the culprits of the ruinous outcomes of financial activity were identified as unscrupulous traders manip-ulating the market. The stigma, however, was also addressed to ordinary investors, who gambled in finance while shunning hon-est toil and engaging in sinful drinking. In the eighteenth century financial delinquency was initially associated to currency fraud, and later entered the debate around luxury and usury. A sepa-ration between productive and inert accumulation was drawn, and this was destined to return periodically in economic reason-ing. Responsibility for financial collapse was laid upon employees and predatory insiders of otherwise honest institutions, but also imputed to fraudsters setting up phony stock companies over-night to then quickly run with the money in the morning. Crashes were accidents, like those inadvertently provoked by gentlemen running over pedestrians while riding their horses. Whether ine-luctable natural events or acts of individual pathology, crises were deemed part of economic growth, which needed dangerous and expensive experiments to progress. For Bentham, such experi-ments had to be coupled with tax exemption for the wealthy, an exhortation which is still faithfully heeded. Finally, prudence was still perceived as a virtue, but virtuous people were deemed lack-lustre individuals, devoid of charm. Conversely, transgressors were regarded as imprudent creators.

As the seventeenth century drew to its close, the blame for financial delinquency shifted more emphatically towards its victims, namely rash and greedy investors. Legislation, it was remarked, could not protect fools from folly. Financial crime, on the other hand, was regarded as a logical impossibility, due to the 'calming' effect finance exercised on operators. Soon after, however, unorthodox operators were included among the range of 'criminaloids', a class of individuals neither solidly honest nor dishonest, just imitators of wealthy people whose behaviour followed a cascade principle. The nineteenth century, the century of scientific examination of crime and criminals, offered glimpses of corrupt elites, adventurous bankers, and robber barons. Later, the return of the 'criminaloid' marked the first attempts to formulate a definition of white-collar crime, which was associated with economic and social values centred on egoistic conduct, encouraged and rewarded in the dominant classes.

Definitions favourable to law violation denoted a form of structural immorality in the analysis of the twentieth century, which looked at financial delinquency through the study of managers, the morally unbound characters servicing organizations. This century offered extraordinary examples of delinquency and a barrage of interpretations revolving around organizational dynamics, criminogenic markets, rape, fraudulent bookkeeping, psychopaths, thrills, suitable targets, and networks of greed. In such networks, the co-presence was detected of financial operators and members of conventional criminal groups.

The current century, finally, sees a symbiosis between these two seemingly different actors engaged in financial delinquency, with criminal entrepreneurs joining their official, legitimate counterparts in hiding the wealth of nations. This century is also witnessing the return of financial crises as accidents, the result of unpredictable dynamics which may cause collateral damage. Such damage, at least in the official rhetoric, is deemed a mere externality, whereby the unfortunate victims are harmed by unintentional criminals.

We have traversed a splendid trajectory: individual culpability turned into organizational dysfunction and completed its course by erasing itself altogether. Guilt shifted from persons to persons influenced by organizations, then to organizations influenced by persons, reaching a stage where it was not precisely assignable (again, as Bentham would postulate) until, ultimately, it evaporated. Coprophilia and necrophilia, namely love for the devil's excrements and dead matter identified by Freud and Hegel respectively, also disappeared, leaving swindlers adored as prophets.

Similarly, sin turned into secular guilt and, in the final stage of its evolution, vanished. Greed morphed into crisis, namely an inexplicable manifestation of human action bereft of criminal intent, on the one hand, and of insatiability, on the other. Crises were depicted as endogenous phenomena accompanying the normal running of economic matters, therefore they were not imputed to specific actors. Old and current financial crises, in this sense, seem to be animated by their own peculiar narrative, in predictable patterns that distinguish them from other crises occurring, for instance, in the realm of security. Think of a violent attack on civil populations: the event unfolds storytelling, whereby the public engages in a cognitive process characterized by the following stages. First, the public requires an account of the incident, its features, dynamics, and development. Second, it inquires about the victims caused by that incident, the persons unfortunate enough to have found themselves at the centre of the event. At this crucial stage, empathy emerges and is addressed to the innocent casualties of someone else's deliberate acts. Third, a 'finger pointing' stage follows, in which precise information is demanded as to who, through their acts, has produced evil consequences. Finally, stage four marks the end of the crisis and the shaping of measures responding to those who caused it, along with the setting up of strategies to prevent it from occurring again.

There are no such stages in the cognitive process accompanying financial crises. While the events and actions causing them may be unveiled, the victims are normally neglected, and the perpetrators as well as the consequences of their behaviour disappear. As for the shaping of responses, the process may result in a dual solution: first, it might lead to increasing uncertainty of the boundaries between acceptable and unacceptable practices in the financial world (see chapters 9 and 10) and, second, it might encourage the conclusion that measures are ineffective if not counterproductive.

Financial crises are not dialectic, but entropic, in the sense that they do not lead to different social and institutional arrangements, rather, they resemble periodical implosions experienced by a sector that has lost its télos, namely its sense of direction and purpose. They do not give rise to questions about the anthropological foundations of economic conduct, leaving the avid to accumulate wealth without a specific goal (Zamagni, 2015). And the paradox of avidity is that it does not only lead to disinterest for others but also for oneself: Hazlitt (2009) argued that misers are not so sorry when they die, because they think they no longer have to provide for themselves.

The financial world shows how the sovereignty of politics and the civil society can be bypassed by a closed private sphere that becomes itself a centre of moral authority. Simultaneously, the language of finance becomes increasingly codified, self-referential, and detached from everyday language, while knowledge is reduced to calculations conducted by banks. Governments are finally redundant, as policies are forged through financial calculations and political representatives are superseded by data analysts. Financial reports do not highlight choices, they simply dictate unquestionable solutions, implying the absence of social actors. Verbs appear in the gerund tense: 'providing, working, sharing, improving and fostering, [so that] an action's completion [remains] undefined, thus depriving it of any definite contour' (Moretti and Pestre, 2015: 99). Policies are always in progress, instability looms, and collapse is always possible. If collapse does occur, however, cynical reason explains that victimization and impoverishment are not the product of social and political choice, but the result of 'the sins of the human race or the fatality of life on Earth' (Jameson, 2015: 125).

This demophobic world is inspired by a morbid philosophy of desire. The 'being' it posits is linked to an idea of 'lacking', referred to as deficit, something we will never attain. To 'be' means to feel the possibility of reaching something that is not there yet, that has not yet become real and never will. Desire, therefore, cannot target precise objects but an indefinite variety and quantity of objects, thus becoming desire of nothing. Hence the importance of idols: we need stability, reference points that only idols can offer. The financial world offers one such idol, in the form of operations apparently bringing stability and tempering anxiety. But how can this be done, if desire is infinite? Instead of trying to possess things, humans may choose to be possessed by them: they become, in this way, prisoners of the things they want, so that anxiety and uncertainty may cease. We then become totally alienated: we dissolve ourselves in the objects we desire, we become objects and things ourselves. Money was initially identified with freedom: freedom from want, independence, and freedom to help others. Now it can easily lead to slavery.

References

Adams, J.R. and Frantz, D. (2000), *Full Service Bank: How BCCI Stole Billions around the World*, London: Simon & Schuster.

Aglietta, M. and Orléan, A. (eds) (2002), *La monnaie entre violence et confiance*, Paris: Odile Jacob.

Ahamed, L. (2009), *Lords of Finance. The Bankers Who Broke the World*, London: William Heinemann.

Akerlof, G. and Romer, P. (1993), 'The Economic Underworld of Bankruptcy for Profit', *Brookings Papers on Economic Activity*, 2: 1–73.

Alibux, A.N.R.N. (2016), 'Criminogenic Conditions, Bribery and the Economic Crisis in the EU: A Macro Level Analysis', *European Journal of Criminology*, 13: 29–49.

Allen, W.H. (1969), *John Law. The History of an Honest Adventurer*, London: W.H. Allen.

Amato, R. and Greco, A. (2015), 'Rivoluzione europea sui fallimenti bancari', *La Repubblica*, 5 November.

Amatrudo, A. (2009), *Criminology and Political Theory*, London: Sage.

Animation Magazine, 1 April 2003, 'Germany's EM.TV Singing Financial Blues, http://www.animationmagazine.net/tv/germanys-em-tv-singing-financial-blues/ (accessed 13 February 2016).

Arendt, H. (2015), 'Socrates', in *The Promise of Politics*, New York: Random House.

Aristotle (1995), *Politics*, Oxford: Oxford University Press.

Arlacchi, P. (1994), 'Corruption, Organized Crime and Money Laundering World-Wide', in Punch, M., Kolthoff, E., van der Vijver, K., and van Vliet, B. (eds), *Coping with Corruption in a Borderless World*, Deventer and Boston: Kluwer.

Armitage, J. and Goodway, N. (2014), 'Co-op Bank Ditches Plans to Float after £400m Loss is Uncovered', *The Independent*, 25 March.

Arrighi, G. (1994), *The Long Twentieth Century*, London: Verso.

Associated Press, 24 November 2000, 'Scandal at Belgian High-Tech Firm', http://www.deseretnews.com/article/795004/Scandal-at-Belgian-high-tech-firm.html?pg=all (accessed 13 February 2016).

Associated Press (2013), 'HSBC Man who Passed Clients' Details to Tax Investigators Escapes Extradition'. Available at http://www.theguardian.com/business/2013/may/08/hsbc-tax-extradition-herve-falciani (accessed 14 October 2015).

Atwood, M. (2009), *Payback. Debt and the Shadow Side of Wealth*, London: Bloomsbury.

Aubert, V. (1952), 'White-Collar Crime and Social Structure', *American Journal of Sociology*, 58: 264–80.

Augustine (2003), *The City of God*, Harmondsworth: Penguin.

Babiak, P. and Hare, R. (2006), *Snakes in Suits: When Psychopaths Go to Work*, New York: Regan Books.

Babiak, P. and O'Toole, M.E. (2012), 'The Corporate Psychopath', https://leb.fbi.2012/november/the-corporate-psychpath (accessed 6 February 2016).

Badiou, A. (1997), *Saint Paul*, Paris: Presse Universitaire Française.

Bakan, J. (2004), *The Corporation. The Pathological Pursuit of Profit and Power*, New York: Free Press.

Bakhtin, M.M. (1981), *The Dialogic Imagination*, Austin: University of Texas Press.

Balzac (de), H. (1966), *Le Père Goriot*, Paris: Garnier-Flammarion.

Barak, G. (2012), *Theft of a Nation: Wall Street Looting and Federal Regulatory Colluding*, Lanham: Rowman & Littlefield.

Barak, G. (ed) (2015), *The Routledge International Handbook of the Crime of the Powerful*, London and New York: Routledge.

Beaumont, R. (2003), *The Railway King*, London: Headline.

Beccaria, C. (1804), *Elementi di economia pubblica*, Milan: Destefanis.

Beccaria, C. (1995 [1765]), *On Crimes and Punishments and Other Writings*, Cambridge: Cambridge University Press.

Begg, I. (2009), 'Regulation and Supervision of Financial Intermediaries in the EU: The Aftermath of the Financial Crisis', *Journal of Common Market Studies*, 4: 2–20.

Beirne, P. (1993), *Inventing Criminology: Essays on the Rise of 'Homo Criminalis'*, New York: SUNY Press.

Benson, M.L. and Simpson, S.S. (2015), *Understanding White-Collar Crime. An Opportunity Perspective*, Second Edition, New York and London: Routledge.

Bentham, J. (1787a) *Defence of Usury*, http://www.econlib.org/library/Bentham/bnthUsl.html (accessed 17 June 2015).

Bentham, J. (1787b), 'Letter XIII: To Dr. Smith', in *Defence of Usury*, http://www.econlib.org/library/Bentham/bnthUsl.html (accessed 17 June 2015).

Bentham, J. (1948), *The Principles of Morals and Legislation*, Darien: Hafner Publishing.

Bentham, J. (1952a), 'Tax with Monopoly', in Stark, W. (ed), *Jeremy Bentham's Economic Writings*, London and New York: Routledge.

Bentham, J. (1952b), 'Proposal for a Mode of Taxation', in Stark, W. (ed), *Jeremy Bentham's Economic Writings*, London and New York: Routledge.

Bentham, J. (1967), *A Fragment of Government*, Oxford: Basil Blackwell.

Bernstein, C. and Woodward, B. (2006), *All the President's Men*, New York: Simon & Schuster.

Bierman, H. (1998), *The Causes of the 1929 Stock Market Crash. A Speculative Orgy or a New Era?*, Westport: Greenwood Press.

Bilginsoy, C. (2015), *A History of Financial Crises. Dreams and Follies*, London and New York: Routledge.

Binswanger, H.C. (1994), *Money and Magic: A Critique of the Modern Economy in the Light of Goethe's Faust*, Chicago and London: University of Chicago Press.

Black, W.K. (2005), *The Best Way to Rob a Bank Is to Own One*, Austin: University of Texas Press.

Blackburn, R. (2002), 'Enron and the Pension Crisis, *New Left Review*, 14: 26–52.

Blake, W. (1994), *The Marriage of Heaven and Hell*, New York: Dover.

Boddy, C.R., Ladyshewsky, R.K., and Galvin, P.G. (2010), 'Leaders without Ethics in Global Business: Corporate Psychopaths', *Journal of Public Affairs*, 10: 121–38.

Boltanski, L. (2014), *Mysteries & Conspiracies*, Cambridge: Polity.

Boltanski, L. and Chiapello, E. (2005), *The New Spirit of Capitalism*, London: Verso.

Bombasaro-Brady, J. (2010), 'Absence of Punishment for White-Collar Criminals', https://www.academia.edu/3881730/Absence_of_Punishment_for_White_Collar_Criminals (accessed 31 October 2015).

Bonger, W. (1916), *Criminality and Economic Conditions*, Boston: Little, Brown and Company.

Bonger, W. (1936), *An Introduction to Criminology*, London: Methuen.

Bowers, S. (2014), 'ICAP Brokers on Libor Charges', *The Guardian*, 29 March.

Bowers, S. (2016a), 'Google's Tax Deals to Boost Offshore Cash Pile to $43bn', *The Guardian*, 27 January.

Bowers, S. (2016b), 'Can Google Say It Pays Close to the Rate of Corporation Tax?, https://www.theguardian.com/technology/2016/feb/11/can-google-say-it-pays-close-to-the-rate-of-uk-corporation-tax (accessed 21 April 2016).

Bowers, S. (2016c), 'Brink's-Mat Heist. Lawyer Who Helped Hide Robbery Millions', *The Guardian*, 5 April.

Box, S. (1983), *Power, Crime and Mystification*, London: Tavistock.

Braithwaite, J. (1985), 'White-Collar Crime', *Annual Review of Sociology*, 11: 1–25.

Braithwaite, J. (1989), 'Criminological Theory and Organizational Crime', *Justice Quarterly*, 6: 333–58.

Braudel, F. (1984), *The Perspective of the World*, New York: Harper & Row.

Brignall, M. (2014), 'Is Opening an Account at Barclays a Passport for International Crooks?' *The Guardian*, 13 September.

Bromberg, W. (1953), 'American Achievements in Criminology', *The Journal of Criminal Law, Criminology and Police Science*, 44 (2): 166–76.

Brooks, J. (1999), *Once in Golconda. A True Drama of Wall Street 1920–1938*, New York: John Wiley.

Brooks, R. (2016), 'We Don't Need to Reform Tax Havens—Just Get Rid of Them', *The Guardian*, 5 April.

Brown, P. (2012), *Through the Eye of a Needle. Wealth, the Fall of Rome, and the Making of Christianity in the West, 350–550 AD*, Princeton: Princeton University Press.

Brown, P. (2015), *The Ransom of the Soul. Afterlife and Wealth in Early Western Christianity*, Cambridge: Harvard University Press.

Buchan, J. (1997), *Frozen Desire. The Meaning of Money*, New York: Farrar Straus Giroux.

Bunyan, J. (1952), *The Pilgrim's Progress*, London: Odhams Press Limited.

Burke, E. (1968), *Reflections on the Revolution in France*, Harmondsworth: Penguin.

Butler, J. (2015), *Senses of the Subject*, New York: Fordham University Press.

Butler, S. (2016a), 'Tesco Delayed Payments to Suppliers to Boost Profits, Watchdog Says', *The Guardian*, 26 January.

Butler, S. (2016b), 'Tesco Made Suppliers Wait Years for Payment', *The Guardian*, 27 January.

Cacciari, M. (1996) 'Dialogo su Agostino', *MicroMega*, 3: 14–29.

Calavita, K. and Pontell, H.N. (1992), 'The Savings and Loan Crisis', in Ermann, M.D. and Lundman, R.J. (eds), *Corporate and Governmental Deviance*, Fourth Edition, Oxford: Oxford University Press.

Calhoun, C. and Derluguian, G. (eds) (2011), *Aftermath: A New Global Economic Order?*, New York: New York University Press.

Capra, C. (2002), *I progressi della ragione. Vita di Pietro Verri*, Bologna: Il Mulino.

Carandini, G. (2012), *Racconti della civiltà capitalista. Dalla Venezia del 1200 al mondo del 1939*, Rome-Bari: Laterza.

Carnegie, A. (1900), *The Gospel of Wealth*, New York: Century Company.

Carnegie, A. (1920), *Autobiography*, London: Constable & Co.

Carpenter, D.S. and Feloni, J. (1989), *The Fall of the House of Hutton*, New York: Holt.

Cavallaro, L. (2004), *Il modello mafioso e la società globale*, Rome: Il Manifesto.

Chemow, R. (2013), *Titan: The Life of J.D. Rockefeller*, New York: Vintage.

Chomsky, N. and Ruggiero, G. (2002), *The Umbrella of U.S. Power: The Universal Declaration of Human Rights and the Contradictions of U.S. Policy*, New York: Seven Stories Press.

Christensen, J. (2011), 'The Looting Continues: Tax Havens and Corruption', *Critical Perspectives on International Business* 7: 177–96.

Christensen, J. (2015), 'On Her Majesty's Secrecy Service', in Whyte, D. (ed), *How Corrupt is Britain?*, London: Pluto.

Cipriani, A. (1989), *Mafia. Il riciclaggio del denaro sporco*, Rome: Napoleone.

Clarke, M. (1990), *Business Crime: Its Nature and Control*, Cambridge: Polity.

Clinard, M.B. (1952), *The Black Market*, New York: Knopf.

Clinard, M.B. (1979), *Illegal Corporate Behaviour*, Washington, DC: US Department of Justice.

Clinard, M.B. (1983), *Corporate Ethics and Crime. The Role of Middle Management*, Beverly Hills: Sage.

Clinard, M.B. and Yeager, P.C. (1980), *Corporate Crime*, New York: Macmillan.

Coleman, J.S. (1982), *The Asymmetric Society*, Syracuse: Syracuse University Press.

Coleman, J.W. (1987), 'Toward an Integrated Theory of White-Collar Crime', *American Journal of Sociology*, 93: 406–39.

Coleman, J.W. (2006), *The Criminal Elite. Understanding White-Collar Crime*, Sixth Edition, New York: Worth Publishers.

Collinson, P. and Osborne, H. (2014), 'FCA Faces Legal Inquiry as Zombie Funds Announcement Sends Shares Plunging', *The Guardian*, 29 March.

Conklin, J.E. (1977), *Illegal But Not Criminal: Business Crime in America*, Englewood Cliffs, NJ: Prentice-Hall.

Craft, N. and Toniolo, G. (eds) (1996), *Economic Growth in Europe Since 1945*, Cambridge: Cambridge University Press.

Cressey, D. (1950), *Other People's Money*, Glencoe: Free Press.

Croall, H. (1992), *White-Collar Crime*, Milton Keynes: Open University Press.

Czarniawska, A. (2008), *A Theory of Organizing*, Cheltenham: Edward Elgar.

Daly, K. (1989), 'Gender and Varieties of White-Collar Crime', *Criminology*, 27: 790–812.

Dante, A. (1965), *La divina commedia*, Florence: Sansoni.

Dash, M. (1999), *Tulipomania: The Story of the World's Most Coveted Flower and the Extraordinary Passions It Aroused*, London: Gollancz.

Davidson Reynolds, P. (2016), *Primer in Theory Construction*, London and New York: Routledge.

Davies, H. (2015), *Can Financial Markets be Controlled?* Cambridge: Polity.

Davies, R. (2016), 'Select Committee Chief Lashes Out at Sir Philip Green over BHS Sale', *The Guardian*, 2 May.

Davies, W. (2012), 'An Interview with Bank of England's Andy Haldane', Available at opendemocracy.net (accessed 4 April 2014).

de Bruin, B. (2015), *Ethics and the Global Financial Crisis*, Cambridge: Cambridge University Press.

de Duve, T (2012), *Sewn in the Sweatshops of Marx: Beuys, Warhol, Klein, Duchamp*, Chicago and London: University of Chicago Press.

DeKeseredy, W.S. (2011), *Contemporary Critical Criminology*, London and New York: Routledge.

Demaris, O. (1971), *Captive City*, London: Sphere.

Dermine, J. (2013), 'Bank Regulations After the Global Financial Crisis: Good Intentions and Unintended Evil', *European Financial Management*, 19: 658–74.

Derrida, J. (1992), 'Force of Law: The Mystical Foundation of Authority', in Cornell, D., Rosenfeld, M., and Gray Carlson, D. (eds), *Deconstruction and the Possibility of Justice*, London: Routledge.

De Sanctis, F.M. (2013), *Money Laundering through Art. A Criminal Justice Perspective*, Dordrecht: Springer.

DeVerteuil, G. and Golubchikov, O. (2016), 'Can Resilience Be Redeemed?', *City*, 20: 143–51.

Dickens, C. (2012), *Little Dorrit*, Oxford: Oxford University Press.

DiMartino, F.J. and Roberson, C. (2013), *An Introduction to Corporate and White-Collar Crime*, London and New York: Taylor & Francis.

Dino, A. (ed) (2006), *Pentiti. I collaboratori di giustizia, le instituzioni, l'opinione pubblica*, Rome: Donzelli.

Dirks, R.L. and Gross, L. (1974), *The Great Wall Street Scandal*, New York: McGraw Hill.

Di Stefano, T.F. (2005), 'WorldCom's Failure: Why Did It Happen?', http://www.ecommercetimes.com/story/45542.html (accessed 4 February 2016).

Dodd, N. (2014), *The Social Life of Money*, Princeton and Oxford: Princeton University Press.

Dodge, M. and Steele, S. (2015), 'A Comprehensive Framework for Conceptualizing Financial Frauds and Victimization', in Barak, G. (ed), *The Routledge International Handbook of the Crime of the Powerful*, London and New York: Routledge.

Dorn, N. (2010), 'The Governance of Securities. Ponzi Finance, Regulatory Convergence, Credit Crunch', *The British Journal of Criminology*, 50: 23–45.

Douglas, J.D. and Johnson, J.M. (eds) (1977), *Official Deviance*, Chicago: Lippincott.

Doward, J. (2012), 'Blair Inc's Baffling 40% Rise in Earnings', *The Observer*, 8 January.

Drucker, P.F (1966), *The Effective Executive*, New York: Harper & Row.

Dunn, D. (2004), *Ponzi: The Incredible True Story of the King of Financial Cons*, New York: Broadway.

Durkheim, E. (1938), *The Rules of Sociological Method*, New York: Free Press.

Edelbacker, M., Kratcoski, P., and Theil, M. (eds) (2012), *Financial Crimes. A Threat to Global Security*, London: Taylor & Francis.

Edelhertz, H. (1970), *The Nature, Impact and Prosecution of White-Collar Crime*, Washington: US Department of Justice.

Ellero, P. (1978), *La tirannide borghese*, Turin: Bocca.

Ellis, C. and de Oliveira, I.S. (2015), *Tackling Money Laundering. Towards a New Model for Information Sharing*, London: Royal United Services Institute.

Ellul, J. (2010), *On Freedom, Love, and Power*, Toronto: Toronto University Press.

Ermann, M.D. and Lundman, R.J. (eds) (1978), *Corporate and Governmental Deviance*, New York: Oxford University Press.

ESMA (European Securities and Markets Authority) (2014), *Trends, Risks, Vulnerabilities*, Paris: ESMA.

Evans, D.M. (1968), *Facts, Failures and Frauds: Revelations, Financial, Mercantile, Criminal*, New York: Augustus M. Kelly.

Evans, D.M. (1970), *The Commercial Crisis 1847–48*, New York: Burt Franklin

Fabian, A. (1990), *Card Sharps, Dream Books and Bucket Shops: Gambling in 19th-Century America*, Ithaca and London: Cornell University Press.

Fahey, D. (2015), 'When a Bank Goes Bust', *The Irish Times*, 5 September.

Farnsworth, K. and Fooks, G. (2015), 'Corporate Taxation, Corporate Power and Corporate Harm', *The Howard Journal of Criminal Justice*, 54: 25–41.

Felson, M. (2002), *Crime and Everyday Life*, Thousand Oaks: Sage.

Ferenczi, S. (1914), 'The Ontogenesis of the Interest in Money', in *First Contributions to Psycho-Analysis*, London: Karnac Books.

Ferri, E. (1967), *Criminal Sociology*, New York: Agathon Press.

Fittipaldi, E. (2015), *Avarizia. Le carte che svelano ricchezza, scandali e segreti della Chiesa di Francesco*, Milan: Feltrinelli.

Folsom, B. and Robinson, R. (2010), *The Myth of the Robber Barons*, Washington: Young America's Foundation.

Forti, G. and Visconti, A. (2007), 'Cesare Beccaria and White-Collar Crimes' Public Harm: A Study in Italian Systemic Corruption', in Pontell, H.N. and Geis, G. (eds), *International Handbook of White-Collar and Corporate Crime*, New York: Springer.

Fowler, A. (1968), 'Introduction', in Milton, J., *Paradise Lost*, London: Longman.

Fox, L. (2003), *Enron: The Rise and Fall*, Hoboken: John Wiley.

Frankel, T. (2012), *The Ponzi Scheme*, New York: Oxford University Press.

Freud, S. (1927), 'The Future of an Illusion', in *The Standard Edition of the Complete Psychological Works of Sigmund Freud*, vol. XXI, London: The Hogarth Press.

Freud, S. (1930), 'Civilization and Its Discontents', in *The Standard Edition of the Complete Psychological Works of Sigmund Freud*, vol. XXI, London: The Hogarth Press.

Frieden, J.A. (1987), *Banking on the World. The Politics of American International Finance*, New York: Harper & Row.

Friedrichs, D. (1996), *Trusted Criminals: White-Collar Crime in Contemporary Society*, First Edition, Belmont: Wadsworth.

Friedrichs, D. (2007), *Trusted Criminals: White-Collar Crime in Contemporary Society*, Third Edition, Belmont: Wadsworth.

Friedrichs, D. (2013), 'Wall Street: Crime Never Sleeps', in Will, S., Handelman, S., and Brotherton, D.C. (eds), *How They Got Away with It. White Collar Criminals and the Financial Meltdown*, New York: Columbia University Press.

Friedrichs, D. (2015), 'Crimes of the Powerful and the Definition of Crime', in Barak, G. (ed) (2015), *The Routledge International Handbook of the Crime of the Powerful*, London and New York: Routledge.

Gaddis, J. L. (2005), *The Cold War: A New History*, Harmondsworth: Penguin.

Galbraith, J.K. (1959), 'Introduction', in Shaplen, R., *Kreuger: Genius & Swindler*, London: World Distributors.

Galbraith, J.K. (1987), *A Short History of Financial Euphoria*, Harmondsworth: Penguin.

Galbraith, J.K. (2004) *The Economics of Innocent Fraud*, London: Allen Lane.

Galbraith, J.K. (2009), *The Great Crash 1929*, London: Penguin.

Gallini, C. (1985), 'Introduzione', in Sighele, S. (1985), *La folla delinquente*, Venice: Marsilio.

Gallino, L. (2005), *L'impresa irresponsabile*, Turin: Einaudi.

Gallino, L. (2011), *Finanzcapitalismo. La civiltà del denaro in crisi*, Turin: Einaudi.

Gallino, L. (2015), *Il denaro, il debito e la doppia crisi*, Turin: Einaudi.

Garber, P.M. (1989), 'Tulipmania', *Journal of Political Economy*, 97: 535–60.

Garber, P.M. (2000), *Famous First Bubbles: The Fundamentals of Early Manias*, Cambridge: MIT Press.

Garofalo, R. (1914), *Criminology*, Boston: Little, Brown and Company.

Garofalo, R. (2012), 'The Natural Crime', in DiCristina, B. (ed), *The Birth of Criminology*, New York: Wolters Kluwer.

Garside, J. (2016), 'The Hidden Deals That Helped David Cameron's Father Avoid Paying UK Tax', *The Guardian*, 5 April.

Gay, P. (2007), *Modernism. The Lure of Heresy from Baudelaire to Beckett and Beyond*, London: William Heinemann.

Geis, G. (2007), 'The Heavy Electrical Equipment Antitrust Cases of 1961', in Geis, G. (ed), *White-Collar Criminal: The Offender in Business and the Professions*, New Brunswick: Aldine Transactions.

Geis, G. (2013), 'Unaccountable External Auditors and Their Role in the Economic Meltdown, in Will, S., Handelman, S., and Brotherton, D.C. (eds), *How They Got Away with It. White Collar Criminals and the Financial Meltdown*, New York: Columbia University Press.

Geis, G. (2016), *White-Collar and Corporate Crime*, New York and London: Oxford University Press.

Geis, G. and Stotland, E. (eds) (1980), *White-Collar Crime. Theory and Research*, Beverly Hills and London: Sage.

Gerber, J. and Weeks, S.L. (1992), 'Women as Victims of Corporate Crime', *Deviant Behavior*, 13: 325–47.

Giddens, A. (1978), *Durkheim*, Glasgow: Fontana/Collins.

Gilchrist, J.T. (1969), *The Church and Economic Activity in the Middle Ages*, New York: Macmillan.

Gill, M. and Taylor, G. (2004), 'Preventing Money Laundering or Obstructing Business?', *British Journal of Criminology*, 44: 582–94.

Gilmore, W.C. (2004), *Dirty Money. The Evolution of International Measures to Counter Money laundering and the Financing of Terrorism*, Third Edition, Strasbourg: Council of Europe.

Gleeson, J. (2000), *Millionaire: The Philanderer, Gambler, and Duelist Who Invented Modern Finance*, New York: Simon & Schuster.

Goethe, J.W. (1999), *Faust*, London: Wordsworth Clascics.

Goldgar, A. (2007), *Tulipmania. Money, Honor, and Knowledge in the Dutch Golden Age*, Chicago: University of Chicago Press.

Goldstein, M. (2014), 'Regulators Ease Volcker Rule Provision on Smaller Banks', *The New York Times*, 14 January.

Goodhart, C.A.E. (2008), 'The Regulatory Response to the Financial Crisis', *Journal of Financial Stability*, 4: 351–8.

Goodway, N. (2016), 'British Banks at Heart of Panama Tax-Havens Leaks', *Evening Standard*, 4 April.

Gori, P. (1968), 'L'evoluzione della sociologia criminale', in *Scritti Scelti*, Cesena: Edizioni Antistato.

Gori, P. (2011), *La miseria e i delitti*, in M. Antonioli, M. and Bertolucci, F. (eds), *Nostra patria è il mondo intero*, Pisa: Biblioteca Franco Serantini.

Gounev P. and Ruggiero, V. (eds) (2012), *Corruption and Organized Crime in Europe*, London and New York: Routledge.

Gov.uk. (n.d.), 'Policy: Bank Regulation', Available at Gov.uk/government/policies/creating-stronger-and-safer-banks (accessed 10 February 2014).

Graeber, D. (2011), *Debt. The First 5,000 Years*, New York: Melville House.

Green, G.S. (1993), 'White-Collar Crime and the Study of Embezzlement', in Geis, G. and Jesilow, P. (eds), 'White-Collar Crime', Special Issue of *The Annals of the American Academy of Political and Social Science*, 525, January.

Greenslade, R. (1992), *Maxwell's Fall*, London: Simon & Schuster.

Hagan, J. and Parker, P. (1987), 'White-Collar Crime and Punishment: The Class Structure and Legal Sanctioning of Securities Violations', *American Sociological Review*, 50: 302–15.

Haldane, A. (2013), 'The Doom Loop', *London Review of Books*, 4 (4): 21–2.

Hall, S. (2012), *Theorizing Crime & Deviance. A New Perspective*, London: Sage.

Harper, T. (2014), 'Lloyds Accused of Short-Changing PPI Claimants', *The Independent*, 25 March.

Harrington, B. (2012), 'The Sociology of Financial Fraud', in Knorr, C.K. and Preda, A. (eds), *The Oxford Handbook of the Sociology of Finance*, Oxford: Oxford University Press.

Hartung, F.E. (1950), 'White-Collar Offences in the Wholesale Meat Industry in Detroit', *American Journal of Sociology*, 56: 25–32.

Harvey, D. (1989), *The Condition of Postmodernity. An Enquiry into the Origins of Cultural Change*, Oxford: Basil Blackwell.

Hatch, M.J. (2011), *Organizations. A Very Short Introduction*, Oxford: Oxford University Press.

Hatch, M.J. and Cunliffe, A.L. (2006), *Organization Theory: Modern, Symbolic and Postmodern Perspectives*, Second Edition, Oxford: Oxford University Press.

Hayek, F.A. (1973), *Law, Legislation and Liberty*, London: Routledge & Kegan Paul.

Hazan, H. (2015), *Against Hybridity: Social Impasses in a Globalizing World*, Cambridge: Polity Press.

Hazlitt, H. (1947), *Will Dollars Save the World?*, New York and London: D. Appleton-Century.

Hazlitt, H. (2009), 'Want of Money', in *Selected Essays*, Oxford: Oxford University Press.

Hebberecht, P. (2010), 'Willem Bonger (1876–1940)', in Hayward, K., Maruna, S., and Mooney, J. (eds), *Fifty Key Thinkers in Criminology*, London and New York: Routledge.

Hegel, F. (1948), *Early Theological Writings*, Chicago: University of Chicago Press.

Hellwig, M. (2010), *Capital Regulation after the Crisis: Business as Usual?* Bonn: Max Planck Institute.

Henwood, D. (1998), *Wall Street. How It Works and for Whom*, London and New York: Verso.

Hickey, S. and Grierson, J. (2015), 'Former City Trader Given 14-Year Sentence for Libor Rigging', *The Guardian*, 4 August.

Hobsbawm, E.J. (1968), *Industry and Empire*, Harmondsworth: Penguin.

Hooper, J. (2008), 'Parmalat Founder Gets 10 Years Prison for Market Rigging', *The Guardian*, 19 December.

House of Lords (2015), *The Post-Crisis EU Financial Regulatory Framework: Do the Pieces Fit?* London: Stationary Office Limited.

Hughes, M. (2012), 'The Stock Market Crash of 1987: What Have We Learned?', www.bbc.co.uk/new/business-19994566 (accessed 15 January 2016).

Hume, D. (2011), *The Essential Philosophical Works*, London: Wordsworth.

Itskevich, J. (2002), 'What Caused the Stock Market Crash of 1987?', www.historynewsnetwork.org/article/895 (accessed 15 January 2016).

Jackson, B. (1988), *Honest Graft: Big Money and the American Political Process*, New York: Alfred A. Knopf.

Jameson, F. (2015a), 'The Aesthetics of Singularity', *New Left Review*, 92: 101–32.

Jameson, F. (2015b), *The Ancients and the Postmoderns*, London and New York: Verso.

Johnson, S. (2009), *Lives of Poets*, Oxford: Oxford University Press.

Johnston, M. (2005), *Syndromes of Corruption: Wealth, Power and Democracy*, Cambridge: Cambridge University Press.

Josephson, M. (1962), *The Robber Barons. The Great American Capitalists 1861–1901*, London: Eyre & Spottiswoode.

Kay, J. (2013), 'Why Business Loves Capital Markets, Even if It Doesn't Need Capital', *Financial Times*, 14 May.

Kerényi, C. (2002), *The Gods of the Greeks*, London: Thames & Hudson.

Keynes, J.M. (1972), *Essays in Persuasion*, London: Macmillan.

Kierkegaard, S. (1983a), *Sickness unto Death*, Princeton: Princeton University Press.

Kierkegaard, S. (1983b), *Fear and Trembling*, Princeton: Princeton University Press.

Kindleberger, C.P. (1984), *A Financial History of Western Europe*, London: George Allen & Unwin.

Kindleberger, C.P. (2002), *Manias, Panics and Crashes. A History of Financial Crises*, Fourth Edition, Basingstoke: Palgrave.

Kindleberger, C.P and Aliber, R.Z. (2005), *Manias, Panics and Crashes. A History of Financial Crises*, Fifth Edition, Basingstoke: Palgrave.

Klein, M. (1923), *The Psychoanalysis of Children*, London: The Hogarth Press.

Kochan, N. and Whittington, R. (1991), *Bankrupt: the BCCI Fraud*, London: Gollancz.

Kristeva, J. (2015), *Teresa, My Love. An Imagined Life of the Saint of Avila*, New York: Columbia University Press.

Krugman, P. (2014), 'I lupi di Wall Street', *Il Sole 24 Ore*, 9 March.

Landes, D. (1969), *The Unbound Prometheus*, Cambridge: Cambridge University Press.

Landesco, J. (1929), *Organized Crime in Chicago*, Chicago, Ill.: University of Chicago Press.

Lange, B. (2007), *The Stock Market Crash of 1929. The End of Prosperity*, New York: Infobase Publishing.

Latour, B. and Lépinay, A. (2009), *The Science of Passionate Interests: An Introduction to Gabriel Tarde's Economic Anthropology*, Chicago: Prickly Paradigm Press.

Laufleur, L.J (1948), 'Introduction: Jeremy Bentham and the Principles', in Bentham, J., *The Principles of Morals and Legislation*, Darien: Hafner Publishing.

Lazerfield, P.F. and Merton, R.K. (1970), 'Mass Communications, Popular Taste and Organized Social Action', in Schramm, W.L. (ed), *Mass Communications*, Urbana: University of Illinois Press.

Le Bon, G. (2008), 'The Crowd', in Ruggiero, V. and Montagna, N. (eds), *Social Movements: A Reader*, London: Routledge.

Leclercq, J. (1959), *Christianity and Money*, London: Burns & Oates.

Leeson, N. (1996), *Rogue Trader. The Original Story of the Banker Who Broke the System*, London: Sphere.

Leeson, N. (1999), *Back from the Brink. Coping with Stress*, London: Virgin Books.

Le Goff, J. (1987), *La borsa e la vita. Dall'usuraio al banchiere*, Roma/Bari: Laterza.

Le Goff. J. (2010), *Le Moyen Age et l'argent. Essai d'anthropologie historique*, Parigi: Perrin.

Leith, S. (2016), 'Hats off to the Brave Panama Whistleblower', *Evening Standard*, 4 April.

Levi, M. (1987), *Regulating Fraud. White-Collar Crime and the Criminal Process*, London: Tavistock.

Levi, M. (2014), 'Money Laundering', in Paoli, L. (ed), *The Oxford Handbook of Organized Crime*, Oxford: Oxford University Press.

Lewis, M. (2011), *The Big Short: Inside the Doomsday Machine*, London: Allen Lane.

Lewis, M. (2014), *Flash Boys: A Wall Street Revolt*, New York: Norton.

Linsboth, C. (2015), 'Crisis in the Highest Circles' (http://www.habsburger.net/en/chapter/crisis-highest-circles-economic-boom-and-stock-exchange-crash), (accessed 24 September 2015).

Lodato, S. (1992), *Potenti. Sicilia anni Novanta*, Milan: Garzanti.

Lombroso, C. (1876), *L'uomo delinquente*, Turin: Bocca.

Lombroso, C. (1902), *Delitti vecchi e delitti nuovi*, Turin: Bocca.

Lombroso, C. (1971), *L'uomo di genio*, Rome: Napoleone Editore.

Lordon, F. (2014), *Willing Slaves of Capital. Spinoza & Marx on Desire*, London and New York: Verso.

Luhman, N. (1985), *A Sociological Theory of Law*, London: Routledge.

Luyendijk, J. (2015), *Swimming with Sharks. My Journey into the World of the Bankers*, London: Guardian Books.

Mackay, C. (2004), *Extraordinary Popular Delusions and the Madness of Crowds*, New York: Barnes & Noble.

Mackay, M. (2013), *Impeccable Connections: The Rise and Fall of Richard Whitney*, New York: Brick Tower Press.

MacKenzie, D. (2013), 'The Magic Lever', *London Review of Books*, 35(9): 16–19.

MacKinnon, D. and Derickson, K. (2013), 'From Resilience to Resourcefulness: A Critique of Resilience Policy and Activism', *Progress in Human Geography*, 37: 253–70.

Mandeville, B. (1989), *The Fable of the Bees*, Harmondsworth: Penguin.

Manes, L. and Dojmi, C. (2015), *Soldi sporchi. Corruzione, riciclaggio, abuso di potere tra Europa e Delta del Niger*, Rome: Round Robin.

Manguel, A. (2015), *Curiosity*, New Haven and London: Yale University Press.

Manning, D.J (1968), *The Mind of Jeremy Bentham*, London: Longmans.

March, J.G. and Simon, H.A. (1958), *Organizations*, New York: John Wiley & Sons.

Marenbon, J. (2015), *Pagans and Philosophers. The Problem of Paganism from Augustine to Leibniz*, Princeton: Princeton University Press.

Marivaux (de), P. (2013), *Le triomphe de Plautus*, Paris: Hachette.

Markham, J.W. (2006), *A Financial History of Modern US Corporate Scandals: From Enron to Reform*, New York: M.E. Sharpe.

Martin, F. (2013), *Money: The Unauthorised Biography*, London: The Bodley Head.

Marx, K. (1853), 'Capital Punishment', *New York Daily Tribune*, 18 February: 3–6.

Marx, K. (1973), *Grundrisse*, New York: Penguin.

Marx, K. (1992), *Early Writings*, Harmondsworth: Penguin.

Mayer, M. (1993), *Nightmare on Wall Street: Salomon Brothers and the Corruption of the Marketplace*, New York: Simon & Schuster.

Mayhew, H. (1968), *London Labour and the London Poor*, New York: Dover Publications.

McBarnet, D. (2006), 'After Enron Will "Whiter than White Collar Crime" still Wash?', *British Journal of Criminology*, 46: 1091–109.

McCarthy, B. and Hagan, J. (2001), 'When Crime Pays: Capital, Competence, and Criminal Success', *Social Forces*, 79: 1035–60.

McLennan, G. (2016), 'Quiddity and Flux', *New Left Review*, 97: 151–7.

McNamara, G. (2013), 'The Gilded Age', http://history1800s.about.com/od/1800sglossary/fl/The-Gilded-Age.htm, (accessed 10 September 2015).

Mead, G.H. (1934), *Mind, Self and Society*, Chicago: University of Chicago Press.

Melville, H. (1984 [1857]), *L'uomo di fiducia*, Milano: Feltrinelli.

Michalowski, R. and Kramer, R. (2006), *State-Corporate Crime: Wrongdoing at the Intersection of Business & Government*, London: Rutgers University Press.

Michelet, J. (1981), *Storia della rivoluzione francese*, vol. IV, Milan: Rizzoli

Middleton, D. and Levi, M. (2015), 'Let Sleeping Lawyers Lie: Organized Crime, Lawyers and the Regulation of Legal Services', *British Journal of Criminology*, 55: 647–68.

Mill, J.S. (1990), *Writings on India*, Toronto: University of Toronto Press.

Millington, B. (1996), 'Das Rheingold', in Sadie, S. and Macy, L. (eds), *Operas*, Oxford: Oxford University Press.

Milton, J. (1968), *Paradise Lost*, London: Longman.

Minsky, H. (1982), *Can It Happen Again? Essays on Instability and Finance*, New York: M.E. Sharpe.

Minsky, H. (2008), *Stabilizing an Unstable Economy*, New York: McGraw-Hill.

Mirowski, P. (2014), *Never Let a Serious Crisis Go to Waste*, London: Verso.

Moggach, D. (2000), *Tulip Fever*, London: Vintage.

Moley, R. (1926), 'Politics and Crime', *Annals of the American Academy of Political and Social Science*, 25: 78–84.

Monroe, A.L. (2014), *Early Economic Thought. Selected Writings from Aristotle to Hume*, New York: Dover Publishers.

Montesquieu (1989), *The Spirit of the Laws*, Cambridge: Cambridge University Press.

Moretti, F. and Pestre, D. (2015), 'Bankspeak. The Language of World Bank Reports', *New Left Review*, 92: 75–99.

Morselli, C. (2009), *Inside Criminal Networks*, New York: Springer.

Mukherjee, R. (1955), *The Rise and Fall of the East India Company*, Bombay: Popular Prakashan.

Murphy, A.E. (1997), *John Law: Economic Theorist and Policy-Maker*, Oxford: Oxford University Press.

Natarajan, M. (2006), 'Understanding the Structure of a Large Heroin Distribution Network: A Quantitative Analysis of Qualitative Data, *Journal of Quantitative Criminology*, 22: 171–92.

NCA (National Crime Agency) (2015), *Money Laundering*, http://nationalcrimeagency.gov.uk/crime-threats/money-laundering, (accessed 2 February 2015).

Neate, R. (2012), 'UN Spent £50m in Food Aid on Wheat from Glencore', *The Guardian*, 7 February.

Nelken, D. (1994), 'White-Collar Crime', in Maguire, M., Morgan, R., and Reiner, R. (eds), *The Oxford Handbook of Criminology*, Oxford: Clarendon.

Nietzsche, F. (1968), *The Genealogy of Morals*, New York: Random House.

Norton, S.D. (2012), 'The Causes of the Banking Crises of the 1920s', *The World Financial Review*, http://www.worldfinancialreview.com/?p=2446 (accessed 30 October 2015).

Nuzzi, G. (2015), *Via Crucis*, Milan: Chiarelettere.

O'Neill, S. (2015), 'City Lauders Billions of Pounds a Day', *The Times*, 29 January.

Palan, R. (2003), *The Offshore World: Sovereign Markets, Virtual Places, and Nomad Millionaires*, Ithaca and London: Cornell University Press.

Palley, T. (2010), 'The Limits of Minsky's Financial Instability Hypothesis', *Monthly Review*, 61: 28–43.

Park, R.E. (1925), 'The City: Suggestions for the Investigation of Human Behaviour in the Urban Environment', in Park, R.E., Burgess, E.W., and McKenzie, R.D. (eds.), *The City*, Chicago: University of Chicago Press.

Parker, S. (2008), *The Great Crash: How the Stock Market Crash of 1929 Plunged the World into Depression*, London: Little, Brown and Company.

Parks, T. (2016), 'The Passion of the Bureaucrats', *London Review of Books*, 18 February: 13–16.

Passas, N. (1990), 'Anomie and Corporate Deviance', *Contemporary Crises*, 14: 157–78.

Passas, N. (1996), 'The Genesis of the BCCI Scandal', in Levi, M. and Nelken, D. (eds), *The Corruption of Politics and the Politics of Corruption*, Oxford: Blackwell.

Passas, N. and Nelken, D. (1993), 'The Thin Line Between Legitimate and Criminal Enterprise: Subsidy Frauds in the European Community', *Crime, Law and Social Change*, 19: 223–43.

Pearce, F. (1976), *Crimes of the Powerful*, London: Pluto.

Pearce, F. and Tombs, S. (1990), 'Ideology, Hegemony, and Empiricism: Compliance Theories and Regulation', *British Journal of Criminology*, 30: 423–33.

Pearce, F. and Tombs, S. (1991), 'Policing Corporate "Skid Rows": A Reply to Keith Hawkins', *British Journal of Criminology*, 31: 415–26.

Pepinsky, H.E. (1974), 'From White-Collar Crime to Exploitation: Redefinition of a Field', *Journal of Criminal Law & Criminology*, 65: 226–38.

Perkin, H. (1971), *The Age of the Railway*, Newton Abbott: David and Charles.

Perry, F. (2013), 'Visionaries or False Prophets?', *Journal of Contemporary Criminal Justice*, 29: 331–50.

Perth Gazette, 21 May 1858 ('Trial of the Royal British Bank Directors').

Petrosino, S. (2015), *L'idolo. Teoria di una tentazione dalla Bibbia a Lacan*, Milan: Mimesis.

Pinna, A. (1999), 'Quelle ville da sogno vendute con lo slogan: La barca sotto casa', *Il Corriere della Sera*, 14 October.

Pinto, D. (2014), *Capital Wars*, London: Bloomsbury.

Plato (2005), *The Collected Dialogues. Including the Letters*, Princeton: Bollinger.

Platt, S. (2015), *Criminal Capital: How the Finance Industry Facilitates Crime*, London: Palgrave Macmillan.

Polanyi, K. (1944), *The Great Transformation*, New York: Farrar & Rinehart.

Pontell, H., Black, W., and Geis, G. (2014), 'Too Big to Fail, Too Powerful to Jail? On the Absence of Criminal Prosecutions after the 2008 Financial Meltdown', *Crime, Law and Social Change*, 61: 1–13.

Porter, T. (ed) (2014), *Transnational Financial Regulation after the Crisis*, London: Routledge.

Praet, P. and Nguyen, G. (2008) 'Overview of Recent Policy Initiatives in Response to the Crisis', *Journal of Financial Stability* 4: 368–75.

Praz, M. (1967), *Storia della letteratura inglese*, Florence: Sansoni.

Presdee, M. (2000), *Cultural Criminology and the Carnival of Crime*, London and New York: Routledge.

Prins, N. (2004), *Other People's Money: The Corporate Mugging of America*, New York: The New Press.

Prins, N. (2014), *All the Presidents' Bankers*, New York: Nation Books.

Proudhon, P.J. (1857), *Manuel du spéculateur à la Bourse*, Fourth Edition, Paris: Librairie de Garnier Frères.

Pugh, D.S. (ed) (1990), *Organization Theory. Selected Readings*, Harmondsworth: Penguin.

Punch, M. (1996), *Dirty Business. Exploring Corporate Misconduct*, London: Sage.

Quetelet, A. (1835), 'A Treatise on Man and the Development of His Faculties', in DiCristina, B. (ed) (2012), *The Birth of Criminology*, New York: Wolters Kluwer.

Quinney, R. (1970), *The Problem of Crime*, New York: Dodd, Mead.

Rabelais, F. (1993), *Gargantua et Pantagruel*, Paris: Flammarion.

Rajan, R.G (2010), *Fault Lines. How Hidden Fractures Still Threaten the World Economy*, Princeton: Princeton University Press.

Rakoff, J.S. (2014), 'The Financial Crisis: Why Have No High-Level Executives Been Prosecuted? *New York Review of Books*, 61(1): 4–8.

Ramesh, R. (2016), 'How Former PM Was Sold as the Man to Unlock Situations for Business', *The Guardian*, 29 April.

Randacio, E. (2015), 'Bocelli, Ramazzotti e altri 65: soldi all'estero e meno tasse', *La Repubblica*, 5 November.

Reichman, N. (1993), 'Insider Trading', in Tonry, M. and Reiss, A.J. (eds), *Beyond the Law*, Chicago: University of Chicago Press.

Reinhart, C.M. and Rogoff, K.S. (2009), *This Time is Different. Eight Centuries of Financial Folly*, Princeton and Oxford: Princeton University Press.

Renehan, E.J. (2005), *Dark Genius of Wall Street. The Misunderstood Life of Jay Gould, King of the Robber Barons*, New York: Basic Books.

Robb, G. (1992) *White Collar Crime in Modern England: Financial Fraud and Business Morality 1845–1929*, Cambridge: Cambridge University Press.

Robb, G. (2006), 'Women and White-Collar Crime: Debates on Gender, Fraud and the Corporate Economy in England and America', *British Journal of Criminology*, 46: 1058–72.

Roebuck, J. and Weeber, S.C. (1978), *Political Crime in the United States*, New York: Praeger.

Ross, D. (2014), *Philosophy of Economics*, London: Palgrave Macmillan.

Ross, E.A. (1907), *Sin and Society. An Analysis of Latter-Day Iniquity*, Boston: Houghton Mifflin.

Ross, I. (1992), *Shady Business: Confronting Corporate Corruption*, New York: Twentieth Century Fund Press.

Ross-Sorkin, A. (2002), 'Top Tyco Executives Charged with $600 Million Fraud Scheme', *New York Times*, 13 September, http://www.nytimes.com/2002/09/13/business/2-top-tyco-executives-charged-with-600-million-fraud-scheme.html?pagewanted=all (accessed 13 February 2016).

Rousseau, J-J. (1993), *Le contract social*, Paris: Gallimard.

Rubin, J. (1971), *We are Everywhere*, New York: Harper & Row.

Ruggiero, V. (1996), *Organized and Corporate Crime in Europe. Offers that Can't Be Refused*, Aldershot: Dartmouth.

Ruggiero, V. (2000), *Crime and Markets. Essays in Anti-Criminology*, Oxford: Oxford University Press.

Ruggiero, V. (2013), *The Crimes of the Economy. A Criminological Analysis of Economic Thought*, London and New York: Routledge.

Ruggiero, V. (2015a), *Power and Crime*, London and New York: Routledge.

Ruggiero, V. (2015b), 'Social Harm and the Vagaries of Financial Regulation in the UK', *International Journal of Crime, Justice and Social Democracy*, 4 (4): 91–105.

Ruggiero, V. (2016), 'Clausewitz in the Boardroom. Legitimacy and Hegemony', in Ruzza, S., Jakobi, A., and Geisler, C. (eds), *Non-State Challenges in a Re-Ordered World*, London and New York: Routledge.

Rushe, D. and Treanor, J. (2012) 'Fears for Jobs Save HSBC from Trial', *The Guardian*, 12 December.

Sassen, S. (2013), 'The Logics of Finance: Abuse of Power and Systemic Crisis', in Will, S., Handelman, S., and Brotherton, D.C. (eds), *How They Got Away with It. White Collar Criminals and the Financial Meltdown*, New York: Columbia University Press.

Schain, M. (ed) (2001), *The Marshall Plan: Fifty Years After*, New York: Palgrave.

Scheinkman, J. (2014), *Speculation, Trading and Bubbles*, New York: Columbia University Press.

Schelling, T.C. (1984), *Choice and Consequences*, Cambridge: Harvard University Press.

Schlesinger, A.M. (1957), *The Crisis of the Old Order: 1919–1933*, Boston: Houghton Mifflin.

Schmidt, M.S. and Lee Myers, S. (2016), 'Leaked Documents Detail Offshore Accounts', *The New York Times*, 4 April.

Schrager, L.S. and Short, J.F. (1977), 'Toward a Sociology of Organizational Crime', *Social Problems*, 25: 407–19.

Schrager, L.S. and Short, J.F. (1980), 'How Serious Is a Crime? Perceptions of Organizational and Common Crime', in Geis, G. and Stotland, E. (eds), *White-Collar Crime: Theory and Research*, London: Sage.

Schuchter, A. and Levi, M. (2015), 'Beyond the Fraud Triangle: Swiss and Austrian Elite Fraudsters', *Accounting Forum*, 39: 176–87.

Schumpeter, J.A. (1954), *History of Economic Analysis*, London: George Allen & Unwin.

Schumpeter, J. (1958), *The Economics and Sociology of Capitalism*, Princeton: Princeton University Press.

Schur, E.M. (1957), 'Sociological Analysis of Confidence Swindling', *Journal of Criminal Law and Criminology*, 48 (3): 296–304.

Schur, E.M. (1972), *Labeling Deviant Behavior. Its Social Implications*, New York: Joanna Cotler Books.

Schwanen, T. (2016), 'Rethinking Resilience as Capacity to Endure', *City*, 20: 152–60.

Schwartz, M. and Watkins, S. (2003), *Power Failure: The Inside Story of the Collapse of Enron*, New York: Doubleday.

Scott, P.D. (2007), *The Road to 9/11. Wealth, Empire and the Future of America*, Berkeley: University of California Press.

Sen, A. (1987), *On Ethics and Economics*, Oxford: Basil Blackwell.

Sen, A. (2015), *The Country of First Boys and Other Essays*, New Delhi: The Little Magazine.

Shapiro, S.P. (1984), *Wayward Capitalists. Target of the Securities and Exchange Commission*, New Haven: Yale University Press.

Shapiro, S.P. (1990), 'Collaring the Crime, Not the Criminal: Reconsidering the Concept of White-Collar Crime', *American Sociological Review*, 55: 346–65.

Shaplen, R. (1959), *Kreuger: Genius & Swindler*, London: World Distributors.

Shaw, J.B. (2010), *The Perfect Wagnerite: A Commentary on the Niblung's Ring*, London: Dover Books.

Shaxson, N. (2007), *Poisoned Wells. The Dirty Politics of African Oil*, London: Palgrave.

Shaxson, N. (2011), *Treasure Islands. Uncovering the Damage of Offshore Banking and Tax Havens*, London: Palgrave Macmillan.

Shaxson, N. and Christensen, J. (2015), *The Finance Curse. How Oversized Financial Centres Attack Democracy and Corrupt Economies*, London: Tax Justice Network.

Shelley, P.B. (1994), *Adonais and Other Poems*, London: Wordsworth.

Shover, N. and Hochstetler, A. (2006), *Choosing White-Collar Crime*, New York: Cambridge University Press.

Sighele, S. (1985), *La folla delinquente*, Venice: Marsilio.

Sikka, P. (2013), 'Why Combatting Tax Avoidance Means Curbing Corporate Power', *Criminal Justice Matters*, 94: 16–17.

Simmel, G. (1978), *The Philosophy of Money*, London: Routledge.

Simon, E. (2009), Money, Money, Money, http://www.torah.org/features/firstperson/a-rod.html, (accessed 16 May 2016)

Simpson, S.S. (2002), *Corporate Crime, Law and Social Control*, New York: Cambridge University Press.

Skidelsky, R. and Skidelsky, E. (2012), *How Much is Enough? The Love for Money and the Case for the Good Life*, London: Allen Lane.

Smith, D.C. (1980), 'Paragons, Pariahs, and Pirates: A Spectrum-Based Theory of Enterprise', *Crime and Delinquency*, 26: 358–86.

Smith, D.C. and Alba, R.D. (1979), 'Organized Crime and American Life', *Society*, 16: 32–8.

Soble, R.L. and Dallos, R.E. (1975), *The Impossible Dream: The Equity Funding Story. The Fraud of the Century*, New York: G.P. Putnam's Sons.

Soll, J. (2014), *The Reckoning. Financial Accountability and the Making and Breaking of Nations*, London: Allen Lane.

Sombart, W. (1915), *The Quintessence of Capitalism. A Study of the History and Psychology of the Modern Business Man*, London: T. Fisher Unwin.

Soros, G. (1987), *The Alchemy of Finance: Reading the Mind of the Market*, London: Weidenfeld and Nicolson.

Spector, M. and Kitsuse, J.I. (1982), *Constructing Social Problems*, Menlo Park: Cummings.

Spencer, J.C. (1965), 'A Study of Incarcerated White-Collar Offenders', in Grygier, T., Jones, H., and Spencer, J.C. (eds), *Criminology in Transition*, London: Tavistock.

Spang, R.L. (2015), *Stuff and Money in the Time of the French Revolution*, Cambridge: Harvard University Press.

Spinoza, B. (1959), *Ethics*, London: Everyman's Library.

Squires, S.E., Smith, C., McDougall, L., and Yeack, W.B. (2003), *Inside Arthur Andersen: Shifting Values, Unexpected Consequences*, New York: Prentice Hall.

Steffens, L. (1904), *The Shame of the Cities*, New York: Hill and Wang.

Stevens, M. (1989), *Sudden Death. The Rise and Fall of E.F. Hutton*, New York: New American Library.

Stigler, S. M. (1986), 'Adolphe Quetelet', in Kotz, S. (ed), *Encyclopedia of Statistical Sciences*, New York: John Wiley & Sons. 1986.

Stiles, T.S. (2010), *The First Tycoon: The Epic Life of Cornelius Vanderbilt*, New York: Vintage.

Strier, R. (2011), *The Unrepentant Renaissance: from Petrarch to Shakespeare to Milton*, Chicago and London: University of Chicago Press.

Sullivan, B.A. (2015), 'Corporate-Financial Crime Scandals', in Barak, G. (ed), *The Routledge International Handbook of the Crime of the Powerful*, London and New York: Routledge.

Sunstein, C.R. (2016), 'Parking the Big Money', *The New York Review of Books*, 14 January: 37–8.

Surowiecki, J. (2014), 'High on Speed', *New York Review of Books*, 61(12): 37–8.

Sutherland, E. (1940), 'White-Collar Criminality', *American Sociological Review*, 5: 1–12.

Sutherland, E. (1983), *White-Collar Crime: The Uncut Version*, New Haven: Yale University Press.

Sykes, G. and Matza, D. (1957), 'Techniques of Neutralization: A Theory of Delinquency', *American Sociological Review*, 22: 664–73.

Szockyi, E. and Fox, J.G. (1996), *Corporate Victimization of Women*, Boston: Northeastern University Press.

Talani, L.S. (2011), *Globalization, Hegemony and the Future of the City of London*, London: Palgrave Macmillan.

Taneja, V. (2014), 'Kirch Media, Germany', http://www.slideshare.net/tanejavinita/kirch-media-scandal (accessed 18 February 2016).

Tarde, G. (1890), *La philosophie pénale*, Lyon: Stock.

Tarde, G. (1893), 'Foules et sects au point de vue criminel', *Revue des Deux Mondes*, 15: 349–87.

Tarde, G. (1898), *Études de Psychologie Sociale*, Paris: V. Giard & E. Brière.

Tarde, G. (1902), 'Psychologie Économique', in Latour, B. and Lépinay, A. (eds) (2009), *The Science of Passionate Interests: An Introduction to Gabriel Tarde's Economic Anthropology*, Chicago: Prickly Paradign Press.

Tarde, G. (1903), *The Laws of Imitation*, New York: Holt and Co.

Tarde, G. (2012), 'Crime: Preponderance of Social Causes', in DiCristina, B. (ed), *The Birth of Criminology*, New York: Wolters Kluwer.

Taylor, J. (2006), *Creating Capitalism: Joint-Stock Enterprise in British Politics and Culture 1800–1870*, Woodbridge: Boydell Press.

Taylor, J. (2013), *Boardroom Scandal: The Criminalization of Company Fraud in Nineteenth-Century Fraud*, Oxford: Oxford University Press.

The Economist, 27 February 2003, 'Ahold: Europe's Enron', http://www.economist.com/node/1610552 (accessed 3 February 2016).

The Guardian, 19 April 2016: 'Offshore in Central London: The Curious Case of 29 Harley Street'.

The Knapp Commission (1972), *Report on Police Corruption*, New York: George Braziller.

The Washington Post (2013), *The Original Watergate Stories*, New York: Diversion Books.

Thompson, P. and Delano, A. (1989), *Maxwell: A Portrait of Power*, London: Bantam Press.

Tillman, R. (2015), 'Bad Banks: Recurrent Criminogenic Conditions in the US Commercial Banking System', in Barak, G. (ed), *The Routledge International Handbook of the Crime of the Powerful*, London and New York: Routledge.

Todorov, T. (2014), *The Inner Enemies of Democracy*, Cambridge: Polity.

Toffler, B.L. and Reingold, J. (2003), *Accounting: Ambition, Greed and the Fall of Arthur Andersen*, New York: Broadway Books.

Tomasic, R. (2009), 'The Financial Crisis and the Haphazard Pursuit of Financial Crime', paper presented at the Cambridge International Symposium on Economic crime, Jesus College, Cambridge University, 15 September.

Tombs, S. (2013), 'Corporate Theft and Fraud: Business as Usual', *Criminal Justice Matters*, 94: 14–15.

Tombs, S. (2015a) 'Crisis, What Crisis? Regulation and the Academic Orthodoxy', *The Howard Journal of Criminal Justice*, 54: 57–72.

Tombs, S. (2015b), 'Corporate Theft and Impunity in Financial Service', in Whyte, D. (ed), *How Corrupt Is Britain?*, London: Pluto.

Tonkonoff, S. (2013), 'A New Social Physics: The Sociology of Gabriel Tarde and its Legacy', *Current Sociology*, 61: 267–82.

Tonkonoff, S. (2014), 'Crime as Social Excess: Reconstructing Gabriel Tarde's Criminal Sociology', *History of the Human Sciences*, 27: 60–74.

Touraine, A. (2014), *After the Crisis*, Cambridge: Polity.

Trefgarne, G. (2002), 'Universal Disaster as Vivendi Crumbles', *The Telegraph*, 3 July, http://www.telegraph.co.uk/finance/markets/2767010/Universal-disaster-as-Vivendi-crumbles.html (accessed 13 February 2016).

Trigilia, C. (1998), *Sociologia economica. Stato, mercato e società nel capitalismo moderno*, Bologna: Il Mulino.

Truell, P. and Gurwin, L. (1992), *BCCI: The Inside Story of the World's Most Corrupt Financial Empire*, London: Bloomsbury.

Turner, B.S. (2013), 'Review Essay: A Capitalist Catastrophe', *The Sociological Review*, 61: 203–8.

Twain, M. and Warner, D. C. (1873), *The Gilded Age. A Tale of Today*, http://www.gutenberg.org/files/3178/3178-h/3178-h.htm (accessed 10 September 2015).

Twyman-Ghoshal, A. and Passas, N. (2015), 'State and Corporate Drivers of Global Dysnomie: Horrendous Crimes and the Law', in Barak, G. (ed), *The Routledge International Handbook of the Crime of the Powerful*, London and New York: Routledge.

UK Parliament (2015), http://www.parliament.uk/business/publications/research/olympic-britain/crime-and-defence/crimes-of-the-century/ (accessed 25 November 2015).

UN (2011), *Human Development Report*, New York: United Nations.

UNODCCP (United Nations Office for Drug Control and Crime Prevention) (1998), *Financial Havens, Banking Secrecy and Money Laundering*, New York: United Nations.

US Government, 24 July 2002, 'SEC Charges Adelphia and Rigas Family with Massive Fraud, https://www.sec.gov/news/press/2002-110.htm (accessed 13 February 2016).

van Duyne, P. and Levi, M. (2005), *Drugs and Money*, London: Routledge.

Van Niel, J.D. (2009), 'Enron: The Primer', in Rapoport, N.B., Van Niel, J.D., and Dharan, B.G. (eds), *Enron and Other Corporate Fiascos: The Corporate Scandal Reader*, New York: Foundation Press.

Vaughan, A. (1997), *Railwaymen, Politics and Money*, London: John Murray.

Verri, P. (1999), 'Elementi di commercio', in Capra, C. (ed), *Pietro Verri e il suo tempo*, Bologna: Cisalpino.

von Lampe, K. (2016), *Organized Crime. Analyzing Illegal Activities, Criminal Structures, and Extra-Legal Governance*, London: Sage.

Wahnbaeck, T. (2004), *Luxury and Public Happiness. Political Economy in the Italian Enlightenment*, Oxford: Oxford University Press.

Wallerstein, I. (1988), *The Modern World System III*, New York: Academic Press.

Weber, M. (1948), 'The Protestant Sects and the Spirit of Capitalism', in Gerth, H.H. and Mills, C.W. (eds), *From Max Weber: Essays in Sociology*, London: Routledge.

Weber, M. (1977), *The Protestant Ethic and the Spirit of Capitalism*, London: Allen & Unwin.

Weber, M. (1978), *Economy and Society: An Outline of Interpretive Sociology*, Berkeley: University of California Press.

Weisburd, D., Wheeler, S., Waring, E., and Bode, N. (1991), *Crimes of the Middle Class: White-Collar Offenders in the Federal Courts*, New Haven: Yale University Press.

Welborn, L.L. (2015), *Paul's Summons to Messianic Life: Political Theology and the Coming Awakening*, New York: Columbia University Press.

Wheeler, S., Weisburd, D., and Bode, N. (1982), 'Sentencing the White-Collar Offender: Rhetoric and Reality', *American Sociological Review*, 47: 641–59.

Whitehead, A.N. (1978), *Process and Reality*, New York: The Free Press.

Whyte, W.H. (1956), *The Organization Man*, New York: Simon & Schuster.

Will, S. (2013), 'America's Ponzi Culture', in Will, S., Handelman, S., and Brotherton, D.C. (eds), *How They Got Away with It. White Collar Criminals and the Financial Meltdown*, New York: Columbia University Press.

Will, S., Handelman, S., and Brotherton, D. (eds) (2012), *How They Got Away with It. White Collar Criminals and the Financial Meltdown*, New York: Columbia University Press.

Williams, J.D. (1954), *The Compleat Strategyst. Being a Primer on the Theory of Games of Strategy*, New York: Dover Publications.

Wilson, H. (2014), 'London Is Money Laundering Capital', *The Times*, 2 September.

Wilson, S. (2014), *The Origins of Modern Financial Crime*, London and New York: Routledge.

Wood, M. (2016), 'At the Movies', *London Review of Books*, 18 February: 35.

Wood, Z. (2014), 'Uphill Task Ahead for Tesco's New Finance Director', *The Guardian*, 24 September.

Woodiwiss, M. (2001), *Organized Crime and American Power*, Toronto: University of Toronto Press.

Wright Mills, C. (1956), *The Power Elite*, New York: Oxford University Press.

Young, J. (1978), 'Foreword', in Pearce, F., *Crimes of the Powerful*, London: Pluto.

Young. J. (2012), 'Bernie Madoff, Finance Capital and the Anomic Society', in Will, S., Handelman, S., and Brotherton, D.C. (eds), *How They Got Away with It. White Collar Criminals and the Financial Meltdown*, New York: Columbia University Press.

Zaidi, D. (2016), 'The Rise of Shadow Banking and the Repeal of the Glass-Steagall Act, http://prn.fm/deena-zaidi-the-rise-of-shadow-banks-and-the-repeal-of-the-glass-steagall-act/ (accessed 17 May 2016).

Zaloom, C. (2012), 'Traders and Market Morality', in Knorr Cetina, K. and Preda, A. (eds), *The Oxford Handbook of the Sociology of Finance*, Oxford: Oxford University Press.

Zamagni, S. (2015), *Prudenza*, Bologna: Il Mulino.

Zola, E. (2014), *Money*, Oxford: Oxford University Press.

Zuckoff, M. (2005), *Ponzi's Scheme: The True Story of aFinancial Legend*, New York: Random House.

Zucman, G. (2015a), *The Hidden Wealth of Nations: The Scourge of Tax Havens*, Chicago: University of Chicago Press.

Zucman, G. (2015b), 'Tax Evasion by Large Corporations is on the Rise—Leading to Greater Inequality', *The Observer*, 11 November.

Index